THE **BIG** BOOK OF
UNITED
GOALSCORERS & CHAMPIONS

ALSO FROM JAMES WARD

HISTORICAL/FACTUAL

Manchester: A Football History (ISBN 9780955812705, published April 2008)
The Big Book Of City (ISBN 9780955812729, published October 2009)
Manchester: A Football History (ISBN 9780955812736, published December 2010)

BIOGRAPHY

Joe Mercer, OBE: Football With A Smile (ISBN 9780955812743, published April 2010)

THE **BIG** BOOK OF
UNITED
GOALSCORERS & CHAMPIONS

Contributors include:

Tim Ashmore, Edward Garvey, Gary James, Iain McCartney,
Paul Nagel & Alex Wormall

PUBLISHED BY

First published in Great Britain in 2011 by
James Ward
PO BOX 822, HALIFAX, HX1 9FX

www.manchesterfootball.org

www.facebook.com/Jameswardpublishing

info@manchesterfootball.org

Designed by Trevor Hartley

ISBN 978-0-9558127-5-0

James Ward 750

Printed and bound in Great Britain by
CPI Antony Rowe, Chippenham, Wiltshire.

CONTENTS

INTRODUCTION

Since we published our first Manchester-based football book in 2008, we have always been keen to develop quality books written with real passion. *The Big Book Of United – Goalscorers & Champions* is our first United specific publication but does follow our highly regarded *Manchester A Football History* which revealed many new facts about the Reds and helped highlight some long forgotten moments of significance.

We recognised however that *Manchester A Football History* is a detailed, in depth study of football in the region and that many fans simply do not get the right amount of time to dedicate to reading books of that type (although we do actively encourage fans to dip in when they get chance). Every so often we simply want to read a book for a few minutes in between other activities. *The Big Book Of United – Goalscorers & Champions* has been developed out of a desire to satisfy that need.

This book provides a mix of entertaining information in an easy to read format. Though it is not simply a miscellany of information. It provides valid, readable content alongside some of the more trivia based material. It also has a couple of key themes – goalscorers and League champions. As we all know United have broken records with their performances in the League and so we wanted to take those seasons of championship success, highlight key points and make comparisons where possible. Alongside this we have produced profiles of every footballer to have topped United's League goalscoring charts for a season. Hopefully these pen pictures help to identify how significant each player was and will also bring interesting reminders of the stars of the past.

Finally, it is absolutely vital that proper acknowledgement is given to the people who have made this book possible. *The Big Book Of United – Goalscorers & Champions* has been produced by a variety of contributors, each adding their own memories, feelings and thoughts on the Reds. The contributors vary in age, location and years of interest in all things United but as publishers we are delighted with the efforts they have made and the support they have given.

PUBLISHER'S ACKNOWLEDGEMENTS

The publishers would like to thank all purchasers and subscribers to this volume. If this publication proves successful and is well received by supporters, further editions of *The Big Book Of United* may be produced.

We would like to record our appreciation to all the contributors to this volume. This book would not have been possible without your support.

Additional thanks to everyone involved with www.unitedkits.com and United Review Collectors' Club.

Significant support has come from officials at the Lancashire FA, the Manchester FA, the PFA and of course United.

With both this book and *Manchester A Football History*, the contributors and ourselves have received great support, assistance and inspiration from (listed in alphabetical order) a variety of sources including: Ron Atkinson, Alessandro Bacci, John Bailey, Len Balaam, Joachim Barbier, Peter Barnes, Julian Baskcomb, Grant Bliss, Alan Brennan, Phil Brennan, Adam Brown, Tony Bugby, Andy Burton, Mark Bushell, Eric Cantona, Doug Cheeseman, Pat Crerand, Jack Crompton, Olivier De Bannes, Andy Dickman, Tommy Docherty, Garth Dykes, Geoff Fisher, Steve Fleet, Ross Hamilton, Frank Hannah, Trevor Hartley, David Johnson, Ian Jones, Paul Jolleys, Stephen Kelly, Brian Landamore, Andy Lyons, David Meek, Leslie Millman, David Moor, David Moore, Kevin Moore, Tommy Nielsen, Athanasios Papathanasiou, Paul Parker, Mike Pavasovic, David Powter, Ken Ramsden, Andy Ritchie, Simon Shakeshaft, Jed Smith, Jules Spencer, Tom Tyrell, Andy Walsh, Mark Wilbraham, Joyce Woolridge, and Mark Wylie.

The following museums, libraries and media organisations have provided support, imagery, and assistance: Action Images, the BFI, Channel M, Granada TV, Manchester Central Library, Manchester County FA, Manchester Confidential, Manchester Evening News, Manchester United Museum, National Football Museum, the newspaper archive of the British Library at Colindale, the People's History Museum, the Pride of Manchester website, the Reporter Group, Tameside Libraries, Unitedkits.com, and the World of Rugby. It is worth stating that this is not an official MUFC publication.

Inevitably, thousands of individual newspaper editions have been consulted during the production of this book, particularly those national and local editions produced in Manchester. These include:

Manchester Courier
Manchester Evening Chronicle
Manchester Evening News
Manchester Weekly Times
Oldham Evening Chronicle
The Reporter (various locally branded versions)
Salford Chronicle
Daily Dispatch
Athletic News
Sporting Chronicle

Plus of course all modern day national newspapers, football magazines, and club-based material. We would also like to take this opportunity to thank supporters of United in general and those fans who dedicate many hours each day to ensuring the views of supporters are recorded, remembered and promoted via fanzines, supporters clubs, forums, message boards and blogs.

Club historians and members of the Association of Football Statisticians have assisted and we are grateful to them all. We would like to thank all the journalists, photographers, and officials who have helped chronicle United throughout the history of football. The majority of photographs come from the archives of the contributors, Action Images, the Manchester Evening News and Edward Garvey.

Trevor Hartley has expertly designed the book and its cover.

Finally, as this book is such a significant volume, it is recognised that some detail, for example United's trophy record may be (probably will be) out of date within a short timescale. It should be stressed however that this book is intended to provide snapshot information on the Reds rather than a detailed review of the modern era.

Football moves on at an incredible rate, but hopefully you'll agree that *The Big Book Of United – Goalscorers & Champions* has managed to capture a few truly memorable moments from over 130 years history of the Club.

LEADING LEAGUE SCORERS

United have a great history and are known worldwide for the quality of their attacking-minded players. Some of the greatest goalscorers in football history have appeared for the Reds. To celebrate the wonderful achievements of those players, The Big Book Of United has profiled the Reds' leading strikers.

Within the pages of this book are profiles of every player to head United's goalscoring charts for each of the Reds' League seasons up to publication. In fact, we actually go back a couple of years before the first League match and include details of those who topped United's charts in the old Alliance League during the 1890s.

United joined the League in 1892 as Newton Heath and the Club's first leading goalscorer was Bob Donaldson, however before 1892 the Heathens did compete in other regular competition. The Alliance League operated in a formal way and was perceived by many as the unofficial Second Division of the Football League. As far as we're concerned, the leading goalscorers for all Alliance League seasons deserve the same recognition as those for modern day League campaigns.

In total we've got the details of over 120 years' worth of leading goalscorers. Some players, inevitably, topped the charts for a few seasons, but how many of the leading scorers can you name?

Before you turn over the page, take a moment to see how many you remember and how far back you can go.

LEADING GOALSCORERS
THE FULL LIST

Here goes... the full list of United's leading League goalscorers:

Year	Division	Number of Goals	Games	Player
1890	Alliance	10	19	Stewart
1891	Alliance	6	20	Sharpe
1892	Alliance	20	22	Donaldson
1893	One	16	26	Donaldson
1894	One	8	18	Farman
1895	Two	19	29	Smith
1896	Two	16	19	Cassidy
1897	Two	17	28	Cassidy
1898	Two	22	30	Boyd
1899	Two	19	34	Cassidy
1900	Two	16	29	Cassidy
1901	Two	14	34	Leigh
1902	Two	11	29	Preston
1903	Two	11	30	Peddie
1904	Two	11	23	Grassam
				Also 11 in 26 for Arkesen & 11 in 30 for Griffiths
1905	Two	17	32	Peddie
1906	Two	20	33	Picken
1907	One	11	38	Wall
1908	One	25	30	Turnbull (Sandy)
1909	One	17	22	Turnbull (Jimmy)
1910	One	14	32	Wall
1911	One	19	35	West
1912	One	17	32	West
1913	One	21	36	West
1914	One	15	32	Anderson
1915	One	10	23	Anderson

Year	Division	Number of Goals	Games	Player
1920	One	14	32	Spence
1921	One	7	15	Spence
				Also 7 in 21 for Sapsford & 7 in 25 for Miller & 7 in 28 for Partridge
1922	One	15	35	Spence
1923	Two	13	22	Goldthorpe
				Also 13 in 34 for Lochhead
1924	Two	14	40	Lochhead
1925	Two	14	22	Henderson
1926	Two	17	34	Rennox
1927	One	18	40	Spence
1928	One	22	38	Spence
1929	One	19	42	Hanson
1930	One	12	40	Rowley (Harry)
				Also 12 in 42 for Spence
1931	One	17	30	Reid
1932	Two	19	37	Spence
1933	Two	11	23	Ridding
1934	Two	8	21	Dewar
1935	Two	18	40	Mutch
1936	Two	21	42	Mutch
1937	One	14	29	Bamford
1938	Two	14	23	Bamford
1939	One	12	27	Hanlon
1947	One	26	37	Rowley (Jack)
1948	One	23	39	Rowley (Jack)
1949	One	20	39	Rowley (Jack)
1950	One	20	39	Rowley (Jack)
1951	One	18	39	Pearson
1952	One	30	40	Rowley (Jack)
1953	One	16	39	Pearson
1954	One	22	35	Taylor
1955	One	20	30	Taylor
				Also 20 in 34 for Viollet

Year	Division	Number of Goals	Games	Player
1956	One	25	33	Taylor
1957	One	26	39	Whelan
1958	One	16	22	Viollet
Also 16 in 25 for Taylor				
1959	One	29	38	Charlton
1960	One	32	36	Viollet
1961	One	21	39	Charlton
1962	One	14	27	Herd
1963	One	23	38	Law
1964	One	30	30	Law
1965	One	28	36	Law
1966	One	24	37	Herd
1967	One	23	36	Law
1968	One	28	41	Best
1969	One	19	41	Best
1970	One	15	37	Best
1971	One	18	40	Best
1972	One	18	40	Best
1973	One	6	36	Charlton
1974	One	6	29	McIlroy
1975	Two	17	31	Pearson
1976	One	13	39	Pearson
1977	One	15	39	Pearson & Hill
1978	One	17	36	Hill
1979	One	11	33	Greenhoff
Also 11 in 42 for Coppell				
1980	One	13	32	Jordan
1981	One	15	33	Jordan
1982	One	13	41	Stapleton
1983	One	14	41	Stapleton
1984	One	13	42	Stapleton
1985	One	16	38	Hughes

Above: **David Herd.**

Right: **Stan Pearson and (inset) Jack Rowley.**

Below: **George Best – leading scorer in five successive seasons.**

1986	One	17	40	Hughes
1987	One	14	39	Davenport
1988	One	24	40	McClair
1989	One	14	38	Hughes
1990	One	13	37	Hughes
1991	One	13	36	McClair
1992	One	18	42	McClair

Left to right: **Ole Gunnar Solskjaer**, *Wayne Rooney and Ruud van Nistelrooy.*

Year	Division	Number of Goals	Number of Games	Player
1993	Premier	15	41	Hughes
1994	Premier	18	34	Cantona
1995	Premier	14	30	Kanchelskis
1996	Premier	14	30	Cantona
1997	Premier	18	33	Solskjaer
1998	Premier	15	33	Cole
1999	Premier	18	32	Yorke
2000	Premier	20	32	Yorke
2001	Premier	15	29	Sheringham
2002	Premier	23	32	Van Nistelrooy
2003	Premier	25	34	Van Nistelrooy
2004	Premier	20	32	Van Nistelrooy
2005	Premier	11	29	Rooney
2006	Premier	21	35	Van Nistelrooy
2007	Premier	17	34	Ronaldo
2008	Premier	31	34	Ronaldo
2009	Premier	18	33	Ronaldo
2010	Premier	26	32	Rooney
2011	Premier	20	32	Berbatov

Those players on **black bands** also topped the relevant division's goalscoring charts for that season.

Profiles of all these players appear throughout the book.

The Football Season Daily Reminder

August

Ever wondered what football anniversaries fall throughout the season? If you have, take a look at the Big Book Of United's Football Season Daily Reminder. Spread throughout this book we have monthly snippets covering some memorable – and some not so memorable - moments in United's history. We don't highlight every anniversary, but we do provide one for every single date in the period 1st August through to 31st May. Let's start with August...

1st August 1999

As United had won both the League and the FA Cup (and the European Champions League of course!) in 1999 the annual Charity Shield was played between United and the Premier League runners-up Arsenal. A Wembley crowd of 70,185 witnessed a 1-0 Arsenal victory.

2nd August 2008

A testimonial for United's Norwegian striker Ole Gunnar Solskjaer was held at Old Trafford. Fraizer Campbell scored the winner against Espanyol while Solskjaer came on for Carlos Tevez in the 68th minute. The attendance was 68,868.

3rd August 1997

Premier League champions United beat FA Cup winners Chelsea 4-2 on penalties after a 1-1 draw in the Charity Shield. Former Red Mark Hughes had scored for the London side.

4th August 2010

United defeated a League of Ireland XI 7-1 with goals from Ji Sung Park (13 & 63), Michael Owen (25), Javier Hernandez (47), Antonio Valencia (60), Jonny Evans (69) and Nani (an 82nd minute penalty). The game was staged in front of 49,861 and was played to mark the opening of Dublin's Aviva Stadium.

5th August 2007

After a 1-1 draw United beat Chelsea 3-0 on penalties in the FA Community Shield at Wembley. The attendance was 80,731. On the same date in 1985 United won the first ever Manchester International Football Tournament. The

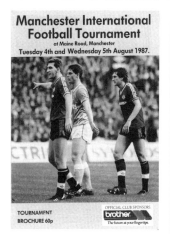

Manchester International Football Tournament
at Maine Road, Manchester
Tuesday 4th and Wednesday 5th August 1987.

TOURNAMENT BROCHURE 60p

OFFICIAL CLUB SPONSORS.
brother
The future at your fingertips.

competition between United, City, PSV Eindhoven and Athletico Mineiro ended with Matt Busby presenting the trophy to the Reds at Maine Road.

6th August 1912

Future United footballer and coach Bert Whalley was born in Ashton-under-Lyne. He made a total of 38 League and Cup appearances but his competitive opportunities were limited by the War. Whalley died in the Munich Air Disaster.

7th August 1993

The Reds won the Charity Shield match with Arsenal 5-4 on penalties after a 1-1 draw (Hughes scored for United) before 66,519 at Wembley Stadium.

8th August 1978

Louis Saha was born in Paris.

9th August 1958

Future United goalkeeper Gary Bailey was born in Ipswich. His father Roy was a goalkeeper with Ipswich Town winning the League title in 1962. Interestingly, Gary made his United debut against Ipswich in November 1978.

10th August 2008

United beat FA Cup winners Portsmouth 3-1 on penalties in the Community (former Charity) Shield at Wembley Stadium before 84,808.

11th August 2010

According to the Daily Star on this date: "Manchester United have signed Vitoria Guimaraes striker Tiago Manuel Dias Correia, better known as Bebe, subject to a medical."

12th August 1972

Despite a goal from Denis Law the first match of the

1972-73 League season ended in a 2-1 defeat at home to Ipswich Town.

13th August 1969

Wilf McGuinness' (above) first home League game as United manager ended in a 2-0 defeat by Everton.

14th August 1971

Goals from Alan Gowling and Denis Law ensured a draw at Derby County on the opening day of the season. United won the return 1-0 (George Best) but Derby ended the season as League champions.

15th August 1993

Goals from Giggs and Robson brought a 2-0

United victory at Norwich City.

16th August 2009

A 34th minute Wayne Rooney goal gave United a 1-0 victory at home to Birmingham City, before 75,062, on the opening day of the 2009-10 season.

17th August 1985

A Mark Hughes brace against Aston Villa helped United achieve a 4-0 opening day victory. Olsen and Whiteside scored the others.

18th August 1951

James Bond (top right) made his first United appearance in the opening game of the season at West Bromwich Albion. The Reds drew the game 3-3 with a hat-trick from Jack Rowley. Although James was Bond's first name he was popularly known as Ernie – his middle name was Ernest.

19th August 1978

Joe Jordan scored the only goal of the opening day fixture against Birmingham City at Old Trafford. It was the third successive season that the two sides met on the opening day. The previous year Lou Macari netted a hat-trick in a 4-1 United victory – it was the Reds' only League hat-trick that season.

20th August 1966

United's 1966-67 title winning season began with an amazing 5-3 victory over West Bromwich Albion. The Old Trafford attendance was 41,343.

21st August 1968

A solitary goal from Jimmy Ryan gave United victory at home to Coventry City in the fourth League game of the season. It was Ryan's first start since 2nd March 1968.

22nd August 1987

Brian McClair and Paul McGrath helped the Reds to a 2-0 victory at home to Watford in front of an Old Trafford crowd of 38,582.

23rd August 1975

United defeated Sheffield United 5-1 in the Reds' first home game of the 1975-76 League season. The return

match (13/12/75) ended 4-1 to United and Stuart Pearson scored twice in each game.

24th August 1974

The first Old Trafford Second Division game since May 1938 ended in a 4-0 victory over Millwall after Gerry Daly had scored a hat-trick. The attendance was 44,756 – almost 9,000 less than the Reds' previous home game in that division.

25th August 1923

United defeated Bristol City 2-1 in the opening game of the Second Division season.

26th August 2007

A solitary goal from Nani (68th minute) gave United their first victory of the season. The Reds beat Tottenham before an Old Trafford crowd of 75,696 in their fourth League game of the season.

27th August 1947

The first United home game of the season ended in a 2-0 victory over League champions Liverpool in front of a crowd of 52,385 (left). Goals from Morris and Pearson set the Reds off at the start of a great season.

WEST HAM UNITED

MANCHESTER UNITED
FOOTBALL LEAGUE — Division One
SATURDAY 19th AUGUST 1961 at 3.0 p.m.

No. 2

OFFICIAL PROGRAMME 6d

CHAMPIONS

By ARCHIE LEDBROOKE

MANCHESTER UNITED 2, LIVERPOOL 0

AN early injury to Harley spoiled the eagerly anticipate tussle between last season's First Division champions an runners-up at Maine-road last night.

Reorganisation of the Liverpool side not only wrecked thei teamwork but spoiled what should have been a titbit of struggle between Carey and Liddell, two of the men who figured on opposite sides in the historic Britain v The Rest match a few months ago. Taylor had to fall back and Harley hobbled about on the wing with an injury which may keep him out of the side for some weeks.

who, while falling over near th penalty spot, performed a gymnast feat to swing his leg at the ball an place it wide of Sidlow.

Nearly Solved

Towards the end Liverpool we plainly disheartened, and th United forward line, moving reall well for the first time, should hav had several more goals. They

Last night's official attendance was 52,385.

PRICE---ONE PENNY

EVERTON F.C.

Official Programme

The only Official Programme issued by the authority of
THE EVERTON FOOTBALL CLUB CO., LTD.

FOOTBALL LEAGUE MATCH

EVERTON v. MANCHESTER UNITED

Saturday, August 29th, 1942.

At Goodison Park.   Kick-off 3-0 p.m.

Right	Everton	Left

Burnett 1

Jones, J. E. 2   Greenhalgh 3

Mercer 4   Jones, T. G. 5   Watson 6

Bentham 7   2Mutch 8   Lawton 9   Stevenson 10   Anderson 11

Mitton 11   Pearson 10   Smith 9   Morris 8   Bryant 7

Whalley 6   Porter 5   Carey 4

Roughton 3   Griffiths 2

Breedon 1

Left   Manchester United   Right

Referee—Mr. W. H. E. Evans (R.A.F.).
Linesmen—Messrs. J. Phillips and W. Cottrill.
(Blue Flag)   (Red Flag)

Liverpool County Combination Match

EVERTON A. v. ST. TERESA'S

Saturday Next, September 5th.

At Goodison Park.   Kick-off 3-0 p.m.

Harry Catterick and Stan Pearson scoring for the Reds. Catterick was a guest player and later found success as the Everton manager. On the same date in 1908 United defeated QPR 4-0 in the Charity Shield replay (below). The first match had ended in a 1-1 draw.

30th August 1926

Two goals from Frank McPherson ensured a point was obtained in the 2-2 draw at Sheffield United. This was the second of three successive games in which McPherson scored twice. McPherson later had spells at Manchester Central and Watford before his sudden death in 1953 at the age of 51 in Davyhulme. On the same date in 1947 Jack Rowley netted four as United defeated Charlton 6-2 in Division One.

31st August 1949

Mitten and Pearson secured a 2-1 victory at Bolton Wanderers in Division One.

28th August 2011

A Rooney hat-trick helped United to a 8-2 victory over Arsenal. After City had defeated Spurs 5-1 the Reds needed to score six more than the Gunners to leapfrog City at the top of the Premier League.

29th August 1942

The fourth season of wartime football opened

with United drawing 2-2 at Goodison Park with

Woeful Arsenal plumb depths as Rooney goes on the rampage

THE Best GOAL

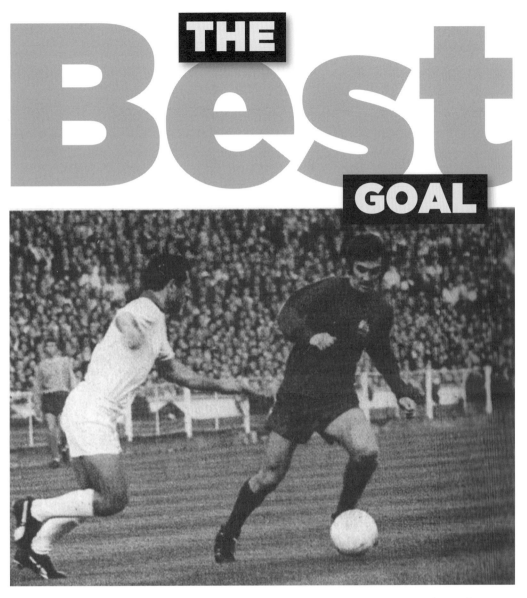

George Best's goal in the 1968 European Cup Final was of course highly significant, but it was also the goal that the United star claimed was his personal 'best'.

Shortly before his United career came to an end he admitted: "Big games always brought out the best in me, if you'll excuse the pun, and they don't come much bigger than European Cup Finals.

"I've had many magic moments, but none stands out more than the one at Wembley in the 1968 Final when I scored against Benfica. Alex Stepney cleared the ball up field and Brian Kidd nodded it on to me. In a flash I was heading for goal with defender Cruz chasing my shadow.

"This was my great chance and as I glanced up I realised only one man stood between me and a goal. But as goalie Henrique came off his line I kept my cool... rounded him... slotted the ball home.

"I'll never forget one moment of that lung-bursting run. It helped bring United the trophy

Above: **The United Review pays tribute to George Best in December 2005.**

they had been so near to winning before. Of course we won 4-1 in the end... but it's the goal that really stands out in my memory."

When Best passed away in 2005 at the age of 59 Brian Glanville, writing for the Guardian, claimed this goal as possibly the player's best, it was certainly one of his most significant goals: "United, initially ahead, had seemed to tire towards the end of normal time and looked in danger of losing. Scarcely had extra time begun, however, than Best had spun past a defender with devastating turn, tacked outside the goalkeeper and run the ball into the net. United went on to win the game with ease, 4-1, becoming the first English team to take the European Cup."

Glanville suggested that Best's greatest game was actually two years earlier: "Was the finest game he ever played not the European Cup Final of 1968 against Benfica, but the time he ran them ragged in Lisbon in the same competition in 1966? As Pat Crerand, the tough Glaswegian right-half who was Best's protector in those days, put it: 'Besty just went

'MY "BEST" GOAL'

daft'. But he did it in the most positive and coruscating way. After six minutes, he headed in a free kick by the United left back, Tony Dunne. When David Herd headed on a long kick from the keeper, Ulsterman Harry Gregg, Best dashed past a formidable centre back and scored again. Gregg must have been particularly pleased. He was wont to recall playing in a training game against the then slender and unknown young Best: 'And he done me'. Which promptly happened again. 'This was our finest hour' said the Churchillian manager Matt Busby as his United ran out 5-1 winners, although the cup eluded them that year, and an injury to Best caused him to miss a tie against Partizan Belgrade, who were surprise semi-final winners."

Two decades after the 1966 meeting with Benfica in Lisbon that Glanville reckoned may have been his greatest game, Best described his memories of the match and his opening goal: "Very early in the game I coasted past a couple of defenders and this seemed to set the pattern. From a Tony Dunne free kick I sneaked into their penalty area and out jumped their defenders to score with a header, then a few minutes later David Herd nodded a big kick from Harry Gregg right into my path, and the defence just seemed to open up for me, to put number two away. We'd hardly had time to realise how well we were playing, when

David Herd again headed the ball on, this time for John Connelly to apply the finishing touch."

Ultimately, everyone who saw him play will have memories and views of George Best's greatest goal. Of course Best himself talked often about his career and appeared on chat shows, sport shows and on tour with Rodney Marsh. During those interviews and talks he often highlighted other goals and other great moments from his career but, as far as we're concerned at "The Big Book Of United", we reckon his views from shortly before he retired – all too prematurely - have to be taken at face value. If Best believed his goal at Wembley in 1968 was his 'best' at that time then we're happy to accept that.

Many fans have memories of that night and, in October 2010, the Daily Mail reported that Best's medal from the European final was sold at auction: "George Best's 1968 European Cup winner's medal has been sold at auction for £156,000. It was arguably the greatest accolade won by the Northern Irish genius during a turbulent football career.

"His goal in extra time of the final at Wembley put Manchester United on course for a 4-1 win against Benfica which helped to create the legend of a club which had suffered so horribly with the Munich disaster 10 years earlier. The European Cup medal was among 13 of Best's awards put up for sale by his sister Barbara McNally, who said she was forced to part with treasured mementos in order to pay off his debts. The items fetched almost £200,000."

George Best and Mike Summerbee outside their fashion store Edwardia in 1968.

Managers
Their First Season

Above: **The United Review welcomes a new manager. Who could have predicted the success that followed?**

It seems a long time ago now, but in May 1987 Alex Ferguson completed his first season with United. It wasn't a full season – he arrived in November 1986 – but it was the start of an amazingly successful career with the Reds.

Ferguson's first season gave little indication of the success that would follow as United finished 11th in the First Division, at that time the highest division in England. Considering what followed, it is worth looking at the statistics of that first season to see how it compares to all previous United managers.

We know that Ferguson has achieved more than any of his predecessors in terms of trophies won, but here we take a look at the other managers and try to identify which manager achieved most in his first season at the Club. As managerial changes often come (but not always!) after a period of failure, success has to be measured differently from times when a manager is well established in his role.

MATT BUSBY
watches the field

Photo. : *Manchester Evening News*

To all United Fans I say " How do you do ? " This is my first opportunity of having a word with you since my arrival here last year, and what better means than by the Club programme ? This represents the written words and thoughts of the Manchester United F.C., and I am certain you and I have an equal interest in it. As it is intended that I have a regular article to discuss football from many view-points I hope it will bring us even closer together. You and I look forward to the opening of the 1946-47 season and what it has in store for us. How often have I felt that tingle run through me, known to all players on the first match of a new season, wondering in what form it would find me and how kindly the ball would run. I am finding all the same reactions as a manager.

A great number of people have asked me about our prospects for the coming season. To this I have replied that our boys are in good heart and excellent physical condition, and will hold their own. Others have remarked that the team should do very well if they start off as they finished last season. Yes, I would be a very happy man if they start off as they finished, but I realise from experience the number of things that can crop up to influence this. After all, each player is human and not a mechanical engine which, when you press a button, goes through its work every minute of the day. I do wish all followers of football would remember this very important point when a player has an " off day."

However, we must get on to the battle which starts this afternoon. We will all find the pace of the game stepping up, the tackling keener and the teamwork improved with a view to getting back to 1939 standards—which is all to the good of the game. Whether we start off on the right foot this afternoon or not, I do feel our boys will provide many happy afternoons for us all.

When I came here, I set out to have a team play methodical and progressive football. Without method a team gets nowhere. Without making progress after creating an opening or a position, the opportunity is lost and the team is back where it started. This will always be my policy, so I leave it to the players to supply the answer, and I hope you will have something good to shout about !

M Busby

Manager.

Walter Crickmer Still Smiling

It is indeed like old times to see Walter Crickmer, our genial secretary, in his usual office. The war years have not left the marks upon him which we might have expected He was on police duty during the blitz and the station received a direct hit by a high explosive bomb. Walter was a lucky one who escaped alive. Also he has been doing tremendously strenuous and important work during the war—of which storage of Government supplies was not the least. In spite of these troubles and trials he is bubbling over with enthusiasm for the old team. His great grudge against the universe is that it has proved impossible to rebuild the stands—thus the games at Maine Road.

Above: **New manager Wilf McGuinness (centre) tries to calm a moment of conflict between George Best and referee Jack Taylor in December 1969**

In terms of actual trophy winning success, none of our managers have won a major trophy in their first season, although Wilf McGuinness guided United to third place in the FA Cup in 1970. That season a third place play-off had been organised for the two losing semi-finalists and United beat Watford 2-0 at Highbury before 15,105.

It should also be remembered that Matt

Dave Sexton
Manager

I was hit by the full force of a Manchester derby soon after my arrival as manager of Manchester United.

For the fixture against Manchester City at Maine Road fell just five games after the start of the season, and I was caught up in excitement and tension.

I was involved in London as both a player and a manager in derby fixtures, and the rivalry was always fairly intense, but I must say that a Manchester derby seems to be out on its own as a special event.

RED AND BLUE
Perhaps it is because the two clubs belong to the same city and therefore football fans tend to divide up red or blue with no room for a neutral! London is slightly more cosmopolitan with several teams in the capital which probably eases the pressures.

Anyway, it is all happening again this evening as we welcome City to Old Trafford for our rearranged match. As a manager I have to remain slightly more detached and no doubt Tony Book is striving for an equally cool approach because no matter how important local prestige might be, the fact is that tonight's match carries just the two points like the rest of the League programme.

We need them after a disappointing run to give ourselves a boost as we blend our new players, Joe Jordan and Gordon McQueen, into the team and try to recapture our rhythm.

This is a critical phase of the season for us, even if some of our targets may now seem to be eluding us. We have got to get our game together for a confident campaign next season.

Busby's 1946-47 side came second to Liverpool in the title race. Busby's Reds were one point behind the Merseyside club although this was not Busby's first year at United (he'd joined the Reds in February 1945), but it was his first competitive season. Busby always felt that James Gibson, the businessman who rescued United in the 1930s, was the man who ensured United developed: "Mr JW Gibson was the man responsible for bringing me to

Managers Alf Albut (top left), Frank O'Farrell (above), Ernest Mangnall (above left) and Matt Busby (left during his playing career).

United in 1945. A businessman, he put the Club on a sound financial footing, before handing over to Harold Hardman."

Busby's arrival transformed United, but what about the first season for United's other appointments?

Have a look at the following records and see which achievement you work out to be the most significant. Incidentally, Matt Busby (the FA Cup) and Ron Atkinson (the FA Cup) are the only United managers to have won a major trophy in their second season, while Dave Sexton guided the Reds to the FA Cup final in his second season. As well as winning the FA Cup Ron Atkinson also took United to the League Cup final in his second season.

Highest placed side after a manager's first season

MATT BUSBY	2nd Division One 1946-47 (first post war League season)*
RON ATKINSON	3rd Division One 1981-82
JOHN BENTLEY	4th Division One 1912-13
WILF McGUINNESS	8th Division One 1969-70
FRANK O'FARRELL	8th Division One 1971-72
DAVE SEXTON	10th Division One 1977-78
ALEX FERGUSON	11th Division One 1986-87
ALF ALBUT	16th Division One 1892-93 *
JOHN ROBSON	18th Division One 1914-15
TOMMY DOCHERTY	18th Division One 1972-73
JOHN CHAPMAN	22nd Division One 1921-22

Note: * Albut managed Newton Heath (United) pre-League as well while Matt Busby managed United prior to the resumption of League football after the war.

Most successful manager in the FA Cup during his first season

WILF McGUINNESS
3rd place play off winners, FA Cup 1969-70

FRANK O'FARRELL
6th round FA Cup 1971-72

Most successful manager in the League Cup during his first season

WILF McGUINNESS semi-final League Cup 1969-70

ALEX FERGUSON 5th round League Cup 1987-88

FRANK O'FARRELL 4th round League Cup 1971-72

Alex Ferguson became manager after the 1986-87 League Cup campaign had ended, so his record for his first season in that competition is included instead.

Most successful manager in Europe during his first season

DAVE SEXTON 2nd round ECWC 1977-78

Sexton was the only United manager to find his side competing in European competition during his first season. The season prior to Alex Ferguson's arrival in 1986 United had ended the season in a place that would ordinarily guarantee a European place, however English clubs were banned from Europe following the Heysel disaster of 1985.

Although he is rarely thought of as a successful manager at United, it is worth highlighting that Wilf McGuinness had a highly successful first season in comparison with most other United managers. In fact his record in domestic cups – semi-final appearances in both – has never been bettered in a manager's first season. In the early 1980s McGuinness was interviewed for "What A Game" by Fred Eyre and Roy Cavanagh. He explained how he became United's manager: "My only regret was that Matt Busby didn't leave it another five years before retiring! The crown was there and I was given it. I was overwhelmed when it happened. They never said 'do you want it'. They just told me it was mine!"

McGuinness took United to a second League Cup semi-final in 1970 but was dismissed a few days later (after a 4-4 draw at Derby County on Boxing Day 1970): "The mention of semi-finals always hurt because we kept losing them! When the sack came it was disappointment following disappointment. I was very hurt at the time, and felt badly let down when it ended. Still, managing Manchester United is an honour open to very few."

UNITED'S LEADING SCORERS

Earlier in The Big Book of United we listed all the players who have topped the seasonal League goalscoring charts for the Reds from the beginning of the Club's spell in the Alliance League through to the start of the 2011-12 season. But what do we know about them? Throughout this book we provide brief biographies, in chronological order, of each of these players. We start with United's first twelve seasonal record holders....

THE PROFILES

1 – WILLIAM STEWART

Willie Stewart was the Club's record goalscorer for the 1889-1890 season, netting ten goals in 19 games. In fact Stewart scored in the Club's first Alliance game when Sunderland Albion were defeated 4-1 at North Road on 21st September 1889. Stewart had joined the Heathens a few weeks earlier from Warwick County.

Born in Perthshire in 1872, Stewart gained a good reputation in Manchester, particularly when he netted the Club's first Alliance hat-trick in the thrilling 9-1 victory over Small Heath (Birmingham City) on 7th April 1890.

By the time the Heathens joined the League in 1892 Stewart was one of the Club's most consistent players, although he was no longer the leading scorer after taking over as the team's half-back during 1891-2. Perhaps he was always more of a defensive player than an out-and-out striker. It's worth noting that he even played one game in goal – 7th January 1893 when the Heathens only fielded ten players against Stoke.

At one point the Manchester Evening News talked positively of his contribution: "There can be little doubt there are few better men in his position in the Country."

After his time at Newton Heath came to

William Stewart

an end in 1899 he had a spell at Thames Ironworks and Dundee. In April 1928 an article in the Topical Times looked back at the early years of the Club and described Stewart as "the elongated Scot who happened one day to take up a partnership with Alf Farman. Stewart found himself when he took over the duties of pivot. He was not a stylist, but he was a fine type of player who afterwards rendered excellent service to Luton."

He died in Dundee in June 1945.

Leading League Scorer in: 1889-1890 - 10 goals, 19 appearances (Alliance League)

2 – WILLIAM SHARPE

William Sharpe's first Alliance League goal came in the 3-1 defeat of Grimsby Town on 18th October 1890 but this was not a particularly great season for strikers. Sharpe netted six goals that season and ended up leading goalscorer.

The following season he only managed three Alliance fixtures and wasn't really seen much in a footballing context again until he appeared for Oldham County in 1896. He had a spell at Oldham Athletic in 1901.

Leading League Scorer in: 1890-1891 - 6 goals, 20 appearances (Alliance League)

3 – ROBERT DONALDSON

After playing for Airdrieonians and Blackburn Rovers, Bob Donaldson arrived at Newton Heath prior to the 1891-92 Alliance season and was an immediate success. He was an ever-present in his first season and also topped the Club's goalscoring charts as the Heathens finished second in the competition.

The following season, the Club's first in the League, saw the player top the charts again. His ratio was not so great but the competition was of course much greater.

On 3rd September 1892 he scored Newton Heath's first League goal and then on 15th October that year he netted the Club's first League hat-trick.

Bob Donaldson

In 1897 he moved to Luton Town, after making 155 League and FA Cup appearances (plus 22 Alliance League games) for the Heathens. Spells at Glossop North End and Ashford followed before he returned to Manchester as a coach (believed to be with Manchester City) in 1900. The following year the Bolton Cricket & Football Field talked of him: "Everybody had a good word for Bob; opponents, though fearing him, respected him."

Leading League Scorer in: 1891-1892 - 20 goals, 22 appearances (Alliance League) 1892-1893 - 16 goals, 26 appearances

4 – ALF FARMAN

Alf Farman joined the Heathens in 1889 with his first known Alliance League appearance coming on 9th November 1889 when he scored against Long Eaton Rangers at North Road. By the end of that season he had scored 5 goals in 17 appearances.

Always popular, by the time he topped the Club's goalscoring charts in 1893-94 he had

Alf Farman

already been given a benefit match. Three decades later team mate Fred Erentz talked of one of Farman's goals in an article in the popular newspaper of the day, the Manchester Evening Chronicle: "I saw Alf Farman hit one shot from close to the touch line. It never rose higher than your knee, and it was in the net in a flash."

Farman's last League game for the Club came on 12th January 1895 at Rotherham Town, but he only managed five appearances that season. His last League goal came at home to Stoke on 23rd March 1894 when he scored twice in the much needed 6-2 Heathens' win (sadly, the season ended in the Club's first relegation).

Leading League Scorer in:
1893-1894 - 8 goals, 18 appearances

5 – RICHARD SMITH

Halliwell-born Dick Smith joined Newton Heath during the summer of 1894 from Heywood Central and made his League debut on 8th September 1894 at Burton Wanderers. Seven days later he netted his first – and second – goal for the Heathens as Crewe were torn apart during a 6-1 Bank Street victory.

Those goals helped establish Smith as a hero, however it was his four goals in the first League Manchester derby that really established his name. The newly-relegated Heathens defeated the reformed Manchester City 5-2 at City's Hyde Road ground on 3rd November 1894. This was the first time a player had netted four for the Heathens and the season ended with Smith as the Club's top scorer.

In following seasons Smith fulfilled a number of different roles as his performances became more limited and other goalscorers took the lead role. He moved to Wigan County in 1899 but returned to Bank Street

Richard Smith

the following February following County's collapse.

He moved from the Club for the last time in January 1901 when he joined Bolton Wanderers. Altogether Smith had made 101 first team appearances for the Heathens and scored 37 goals.

Leading League Scorer in:
1894-1895 - 19 goals, 29 appearances

6 – JOE CASSIDY

Joe Cassidy was a 'strong and burly' forward who had provided Newton Heath with much needed attacking options during the final weeks of the 1892-93 season and the subsequent Test Matches, helping to prolong the club's First Division status for one more season. His initial stay at Newton Heath was fairly brief – he arrived in March 1893 and had moved to Celtic in May – but after a successful time in Glasgow he returned to the Heathens in March 1895. On his second debut for the Club he netted both goals as the Heathens beat Grimsby Town 2-0 and ended that season with 8 goals from 8 games.

The following season saw him make 19

Joe Cassidy

As you would expect Cassidy topped the goalscoring charts at his new club, but the football committee at City decided that despite his record he was not worth the £4 a week they were paying him. Against the wishes of City's secretary-manager Sam Ormerod Cassidy was sold to Middlesbrough in May 1901 for the ridiculously low figure of £75, thereby creating a loss of £175 on the deal.

At Middlesbrough Cassidy became a hero at his new club when he scored the first ever League goal at Ayresome Park. A spell as player-coach at Workington followed in 1906, but ten years later, in April 1916 the Manchester Football News reported the distressing news that: "Joe Cassidy, whose connection with Manchester football extended over such a long period, has had a mental breakdown."

Leading League Scorer in:
1895-1896 - 16 goals, 19 appearances
1896-1897 - 17 goals, 28 appearances
1898-1899 - 19 goals, 34 appearances
1899-1900 - 16 goals, 29 appearances

consecutive appearances from the start of the season with another fantastic goals to game ratio – he topped the charts with 16 goals despite missing the final 11 matches.

Cassidy was, without doubt, the first consistent striker for the Heathens in the League. Game after game, season after season, he demonstrated his qualities and was loved by Bank Street regulars. Sadly, in April 1900 financial difficulties caused the Heathens to sell him.

He moved to Manchester City for a weekly wage of £4, causing the Newton Heath directors to admit that he was the best forward they had ever had, and that it was only because the club was in such dire financial straits that they were prepared to let him go. The Heathens sold Cassidy to the Blues for £250 to ease their debts.

Shortly afterwards a Football Who's Who profiled him as: "the most useful man for several seasons in the Newton Heath team. He is one of the most difficult men to stop, and is a capital shot."

7 - HENRY BOYD

The first player to pass the twenty goals a season mark for the Heathens in the League, Scotsman Henry Boyd arrived at Bank Street in January 1897. Previously he had developed a decent reputation at West Bromwich Albion and Royal Arsenal.

He made his Newton Heath debut on 6th February 1897 against Loughborough Town a memorable one as he scored one of the Heathens goals in a 6-0 victory. He ended his first season with five goals from ten appearances but it was the following season when he really made his mark.

Boyd's hat-tricks in the opening two games of the 1897-98 season set the standard, and he ended the campaign with 22 goals from 30 games (he was an ever-present) overshadowing hero Joe Cassidy who had netted 14.

Despite the positives behind the scenes there were a few issues with the Club's

He made his debut in snowy conditions at Bank Street against Barnsley on 17th March 1900. He scored in a 3-0 win (Joe Cassidy netted twice) before a crowd of about 6,000.

The following season Leigh was the Club's top League scorer but his overall record was not as impressive as Cassidy or Boyd and he was released at the end of the season. According to author Garth Dykes Leigh had been criticised in the local press for his habit of 'fisting the ball, instead of heading it!' – maybe that's the reason he was released.

Leading League Scorer in:
1900-1901 - 14 goals, 34 appearances

9 – STEPHEN PRESTON

Mancunian Stephen Preston was, apparently, playing football near the New Inn, Ancoats, when United official Fred Palmer was walking by. Palmer stopped to watch and was impressed with centre-forward Preston. The player was signed up and on 7th September 1901 he made his mark with two goals on his debut against Gainsborough Trinity.

Stephen Preston

These were difficult times for the Heathens and Preston was one of the few reasons for watching the Club as they struggled in Division Two. They ended the season 15th (out of 18) and off the pitch financial issues dominated activities. Preston ended the season as top scorer but he was an unfortunate victim of the Club's re-birth as Manchester United in 1902.

He stayed with the new Reds for most of 1902-03 but only managed 4 appearances – he did score 3 goals though! – as new players were brought in. He moved to

Henry Boyd

new goalscoring star. He missed training at the start of 1898-99 and was suspended for a week as a result. The story goes that he was so appalled at the suspension that he went missing with the Club only learning of his whereabouts when he sent officials a telegram from Glasgow. Further suspensions followed and he was placed on the transfer list.

In August 1899 he became a Falkirk player. His last season at Bank Street had seen him make 12 appearances and score five goals. His last goal came in the 2-0 defeat of Small Heath on 25th February 1899.

Leading League Scorer in:
1897-1898 - 22 goals, 30 appearances

8 – TOM LEIGH

After a career that had seen him play for Burton Swifts and New Brighton Tower Tom Leigh joined Newton Heath in March 1900.

Stockport County in February 1903 but did become a Red once more the following September. He then spent a season in the United reserve team.

Leading League Scorer in:
1901-1902 - 11 goals, 29 appearances

10 - JOHN PEDDIE

'Jack' Peddie had developed a good goalscoring record while playing for Third Lanark in Scotland and for Newcastle during 1897-1902. However, the press of the day had also been quite critical of his speed (while at Third Lanark) and his moods (at Newcastle). United clearly ignored those aspects and focused on his goalscoring ability – everyone recognised he had an excellent and accurate shooting style.

John Peddie

He made his debut in the first League game under the new name of Manchester United (at Gainsborough Trinity on 6th September 1902) but it wasn't until his seventh League game that he found the net. That day he scored twice at Lincoln as the Reds won 3-1. He ended the season as the Club's leading goalscorer but moved to Plymouth in May 1903. That summer a football who's who described Peddie as "a clever dribbler with a tricky style, and a dead shot."

Although United managed a third place finish in 1903-04 new manager Ernest Mangnall felt Peddie could add value once more and the player returned to Bank Street in May 1904. The move proved successful again as Peddie topped United's charts again in 1904-05 as Mangnall's side once again finished third.

1905-06 saw Peddie improve his goals tally by netting 18 in 34 appearances but overall improvements in United's attack meant he was not the top scorer. Nevertheless, Peddie's record was a key aspect of United's first promotion winning season.

When the 1906-07 First Division season opened Peddie was 29 and, on the face of it, had much to offer but scandal across at Manchester City was now causing manager Mangnall to make a few audacious enquiries about the Blues' banned players. The message coming back to him was that City would be delighted to see some of their biggest stars move to United in preference to moving outside of the city.

Mangnall ultimately signed some of City's stars at the end of 1906 but a month or so earlier he had also brought Alex Menzies from Hearts. Menzies replaced Peddie as centre-forward initially, and then when Billy Meredith, Sandy Turnbull and Jimmy Bannister arrived from City Peddie's opportunities suddenly ended. Within a month of Sandy Turnbull's debut Peddie was transferred to Hearts. Some suggested it was linked to Menzies earlier move.

Peddie emigrated to Canada a short while later and was living in Detroit when he died at the age of 51 in 1928.

Leading League Scorer in:
1902-1903 - 11 goals, 30 appearances
1904-1905 - 17 goals, 32 appearances

11 - WILLIAM GRASSAM

After netting four for West Ham in their first Southern League fixture in 1900, Billy Grassam became recognised for his goalscoring exploits in several leading newspapers of the day. He arrived at Bank Street in September 1903 after a brief spell with Celtic and made his debut replacing the popular Alf Schofield on 3rd October 1903 against Woolwich Arsenal. Schofield returned for the following game but Grassam had done enough to retain a place in the side.

Grassam's first league goal for the Reds came in his fourth match when Gainsborough Trinity were defeated 4-2 on 19th December 1903. He scored several important goals that season as United pushed for promotion, these included two doubles that helped the Reds to 3-1 victories at home to Blackburn and Burnley. That season he was described as "a most conscientious player; keen and clever."

Despite ending the season as the Club's leading scorer, the return of Jack Peddie in 1904 limited Grassam's opportunities and he moved to Leyton in the close season. His last United season saw him score twice in six League games.

After Leyton he moved back to West Ham in December 1905 and re-established his career.

Leading League Scorer in:
1903-1904 - 11 goals, 23 appearances*

*Note: * Grassam's goalscoring ratio in 1903-04 was better than two other players who scored 11 League goals that season – Tom Arkesden (11 in 26 appearances) and Billy Griffiths (11 in 30 appearances).*

12 – JOHN PICKEN

Scotsman 'Jack' Picken was an instant hit as he scored on his debut as the Reds defeated Bristol City 5-1 on the opening day of the 1905-06 Division Two season. By the season's end he had netted 20 goals in 33 games and helped the Reds to promotion in second place. With fellow prolific goalscorer Peddie in the side, as well

Billy Grassam

as Charlie Sagar who scored 16 goals in 20 appearances, United's attack was impressive and there were a few high scoring games along the way (including a 6-0 win on the final day of the season when Picken scored twice). Picken also netted a hat-trick in the 4-1 victory over Chesterfield in March 1906.

In Division One Picken started well with a goal in the opening game of the season, but it's fair to say life was a bit more difficult for the Reds following promotion. Then the arrival of the former City stars, most notably Sandy Turnbull, at the start of 1907 limited his opportunities a little. Nevertheless Picken managed 26 appearances but only scored four goals.

In 1907-08 as United were storming their way towards their first League title Picken found it impossible to dislodge Turnbull and he only managed 8 appearances and one goal. He still remained an important member of the squad and after 13 League appearances (3 goals) in 1908-09, and 19 (7 goals) in 1909-10 he managed 14 appearances (4 goals) in the title winning season of 1910-11.

Picken's last United League appearance came on 18th March 1911 at Notts County and the following December he moved to Burnley. A spell at Bristol City followed before League football was suspended in 1915.

Picken died in Plymouth on 31st July 1952.

Leading League Scorer in:
1905-1906 - 20 goals, 33 appearances

John Picken

UNITED'S EUROPEAN CUP SUCCESSES

In 2008 United won the Champions League (European Cup) for the third time, forty years after the Reds' first success. It was the second time Alex Ferguson had won the trophy.

The following table shows each of United's European Cup successes and, to give an indication of how United's record rated, we include the side with the most number of European Cup wins at the time of each of those successes.

Season	Score	Runners-up	Attendance	Venue	Total European Cup Wins	Team with most European Cup Successes	English team with most European Cup successes
1967-68	4-1 (aet)	Benfica	100,000	Wembley	1	Real Madrid 6	United 1
1998-99	2-1	Bayern Munich	90,000	Barcelona	2	Real Madrid 7	Liverpool 4
2007-08	1-1 (aet*)	Chelsea	69,552	Moscow	3	Real Madrid 9	Liverpool 5

(*United won 6-5 on penalties)

■ By the end of 2011 the twelve most successful sides in the European Cup/Champions League (with the number of times each has been European Cup final runners-up in brackets) were:

Real Madrid 9 (3)

AC Milan 7 (4)

Liverpool 5 (2)

Bayern Munich 4 (4)

Barcelona 4 (3)

Ajax 4 (2)

Inter Milan 3 (2)

United 3 (2)

Benfica 2 (5)

Juventus 2 (5)

Nottingham Forest 2 (0)

Porto 2 (0)

■ United's record home attendance in the European Cup/Champions League stands at 75,598 for the 17th October 1956 meeting with Borussia Dortmund at Maine Road. This remains the largest home crowd for any English side in European competition. In 1998 Arsenal became the first side to challenge this figure when they staged their Champions League game with Lens at Wembley Stadium. Ultimately, that game was watched by 73,707 which was, at the time, the second highest European home attendance achieved by an English club.

■ *The highest attendance for a United Champions League game at Old Trafford is 75,520 for the 4th March 2008 meeting with Olympique Lyonnais.*

■ The highest crowd United have ever played in front of in European competition is 135,000 for the April 1957 semi-final at Real Madrid. In 1968 125,000 watched the next semi-final between the two sides in Madrid.

■ **United were the first English side to enter the European Cup. It is often assumed they were the first English side to play in European competition however this is not true. A representative London side and Birmingham City had already appeared in the Inter-City Fairs Cup in 1956 before United's first European Cup game.**

■ During the final decade of his life, Matt Busby looked back on United's first season of European football and the pioneering role he played in ensuring English participation: "There was strong opposition from the League, but I realised, as we moved into the mid-fifties, that football was not just an English game, but a world game. Sir Stanley Rous at the Football Association said they had no objection, so we decided to go ahead and compete."

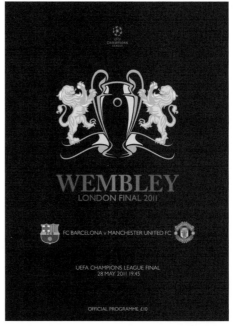

WEMBLEY
LONDON FINAL 2011

FC BARCELONA v MANCHESTER UNITED FC

UEFA CHAMPIONS LEAGUE FINAL
28 MAY 2011 19:45

OFFICIAL PROGRAMME £10

Busby says it: We must win European Cup now

Above: As the 1967-68 League campaign ended Busby vowed to find success in Europe. His team went on to become the first English European Cup winners.

Left: Bobby Charlton with the Champions Cup.

■ That first season United's games were:

12/9/56 **Preliminary Round (1st leg)**

RSC Anderlecht 0-2 United

Attendance 35,000
United scorers Viollet & Taylor

According to Matt Busby Anderlecht came close to scoring when they were awarded a penalty. The ball hit the post and bounced away from the goal instead of into it because the Anderlecht posts were square.

26/9/56 **Preliminary Round (2nd leg)**

United 10-0 RSC Anderlecht

Attendance 40,000 (Maine Road)
United scorers Viollet 4, Taylor 3, Whelan 2 & Berry

Matt Busby's view: "The second leg was an amazing night. We ran up a total of ten goals and allowed many chances to go begging, as the team tried to get David Pegg's name on the scoresheet! Anderlecht were a very good side, but we reached perfection in that match."

17/10/56 **Round 1 (1st leg)**

United 3-2 Borussia Dortmund

Attendance 75,598 (Maine Road)
United scorers Viollet 2 & Pegg

21/11/56 **Round 1 (2nd leg)**

Borussia Dortmund 0-0 United

Attendance 44,570

Matt Busby: "Salford born actor Albert Finney joined us for that second leg match, and he was as delighted as the rest of us when we survived a terrible night to draw and go through to the quarter-finals."

16/01/57 **Quarter-final (1st leg)**

Athletic Bilbao 5-3 United

Attendance 60,000
United scorers Taylor, Viollet & Whelan

Matt Busby: "Throughout our stay in Bilbao we had torrential rain, which turned the pitch into a swamp and I doubted very much if the game would actually finish. We struggled all afternoon and as the game neared its end we were 5-2 down, when Billy Whelan picked the ball up in his own half. He set off on a lazy, mazy, dribble that took him past man after man, I lost count of how many players he beat with that casual loping style of his, eventually he got a clear sight of goal and I kept saying to myself 'hit it Billy! Hit it! Go on hit it!'

"But no, on he went, until the chance was actually clear cut and finally, with a casual air about him, he slipped it past the 'keeper."

6/02/57 **Quarter-final (2nd leg)**

United 3-0 Athletic Bilbao

Attendance 70,000 (Maine Road)
United scorers Taylor, Viollet & Berry

Matt Busby: "What an unforgettable night that was. The referee controlled the match magnificently even though he disallowed two goals for us, early in the second half!"

When Johnny Berry scored the winner near the end of the match: "There was pandemonium on our bench. It was the same on the terraces and apparently even outside the ground, when the thousands locked out, realised we'd done it."

11/04/57 **Semi-final (1st leg)**

Real Madrid 3-1 United

Attendance 135,000
United scorer Taylor

25/04/57 **Semi-final (2nd leg)**

United 2-2 Real Madrid

Attendance 65,000 (Old Trafford)
United scorers Taylor & Charlton

Old Trafford now had floodlights and so the game became the first European tie at United's traditional home. Busby: "All the new pylons did was to highlight the skills of that marvellous Real Madrid team – Di Stefano, Kopa and Gento were all world class forwards and they really cut us open,

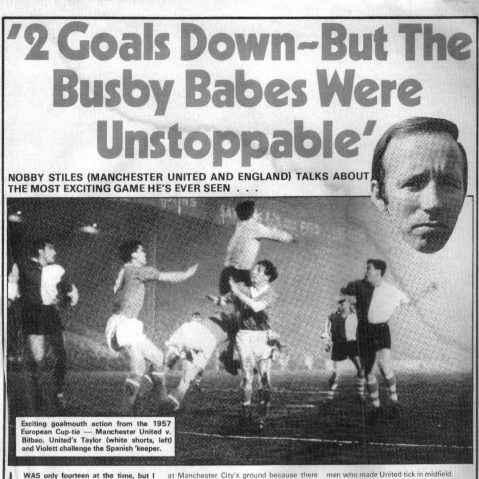

'2 Goals Down~But The Busby Babes Were Unstoppable'

NOBBY STILES (MANCHESTER UNITED AND ENGLAND) TALKS ABOUT THE MOST EXCITING GAME HE'S EVER SEEN . . .

Exciting goalmouth action from the 1957 European Cup-tie — Manchester United v. Bilbao. United's Taylor (white shorts, left) and Violett challenge the Spanish 'keeper.

I WAS only fourteen at the time, but I don't think I'll ever watch a more exciting game than Manchester United's match against Atletico Bilbao in the European Cup back in 1957. For tension and atmosphere I've never known its equal.

It was the second-leg of the Quarter-Finals, United having lost 5-3 in Spain to the club now managed by former Wolves boss Ronnie Allen. United were reaching a peak with the great Duncan Edwards, Johnny Byrne and Tommy Taylor in the line-up . . . all to be so tragically killed in the Munich air disaster exactly one year afterwards in February, 1958.

I signed for the club three months later and was lucky enough to know these great footballers. But this night I was on the terraces wondering if United could possibly pull back such a defit against one of the world's finest teams. A side which contained seven full internationals.

There were about 65,000 people packed into Maine Road to watch the game — held

at Manchester City's ground because there were no floodlights at Old Trafford in those days. The atmosphere was electric.

For most of the first-half it seemed that Bilbao, who flung seven or eight men into defence, would hold out. But three minutes before the interval United scored.

ALL-OUT ATTACK

Bill Whelan collected the ball in midfield and sent Edwards surging through the middle. His pass to Tommy Taylor rebounded to Dennis Viollet who slammed the ball into the net. So United had cut the arrears to one goal and hopes for a place in the Semi-Final grew.

United flung everything into the attack in the second-half, but for a time it looked as though the ball just would not go into the net. Then 20 minutes from the end Taylor scored from an Eddie Colman free-kick.

I idolised Eddie who, with Duncan Edwards, both only 20-year-olds, were the

men who made United tick in midfield.

With both teams all square on aggregate, the game built up to a terrific climax.

Just one more goal would take United through to the Semi-Final of the European Cup — the first English club ever to reach that stage of the competition.

Five minutes from the end Edwards gave Tommy Taylor possession, the England striker took the ball to the by-line and pulled it back for Johnny Berry to hammer home. What a moment! The whole crowd erupted. We knew United had won.

Yes, despite all the matches I have seen since then, none compares with that one. I don't think anyone who was at Maine Road that night will ever forget it.

But if that was a match to remember, there's another game I want to forget — the England v. West Germany World Cup game in Mexico. I didn't play, but it was agony watching the Germans pull back from two goals down. I wouldn't like to see that again!

23

as we tried to pressure them in the first half."

"We were 2-0 down at half-time and in reality, out of the European Cup, but my boys never lie down and in the second half

they threw everything at Madrid and we eventually drew the match but couldn't retrieve the deficit from the first leg.

"My consolation at the time was that Real Madrid was a genuine world class team,

In front of 135,000 Tommy Taylor (9) celebrates scoring at Real Madrid, April 1957.

whereas we were a wee bit short, but we'd done well, gone so close to matching them, that I thought, another year should see us ready to take them on again...."

Sadly, the Munich Air Crash was to bring an end to the possibility of that great United side meeting the magnificent Spanish team.

Inevitably, the disaster had an impact on how the Reds viewed the European Cup. In the years that followed it became something the Club desperately wanted to win as a tribute to those players killed or injured in the crash. During the 1970s George Best looked back to a decade earlier when he first joined United and remembered: "The European Cup was a subject that was always on everybody's minds at Old Trafford. They were for ever talking about it. I would say they even had an obsession about it. I often wondered if we'd ever win it."

United, of course, won the trophy in 1968 with Best one of the star men: "We were fated to win the European Cup. There is no doubt in my mind about that, but it seemed that, that evening in May was the end of the Club's dream. Manchester United had climbed the mountain and it now appeared to be content to slither down the other side. That should have been the start for Manchester United, the beginning of their domination of European football, as it turned out, it was the end."

Those words were a little harsh, but it is fair to say that until the arrival of Alex Ferguson in 1986 and, significantly, the restructuring of English football and European competition in the 1990s, United's opportunity for European glory seemed faint to say the least. Under Ferguson, however, the Reds have become a true European force, proved by their appearance in the Champions League final in 2011. Although the Reds were defeated by Barcelona, they have proved to be the most consistent of all British sides in European competition during the last decade.

44

The Football Season Daily Reminder
September

1st September 1896

The Club's first ever League game played on 1st September ended in a 2-0 win over Gainsborough at Bank Street, Clayton. On this same date in 1948 United were defeated 4-3 in the League by Blackpool in a re-match of the previous season's FA Cup final (right).

2nd September 1989

United defeated Portsmouth 3-2 in the second round League Cup first leg with goals from Ince (2) and Wallace. The return leg ended goalless before an Old Trafford crowd of 26,698.

3rd September 1892

Newton Heath lost their opening game in the Football League 4-3 at Blackburn Rovers.

4th September 1985

Goals from Frank Stapleton (2) and Mark Hughes brought a 3-0 victory at home to Newcastle before a crowd of 51,102.

5th September 1979

After losing the first leg 2-1, United defeated Spurs 3-1 in the two-legged second round League Cup tie meaning a 4-3 aggregate victory.

6th September 1913

An own goal from Sheffield Wednesday's Spoors helped United to a 3-1 victory at Hillsborough.

7th September 1908

Jimmy Turnbull scored both United's goals as they defeated Bury 2-1 at Bank Street. In the first three games of the season he netted 8 goals.

8th September 1984

Newcastle were thrashed 5-0 at Old Trafford with goals from Strachan (2), Hughes, Moses and Olsen.

9th September 2006

The Reds won 1-0 at Old Trafford in the Premier League meeting with Tottenham Hotspur. The United goalscorer was Ryan Giggs and the attendance was 75,453.

10th September 1927

Despite a goal from the popular Joe Spence United suffered an astounding 7-1 defeat at home to

Newcastle. There was better news on this date in 1898 however. Newton Heath defeated Manchester City 3-0 in Division Two.

11th September 2010

United drew 3-3 at Everton in the Premier League with goals from Berbatov, Fletcher and Vidic. Attendance was 36,556.

12th September 1925

The first Maine Road Manchester derby ended 1-1 in front of a crowd of 62,994. City had moved to the stadium in 1923 but as United were a Second Division outfit at the time, Manchester had to wait until the ground's third season for a derby match. Eleven years later the Reds beat the Blues 3-2 before an Old Trafford crowd of 68,796 in the first derby of the 1936-37 season. It remained the largest Old Trafford derby attendance until December 2006.

13th September 1968

Highly controversial half-back Frank Barson died in Birmingham at the age of 77. Barson was a United star between 1922 and 1928 and loved by Reds everywhere but he also displayed a physical approach during play. He was banned in 1926 for a couple of months after an incident in the 1926 FA Cup semi-final with Manchester City. The City captain Sam Cowan was knocked out and subsequent investigations by the FA pointed the finger at Barson. He captained United back to the First Division in 1925 after being promised a pub if he could achieve the return. On the same date in 1890 Newton Heath were defeated 3-1 at Grimsby in the Alliance League.

14th September 1972

Forward Wyn Davies made a surprise £60,000 move across Manchester from City to United. He made his League debut nine days later a memorable one with a goal in the 3-0 victory over Derby County before an Old Trafford crowd of 48,255.

15th September 2007

A tense Premier League match with Everton turned United's way when Vidic scored the only goal in the 83rd minute at Goodison Park.

8   BLUE AND WHITE.

For MOTORING, SPORTS, and all OUTDOOR WEAR.

THE

"KUSHY-PEAK" CAP

(PATENTED)

Will be found IDEALLY COMFORTABLE, being made on SCIENTIFIC LINES, and Soft Fitting on the Forehead.

OBTAINABLE AT ALL OUTFITTERS ———— ANYWHERE.

SATURDAY, SEPTEMBER 12th, 1925.

MANCHESTER CITY

1
J. F. MITCHELL
Goal

2   COOKSON   3   M'CLOY
Right Back   Left Back

4   SHARP   5   COWAN   6   PRINGLE
Right Half-Back   Centre Half-Back   Left Half-Back

7   AUSTIN   8   WARNER   9   ROBERTS   10   JOHNSON   11   HICKS
Outside Right   Inside Right   Centre   Inside Left   Outside Left

KICK-OFF 3-15 P.M.   THE PUBLIC GOAL MANCHESTER HIPPODROME

Referee:
I. JOSEPHS, Boldon.
Linesmen:
O. Reece and C. W. Schofield.

12   MACPHERSON   13   RENNOX   14   HANSON   15   SMITH   16   SPENCE
Outside Left   Inside Left   Centre   Inside Right   Outside Right

17   MANN   18   BARSON   19   BENNION
Left Half-Back   Centre Half-Back   Right Half-Back

20   SILCOCK   21   MOORE
Left Back   Right Back

22
STEWARD
Goal

MANCHESTER UNITED

SLACK & COX LTD.

FOR

Bass, Worthington, Guinness & Mineral Waters

Authorised Bottlers of VI-TONICA and VI-MALTO.

HYDE ROAD, MANCHESTER.

MONDAY, SEPTEMBER 21. 1908.

Manchester United's Supremacy.

Thornley opened the score for City.

Whose ball? An altercation between Blair and Meredith.

Ross worked head and foot.

Turnbull's header made the game all square.

Roberts rose to the occasion.

16th September 1967

A crowd of 47,274 witnessed a 1-1 draw at Sheffield Wednesday with George Best scoring for the Reds.

17th September 1892

The Gorton Reporter gave a brief comment on the previous Saturday's (10/09/1892) game against Burnley: "Newton Heath seem to have been lucky with their new Scotchmen, as all are giving great satisfaction. On Saturday A. Mitchell (late Airdrieonians) was the best back of the field, whilst the forwards made rings round the Burnley halves, but failed with Hillman [the goalkeeper]."

The game had ended 1-1 with Scotsman Robert Donaldson scoring for the Heathens. Donaldson had scored the Club's first ever League goal on 3rd September 1892. Full back Andrew Mitchell proved to be a consistent performer during two seasons with the Club.

18th September 1968

In the first European match after winning the European Cup a Denis Law hat-trick gave United a 3-1 victory at Waterford. The return leg at Old Trafford ended in a 7-1 victory before 41,750.

19th September 1908

Goals from Harold Halse and Jimmy Turnbull gave United a 2-1 victory in the Hyde Road Manchester derby before a crowd of around 40,000 (above). City had taken the lead through Irvine Thornley before Turnbull's header brought the equaliser.

20th September 1947

A crowd of approximately 78,000 witnessed the first post-war Manchester derby. A tense match ended goalless. This was the record crowd for an all-Manchester match until the 2011 FA Cup semi-final at Wembley stadium.

MANCHESTER CITY

1
THURLOW
Goal

2
SPROSTON
Right Back

3
WESTWOOD
Left Back

4
WALSH
Right Half-Back

5
FAGAN
Centre Half-Back

6
EMPTAGE
Left Half-Back

7
WHARTON
Outside Right

8
SMITH
Inside Right

9
McMORRAN
Centre

10
CAPEL
Inside Left

11
CLARKE
Outside Left

Referee :
C. FLETCHER (Northwich)
Kick-off 3-0 p.m.

Linesmen :
A. C. DENHAM (Red Flag)
A. N. SHAKESPEARE (Blue Flag)

11
MITTEN
Outside Left

10
PEARSON
Inside Left

9
ROWLEY
Centre

8
MORRIS
Inside Right

7
DELANEY
Outside Right

6
McGLEN
Left Half-Back

5
CHILTON
Centre Half-Back

4
WARNER
Right Half-Back

3
ASTON
Left Back

2
CAREY
Right Back

1
CROMPTON
Goal

MANCHESTER UNITED

5

The return fixture, also played at Maine Road, was watched by 71,690.

21st September 2008

Despite an 18th minute opener from Park, United ended up drawing 1-1 at Chelsea. At the time the Reds lay in 15th place and some were already suggesting United would miss out on the title – they of course ended up winning their 18th title that season.

22nd September 1984

A crowd of 56,638 witnessed a 1-1 draw between United and Liverpool. Gordon Strachan scored for the home side.

23rd September 1964

Clayton Blackmore was born in Neath. He went on to make his United debut on 16th May 1984 at Nottingham Forest. He appeared in 200 (plus 44 substitute) first team games and scored 25 goals.

24th September 1983

Frank Stapleton ensured a successful day as he scored the only goal of the United-Liverpool League game at Old Trafford.

25th September 1963

United's first game in the European Cup Winners' Cup ended in a 1-1 draw at Willem II. David Herd was the Club's historic first goalscorer. The Reds won the return 6-1 in front of an Old Trafford crowd of 46,272.

26th September 1896

Goalkeeper Frank Barrett made his debut in the 4-0 victory over Newcastle before a Bank Street crowd of around 7,000. He stayed with United for

Joe Jordan netted the only goal against City on 30 September 1978.

THE BIG BOOK OF UNITED

almost four years before moving to New Brighton Tower. He died in 1907 at the relatively young age of 35. Officials sent £14 to his widow.

27th September 2008

A 60th minute Ronaldo penalty gave United the lead at home to Bolton and then 17 minutes later

Wayne Rooney made it 2-0 to ensure victory. These were the first League goals by either player that season.

28th September 1985

Mark Hughes scored the only goal at home to Southampton before 52,449.

29th September 1906

Half-back Frank Buckley made his United debut in a 1-1 draw with Derby at Bank Street. Although Buckley only managed 3 appearances with United he did go on to become a renowned manager in the game, most notably with Wolverhampton Wanderers between 1927 and 1944. 104 years after Buckley's debut, the Reds won at Valencia in the Champions League. Substitute Hernandez provided the only goal.

30th September 1967

United defeated City 2-1 with goals from Bobby Charlton (left) in the Maine Road derby match. The game was watched by 62,942 (above).

UNITED'S LEADING SCORERS

Our story of all the players who have topped the seasonal League goalscoring charts for the Reds through to the start of the 2011-12 season moves on to 1906-07.

THE PROFILES
(PART TWO)

13 – GEORGE WALL

Born in a coal mining area near Sunderland George Wall had played for several local clubs, including Jarrow in the Northern Alliance, before he signed for Barnsley in 1903. In Yorkshire he developed at a rapid rate and in 1907 a football who's who claimed: "Towards the end of his first season with the Yorkshire club his reputation was such as made it impossible for him to stay there. Stoke were offered the first chance, Manchester United completed the transfer on March 31, 1906. The sum paid was £175."

Wall made his debut at Clapton Orient on 7th April 1906 a memorable one by scoring the only goal of the match. The new signing had added a new edge to the Reds' promotion challenge and United only dropped one point in the final seven games of the season with Wall scoring three goals in six appearances.

The following season, despite a few struggles for United, Wall proved he was more than capable of adapting to life in Division One as he netted 11 goals in 38 appearances, ending the season as the Reds' top League scorer. He was an ever-present and, unlike some of his contempories, he survived the arrival of the new stars. Those that had been banned from playing for City. He played on the opposite wing to Billy Meredith and helped

G. WALL
MANCHESTER UNITED F.C.

make United's attack highly potent in the years that followed.

Wall improved his goals tally in 1907-08, scoring 19 in 36 League games, but Sandy Turnbull was the leading scorer as United won the League title. The Reds won the title by an impressive nine points (remember it was only two points for a win back then) that season and Wall had scored some very important goals (he was United's only scorer in three games, but also scored in games where only one goal separated the Reds from their losing opponents). He missed only two games that season with one of those ending in defeat. Only Billy Meredith had appeared in more League games for the Reds during their Championship winning season.

In 1908-09 United found it more difficult as opponents seemed to raise their game against the Champions and, as a result, opportunities became more limited. In the circumstances Wall's 11 goals in 34 appearances was a highly impressive tally. Of course, while United were inconsistent in the League their FA Cup form was outstanding as they won the FA Cup for the first time. While Wall somehow failed to find the net during the Cup run, it is fair to say he contributed a great deal to the Reds' attacking options and thoroughly deserved his FA Cup winner's medal.

Away from Bank Street, this period also saw Wall make his first England appearances. On 18th March 1907 he made his international debut in a 1-1 draw at Craven Cottage against Wales and followed this with an appearance against Ireland in Belfast the following February. He went on to make a total of seven international appearances, scoring twice (both coming in the 2-0 victory over Scotland on 3rd April 1909 which brought England success in the British Home International Tournament).

This was a great time for Wall and in 1909-10 he topped United's goalscoring charts for a second time as the Reds finished fifth in Division One, and then he won another League Championship medal the following

season. By that time he had also scored in Old Trafford's opening game (V Liverpool, 19th February 1910).

By the outbreak of war Wall was still a key member of United's attack, although in 1914-15 his appearances had reduced (he played 17 League games that season). As with so many players he joined the Forces, wearing the uniform of the Black Watch Regiment, and making occasional footballing appearances when he could.

Once the war ended he joined Oldham Athletic (his former United colleague Charlie Roberts was there and ultimately became the Latics' manager) and netted 12 goals in 74 League games. At this time Oldham were a Division One side that had narrowly missed out on the title in the final pre-war season, so the move was not seen as a step down by any stretch of the imagination.

Spells at Hamilton Academical, Rochdale and the progressive Ashton National followed. His last recorded playing performances came for the Manchester Ship Canal team.

George Wall passed away in Manchester in 1962.

Leading League Scorer in:
1906-1907 - 11 goals, 38 appearances
1909-1910 – 14 goals, 32 appearances

14 – ALEXANDER TURNBULL

Born in the strong footballing community of Hurlford near Kilmarnock, Sandy Turnbull first made his name with his local side Hurlford Thistle. In July 1902 Manchester City signed the forward and he was an immediate success, playing alongside the nation's biggest footballing star of the period Billy Meredith.

Turnbull and Meredith combined superbly with the Scotsman often benefitting from the Welshman's amazing work on the wing. He had a wonderful career at City, netting 60 goals in 119 League and FA Cup appearances and was a key member of City's 1904 FA Cup winning side.

These were great days for City. All

Mancunians celebrated City's success but their rapid development was ultimately to have a major impact on the Reds and on Turnbull. To understand the Red significance it is vital to explain what happened to the Blues. The FA felt that the Blues had developed too quickly as a football side and they performed investigations into the club's finances following the Cup success. They found a few anomalies and issues, but nothing the FA could really get their teeth into. Locally, all Mancunians and most northern journalists felt the southern-based FA were simply pursuing City because they were one of a new breed of professional sides who were starting to direct the way the game should evolve – the Football League tended to support City's interests at this time recognising that some of their more ambitious member clubs were being held back by the more traditional amateurish viewpoint that still dogged the FA.

For Sandy Turnbull none of this was of much concern until City faced Aston Villa, a side still viewed as one of football's aristocracy by the FA, in a game that could set City up for Manchester's first League title success in 1904-05 (City had finished third in their Cup winning season the previous year).

The Villa-City game was full of incident and, unfortunately, gave the FA an excuse to investigate once again. With thirty minutes to go City were losing 3-2 but were now in control after a disastrous first half had seen them concede three goals. Sandy Turnbull had scored the Blues second and was a real handful, particularly for the Villa captain, England international Alec Leake.

During those final thirty minutes the game became progressively more violent with Sandy Turnbull seemingly upsetting Leake time and time again. The Bolton Football Field reporter outlined his view: "Turnbull was in his dourest dribbling mood, dashing about the ball with his whole heart set on victory. Leake found him a real hard opponent and, becoming annoyed at the rough impact, gathered up a handful of dirt and hurled it at the City man. Turnbull was not hurt and responded with an acknowledgement favoured by the bourgeoisie - thrusting two fingers in a figurative manner at the Villa man. He then says that Leake appeared to look towards the referee as though appealing, and not catching his eye, 'gave Turnbull a backhander'. The latter immediately responded with his fists and Leake was restrained by his fellow players from retaliating further."

Although Turnbull had developed a reputation for a rough style of play it appears that he was not the guilty one this time. Unfortunately, Leake was viewed as a gentleman and many were convinced that he would only react, not provoke. The Villa biased Sports Argus tried to convince its readership that Leake was entirely innocent and that he had merely enquired what Turnbull was doing rather than throw dirt at him and give him a 'backhander'. It also stated that the City man had hit Leake at least twice although no one else saw this or reported it.

The game continued but frequent fights broke out, ending any chance City had of equalising. When the final whistle went the controversy continued. The Bolton Football Field reported: "Turnbull was coming off the ground (I think he was almost the first of the City players) and was going down the covered passage to the visitors' dressing room when someone, not a player, sprang out from the urinal and grabbed Turnbull, pulled him inside the Villa dressing room and the door was shut behind him. I thought the whole thing was in fun until, within a few seconds, the door was opened and Turnbull was pitched out heavily, by whom I could not see. He was yelling with pain and fright, and he had obviously been badly handled for his right cheek was grazed with a black mark or dirt (something like a cyclist describes as a cinder rash) and he had a mark on his ribs where he had been kicked."

Nobody disputed that Turnbull had been the victim of a deliberate attack by Villa men, but incredibly the Birmingham Sports Argus tried to justify it, thus causing further insults to fly from Manchester to Birmingham and vice versa. Significantly, it wasn't merely the Villa players and employees who were attacking the Blues as police had to be called into the ground to protect the City players. Leaving Villa Park was also a nightmare as an angry mob stoned the City party.

The evidence was clear – Turnbull had been deliberately attacked and was the innocent party. Sure he retaliated and that had to be investigated but the part England international Leake played in the matter was the main issue. Despite the evidence the FA astounded northern football fans and the media when they chose to focus on Turnbull's role and not Leake's. Then rumours started to circulate that City's captain Billy Meredith was supposed to have offered Leake a pre-match £10 bribe to throw the game. Initially Leake laughed at those suggestions when the FA first approached him but for some reason his story changed as the investigations progressed. Leake's part in the whole affair was not investigated after this point and many journalists suggested this was because of the FA's view that he was a respectable England international, while Welshman Meredith and Scotsman Turnbull were from a professional northern club.

The FA didn't even bother to consider what happened to Turnbull in the Villa dressing room. The media viewed this as deeply unfair, while no one from the FA seemed to be doing anything to recognise that Turnbull was clearly the victim.

From that point on the FA had found the excuse they had been looking for to investigate City further. This time they were more thorough and found the Blues had made illegal payments to their star players, although the northern media continued to explain that none of the Country's leading clubs were innocent and that a review of any side's finances would prove the same.

Ultimately City were punished severely

with 17 players banned along with various officials. Sandy Turnbull was one of the banned players and it was decided that once his ban was over he had to move away from City. The Blues, dismayed by the FA's findings, wanted the players' suffering to end and they encouraged some of the biggest stars, including Turnbull, to sign for United. It was the sensible thing to do and the relationship between the two Manchester sides was such that everyone felt this was right and proper (and one in the eye for the FA!).

Four star players – Bannister, Burgess and Meredith joined Turnbull - all made their United debuts on New Year's day 1907 against, ironically, Aston Villa. It was with some satisfaction that Turnbull, the man who had been a central figure on the day of the infamous Villa-City match of 1905, netted the only goal. Meredith had set the goal up of course with a terrific cross.

The impact on the Reds was huge. Turnbull

Sandy Turnbull

and the others helped transform the side. Prior to his arrival the Reds' record was not a great one as they struggled to establish themselves in the top division. They were on 18 points after winning 6 games, drawing 6 and losing 9, while with Turnbull and the others they achieved 11 victories, 2 draws, and only 4 defeats.

In 1907-08 the Reds won the title for the first time, becoming the first Manchester side to win the League, and Turnbull, alongside the ever-popular Meredith, was a star. He was the leading goalscorer with 25 goals from 30 games – this made him United's record goalscorer with a figure not bettered until Rowley netted 26 in 37 games during the 1946-47 season.

The following season Turnbull only managed five goals in 19 League appearances but the story of the season was United's first FA Cup success. Turnbull, of course, was vitally important to that trophy win, scoring the only goal of the final. In 1924 the Topical Times looked back on the final and Turnbull's goal: "A little more than twenty minutes had gone when the United forwards, on one of the very few occasions, were able to attack in a body and, following nearly perfect combination, Halse took a shot from rather close range and set the crossbar shivering.

"Sandy Turnbull, bland and childlike (there was much that was strangely reminiscent in the ways of Ah Sin [a character in a play co-written by Mark Twain] in the ways of Turnbull) seemed to anticipate what would happen, and when the ball flew back into play he was all readiness to pounce upon it, and flying into the far corner of the net did he send it.

"Clay was powerless to save. And we all said the goal was precisely what might have been expected from Turnbull."

Turnbull had cemented his place in the Reds' history and, like Meredith, was one of the first true stars to be idolised at both City and United.

In 1910-11 Turnbull scored 18 goals from 35

League appearances as the Reds won the title once more. By the time the Football League was brought to a halt in 1915 due to the First World War, he had appeared in 245 League and FA Cup games for the Reds, netting 100 goals. Unfortunately, his United career ended in disgrace as he was punished for his part in the match-fixing scandal of 1915 which saw United beat Liverpool 2-0 in suspicious circumstances. The following game (Newcastle, 3rd April 1915) was his last League match.

During the war years he took part in military action in northern France. Sadly, on 3rd May 1917 he was killed in action with his name being recorded on the monument at Arras. Some historians claim he participated in the famous Christmas Day battlefield match against the Germans.

Despite the two FA investigations during his career, it is fair to say that Turnbull will always remain a highly significant early star. Without him the Reds (or the Blues for that matter) may never have found their first successes.

Leading League Scorer in:
1907-1908 - 25 goals, 30 appearances

15 – JAMES TURNBULL

Jimmy Turnbull, often incorrectly assumed to be Sandy's brother, joined the Reds from Southern League club Leyton in May 1907. Previously he had been a successful forward with Dundee, Falkirk and Rangers in Scotland. His arrival at Leyton in May 1906 was viewed positively as, at this time, many of the Southern League clubs viewed their competition as a rival for the League, or at least the Second Division.

At United Turnbull made his debut in the 4-1 victory at Chelsea on 28th September 1907 and his first goal came the following week as the Reds beat Nottingham Forest 4-0 at Bank Street. By the end of the Championship winning season he had scored 10 goals in 26 games.

As Champions the pressure was on when the Reds started the 1908-09 season but Turnbull made sure they opened the campaign in style. He scored an astounding ten goals in the first five League games, including four against Middlesbrough on 12th September 1908. However, United's form dipped. Significantly, the first defeat of the season came in a game Turnbull missed and they also lost the next two matches he was absent from.

By the end of the season Turnbull was top scorer with 17 goals from only 22 League games (in a 38 game season) as the Reds finished 13th. Who knows how the side would have progressed had Turnbull managed more games.

In 1909-10 Turnbull appeared in 19 League games, scoring 9, and the following summer he returned to Scotland briefly as agreement on a new contract was not reached. He moved to Bradford and then Chelsea, before returning to the Reds in September 1914.

His second spell was only brief as United gave him a one month trial. Chelsea asked for a transfer fee of £300 but the Reds felt they could not afford the fee due to the wartime situation. Inevitably, Turnbull was on the move again, this time to Hurst – the Ashton-under-Lyne club that the Reds had often competed against in the early days of Newton Heath.

In 1924 the Topical Times talked of Turnbull's approach to the game and gave an indication as to why he returned to Scotland in 1910 and perhaps also the reason he missed some League games: "If Turnbull had not been so impetuous he would have won higher fame than he did."

Interestingly, a who's who once claimed his occupation was 'Builder' and his hobby was 'Shooting'.

Leading League Scorer in:
1908-1909 - 17 goals, 22 appearances

16 – ENOCH WEST

'Knocker' West was a popular player with Nottingham Forest before he arrived at Old Trafford in June 1910. In 1907-08 he was the First Division's leading goalscorer with

26 in 35 appearances and so, by the time he joined United, he already had a nationwide reputation for his goalscoring.

Known as a particularly fast player – one of his hobbies was athletics – West was also employed in the coal mining industry while at Forest.

On 1st September 1910 he made his United debut at Woolwich Arsenal on the opening day of the season. The Reds won 2-1 with, of course, West opening his account. This was the first of 19 League goals that season as West became the Club's leading scorer and a worthy replacement for Jimmy Turnbull. His goals helped United win their second League title and ensured he became one of Old Trafford's first heroes.

He led the United goalscoring charts again in the two following seasons, with his best tally coming in 1912-13 when he scored 21 in 36 games.

The 1913-14 season was not so great for

Enoch West

West – he only managed 6 goals in 30 games – and then 1914-15 ended in disgrace as he was banned from football for life for his part in the infamous match fixing scandal of April 1914. West always proclaimed his innocence (unlike some of his fellow players) and even took legal action against the FA and the Daily Sketch newspaper. He also appealed against the findings but because he maintained his innocence it seems he was treated harshly.

Years later, in fact right up until his death in 1965, he continued to stress his innocence. By that time he could have admitted his guilt and it would not have been an issue, after all he had already been punished more than the others, but the fact he did not perhaps proves he really was innocent.

In 2003 West's story was covered extensively in the wonderful "Free The Manchester United One" book by Graham Sharpe.

Leading League Scorer in:
1910-1911 - 19 goals, 35 appearances
1911-1912 – 17 goals, 32 appearances
1912-1913 – 21 goals, 36 appearances

17 – GEORGE ANDERSON

Born in Cheetham during the 1892-1893 football season George Anderson joined United in September 1911 from Bury. He made one League appearance for the Reds during 1911-12 when he played as centre-forward in the 2-1 victory over Everton on 9th September, but spent most of the year in the reserves.

The following season he didn't get his chance to impress until the tenth match of the season at home to Notts County on 2nd November 1912. He took his chance well and scored as the Reds won 2-1. He remained first choice for most of the season and by the end of the season his goalscoring ratio of one goal every other game made him the Club's second highest scorer (12 goals in 24 games).

Anderson topped the goalscoring charts in 1913-14 and 1914-15 but his career was suddenly the focus of much attention as he was the player who scored twice in the match-fixing game between United and Liverpool in April 1915. He was not however one of the players banned for life (indeed he gave evidence against Enoch West) and did in fact make some United appearances during the 1915-16 wartime competition.

In February 1916 he angered United when he moved to Ireland to play for Belfast United without permission. The Reds contacted the Football League and Anderson was forced to return to Old Trafford.

As the First World War neared its end Anderson hit the headlines again as a result of further match-fixing allegations. In March 1918 he was charged by the police with

George Anderson

"having conspired with persons unknown who had made bets on the results of various matches."

The games the charge referred to were a 1-0 home victory over Burnley on 29th December 1917 and an Everton-Blackpool game of 12th January 1918. The matter came to light when some of his teammates discussed the Burnley game with United officials. On 8th January Anderson had been banned from attending Old Trafford by officials and then, after the Everton-Blackpool game, the Football League are reported to have given him an indefinite ban.

On 24th March 1918 the News Of The World reported: "Allegations of attempting to bribe certain football players into 'squaring matches' in order that bookmakers might reap the benefit were made at Liverpool, when George Anderson, formerly a Manchester United footballer was charged with having conspired to defraud unknown persons who had wagered upon the result of certain football matches. Mr Wingate Saul [Everton FC, the prosecutors], said it was alleged that the defendant on behalf of bookmakers, attempted to bribe Everton players when they met Blackpool on January 8th. He offered £10 to Fleetwood of the Everton team, and later increased this sum to £60, to be divided between six members of the team."

The newspaper went on to describe the scene further: "Another player Gault, was brought in, who said to Anderson, 'Why do we receive £60 for losing the match?'. Anderson replied 'This is the only way players have of getting a living as they are not paid for playing. Don't be afraid as there are no names mentioned'.

"Anderson added 'I was at Bolton last Friday

paying out money for the match squared the week before. Bolton and Port Vale'."

Using terminology that today suggests prejudice and discrimination the newspaper continued: "In an interview with a Jew, who had not been traced, Fleetwood said 'the boys wanted £20 to be going on with', and this sum was to be handed over on the Friday night by Anderson."

Everton's players had reported the discussions directly to Everton's Will Cuff, who was also a senior figure within the Football League, and they passed on to him the money they had been given. The News Of The World: "After Everton had won 7-2, Anderson called at Fleetwood's house and demanded [the money's] return. He said that this man would lose a terrible lot of money. Dealing with other charges, Mr Saul said that Anderson and the Jew [their terminology] called upon the Oldham captain and offered to make it 'worthwhile' for Blackburn to beat Oldham. They offered to provide him with 'a goalkeeper who could let the ball through'. What the defendant was doing was acting for a professional bookmaker and attempting to 'square' matches to suit the book of the bookmaker on the particular match involved.

"In respect of the Manchester United and Burnley match, Anderson unsuccessfully approached Silcock, Meehan and Woodcock. The hearing was adjourned to Tuesday. Anderson being granted bail."

Inevitably, Anderson denied the charges and, although seven professional footballers gave evidence against him, no hard evidence could be produced. It was suggested that Anderson was working for a Scottish bookmaker but the player denied this.

Despite Anderson's proclaimed innocence he was found guilty and sentenced to eight months imprisonment with hard labour. Some suggested this indicated that the player may have given false evidence as part of the investigations into Enoch West. As recently as 2003 author Graham Sharpe wrote: "Anderson's conviction for match fixing must cast doubt on his own evidence against West. He may well have been looking to implicate West as a scapegoat and so draw attention away from his own dodgy dealings."

His younger brother Thomas signed for Bolton Wanderers in 1921.

There are conflicting stories on what happened to Anderson after his prison sentence came to an end. Some reports suggest he remained in the Manchester area and died in the region in 1959 while others claim he died in Elk City, Oklahoma in October 1931. There is clearly some confusion between players with similar names.

Leading League Scorer in:
1913-1914 - 15 goals, 32 appearances
1914-1915 – 10 goals, 23 appearances

18 – JOE SPENCE

"Give it to Joe" was a poplar expression on the Old Trafford terraces during the mid-twenties when Joe Spence was at his United peak. The view was that if Spence had the ball United would score and, considering that he topped the Reds' goalscoring charts for five out of nine seasons during that decade, it seems as if the shout was accurate. At the 1926 FA Cup semi-final a United fan even held up a placard saying 'Play Up United – Give It To Joe'.

Northumberland born Spence arrived at United in March 1919. He was twenty at this point, and had played for Scotswood in the Northern Victory League during 1918-19 after first being noticed at school where he scored 42 of his side's 49 goals in his first season. Considering his age he had already packed a lot into his life – he'd been a coalminer at the age of 13; served with the Machine Gun Corps at the age of 17; and had made wartime guest appearances for sides such as Liverpool reserves.

At Old Trafford he first played during the final season of wartime competition, making his debut on 29th March 1919 where he scored four in a 5-1 win against Bury. The

Joe Spence

following August he appeared in the first United Football League game since the end of the war, and on 8th September 1919 he scored his first actual League goal in the 3-1 victory at Sheffield Wednesday.

He ended the season as United's top scorer with 14 goals from 32 League games but these were not great seasons for the Reds. Although there was always hope of repeating the pre-war successes the truth was that United had been unable to properly replace players of the calibre of Sandy Turnbull, Enoch West and Charlie Roberts. Billy Meredith was still at United, but only just as he was often in disagreement with the Club about benefit payments and had made it clear that he wanted to return to City (he had spent most of the war years there). United were desperate for a new hero and the time was right for Spence to become the new face of the Reds.

In 1929 Meredith looked back on this time and talked of a practical joke played at Spence's expense: "Joe once had a whippet of which he was very proud, and which he

tended with the greatest care. I may say it was a prize dog and worthy of Joe's efforts. We were staying at Whitley Bay at the time and Joe had brought his whippet along with him for the chief reason that he wanted his father to see it.

"It must be explained now that red and raw meat is the only kind a whippet should have. White meat and bones are absolutely taboo for the welfare of the dog. Well, one day, Joe was out and Jack Pullar, the United trainer, and I put our heads together and conceived a pretty plot. We went out into the yard where Joe's whippet was kept and bandaged it up in cotton wool and got it to lay down on its side, after which we artistically spread some chicken bones around the dog and his kennel.

"The whole effect was to make it appear as if the dog was in a bad state of sickness after having had a 'gorge' of chicken. When Joe returned the whole place was soon in an uproar. Joe went absolutely stark, staring mad, and stamped around breathing fire and vengeance, and you can bet our laughter did not help matters. Nor did he seem pleased when we suggested that the whippet should be given a dose of opium pills!"

The story obviously has no direct relationship with Spence's footballing ability, but it does give an indication of the relationships and humour enjoyed at United during this period.

In 1920-21 Spence was one of four players who shared the honour of being United's leading League scorer, but he had only managed seven goals as the Reds ended the season 13th. Personally, Spence had a better season in 1921-22 (scoring more than double his previous season's tally) but United were relegated for only the second time in their history. At Old Trafford in October 1921 Spence had netted all United's goals as they beat City 3-1 in the Manchester derby – only the third hat-trick recorded in the fixture at this point.

Bizarrely, despite his great reputation, fantastic play and fast pace Spence did not top United's scoring charts during the following Division Two seasons. In fact it wasn't until 1926-27 when, in Division One, he topped the chart again with 18 goals (more than the previous two seasons combined).

In May 1926 Spence made his international debut as he helped England to a 5-3 victory in Belgium and the following October he scored in the 3-3 draw with Ireland at Anfield. Sadly, those two appearances were the only ones he made and some suggested that United's struggles had limited his international opportunities. It is fair to say that had he been playing in a title-challenging side it is likely he would have enjoyed a better run in the national side.

At Old Trafford Spence remained a familiar and popular player season after season but unfortunately, apart from promotions, these were unsuccessful years. When he made his final United League appearance on 1st April 1933 he had managed a total of 481 League games and had netted 158 goals. This was a United record and wasn't broken until Bill Foulkes passed the total during 1965-66.

Spence's total tally of League & FA Cup appearances came to an impressive 510 with 168 goals.

After United Spence helped Chesterfield win the Third Division (North) title and when his career ultimately came to an end his final total of 613 League appearances was a Football League record. It is worth noting that he had played in 19 of the 20 inter-war seasons – also a record!

Post-war Spence returned to Old Trafford as a member of Matt Busby's coaching staff. He passed away on New Year's Eve 1966.

Leading League Scorer in:
1919-1920 - 14 goals, 32 appearances
1920-1921 - 7 goals, 15 appearances*
1921-1922 – 15 goals, 35 appearances
1926-1927 - 18 goals, 40 appearances
1927-1928 - 22 goals, 38 appearances
1931-1932 – 19 goals, 37 appearances

*Note: * Spence's goalscoring ratio in 1920-21 was better than three other players who scored 7 League goals that season – Sapsford (7 in 21 appearances), Miller (7 in 25) and Partridge (7 in 28).*

19 - ERNEST GOLDTHORPE

Leeds born Ernie Goldthorpe was from a well-known family who excelled at Rugby. A bit like the Milburn-Charlton family, the Goldthorpes were significant members of the Rugby community and Ernie's father

Ernie Goldthorpe scoring a penalty against Leicester in 1924.

and uncles were well-known and respected players. Their name is remembered with the Goldthorpe Cup – a competition competed for by schools in Leeds. In fact Ernie Goldthorpe also excelled at the game during his schoolboy days, but it was football that he was ultimately to focus on.

During World War One Goldthorpe had guested for Tottenham and went on to join Bradford City in June 1919. Despite a serious knee injury he managed to develop his abilities and made history when he appeared in Leeds United's first ever League game. Unfortunately, injury restricted his appearances for Leeds – this was to be a recurring theme – and he returned to Bradford City.

In November 1922 he signed for United initially on a month's trial. His impressed immediately scoring on his debut (at Clapton Orient, 11th November 1922) and then netting twice in his second match (a 2-2 draw at Bury).

By the end of his first season he topped the scoring charts with 13 goals – four of those goals had come in a 6-1 victory at Notts County on 10th February 1923 when he netted a hat-trick in only 270 seconds.

Despite his great record the season ended frustratingly after Goldthorpe dislocated a collar-bone in a collision with the opposition 'keeper at home to Blackpool on 7th April.

The following season he only managed four appearances (scoring once) as injury limited his opportunities. Then in 1924-25 he scored in the opening day 1-0 victory over Leicester City, but that turned out to be his only League appearance of the campaign.

In October 1925 he was transferred to Rotherham leaving United fans, and no doubt the player himself, wondering about what might have been had injury not restricted his United career.

Away from football he worked in a bank and also had farming interests but, sadly, his life was cut short only four years after leaving United. Goldthorpe died at the age of 31 leaving a wife and daughter Beryl who was a

month short of her fourth birthday when her father passed away.

The Yorkshire Evening Post (6th November 1929) reported, under the headline "Famous Footballer Drops Dead in Street": "One of the second generation of the famous Goldthorpe family of Hunslet died with tragic suddenness, and his death was the subject of an inquest by Leeds deputy coroner this afternoon. Dr Hoyland-Smith said death was due to heart failure following acute double pneumonia from which he had been suffering for only 24 hours. Severe exertion while playing badminton would be, he said, a secondary cause of collapse. Death from natural causes was the verdict."

The newspaper explained: "Ernest Goldthorpe son of Walter, nephew of Albert and James, had been playing badminton at St Oswald's Institute, Hunslet, last night, and was on his way home when he died. His home was at Woodville Mount, Hunslet Carr and he ran up Belle Vue Road in order to attend to his poultry before going home, 150 yards away, but he died before a doctor could be called."

Leading League Scorer in:
1922-1923 - 13 goals, 22 appearances*

*Note: * Goldthorpe's goalscoring ratio in 1922-23 was better than Lochhead who scored 13 League goals in 34 games that season.*

20 – ARTHUR LOCHHEAD

Born in Busby, Lanarkshire, on 8th December 1897 Arthur Lochhead arrived at Old Trafford from Hearts in July 1921. As with so many footballers at the time he was also pursuing a career in another profession and was studying engineering. By the time he left United four years later he had become a teacher.

Lochhead made his debut in the opening game of the following season at Goodison Park when Everton achieved a 5-0 victory.

By the end of the difficult 1921-22 season – United were relegated in 22nd place - Lochhead had become a regular in the

Arthur Lochhead

many Reds and a local journalist, using typical football hyperbole, summed up the mood: "The transfer of Lochhead is in the nature of a tragedy to the thousands who have delighted in the skilled footwork, long stride, and beautiful body swerve the young Scottish school-master showed."

Interestingly, Lochhead's last goal for United was against Leicester on 16th September 1926. The following month he arrived at Filbert Street for a fee of £3,300 – Leicester's record at the time – and became a popular player for his new side. Exactly nine years after his debut he was appointed Leicester manager after the death of Peter Hodge. After about 18 months in the role he resigned and returned to Scotland.

By the middle of 1938 he was running the Border Hotel at Yetholm near Kelso. He passed away on 30th December 1966 in Edinburgh.

Leading League Scorer in:

1923-1924 - 14 goals, 40 appearances

side, scoring 8 goals in 31 League games. The following season he netted 13 in 34 appearances and, alongside Goldthorpe, headed United's scoring charts. That form continued into 1923-24 and he ended the season as leading scorer in his own right on 14 goals from 40 League appearances, but it's fair to say he was the star man in a poor season as the Reds finished 14th in Division Two.

1924-25 was a much better season for the Reds and Lochhead once again delivered both as a marksman and a playmaker. He wasn't the club's top scorer but his consistency ensured he netted 13 goals in 37 appearances. Many of these goals were highly significant – his goals in five of those games ensured a Red victory while others ensured United maintained the upper hand.

Back in Division One United had a fair season in 1925-26 and reached the FA Cup semi-final, however Lochhead only appeared in five of the opening seven games before he was transferred to Leicester City in October. It was a disappointing move for

21 – WILLIAM HENDERSON

After scoring 36 goals in 39 appearances for Airdrieonians and becoming the highest scorer in Division One of the Scottish League system in 1920-21 it was fairly clear that he would attract the attention of English sides, particularly those in the north. United, City and to some extent the Merseyside clubs regularly raided Scotland looking for potential new stars and so it was inevitable when Henderson moved south in November 1921.

United paid a fee of £1,750 and Henderson netted on his debut against Aston Villa on 26th November 1921. He also scored in his third game (a 1-1 draw at home to

William Henderson

Bradford City) but only managed to appear in a further seven games as United - and Henderson - struggled to find the net.

Appearances were few and far between in the next couple of seasons – he scored once in two League appearances in 1922-23 and made no League appearances the following season. In 1924-25 he returned to the first team and his return coincided with United's surge for a promotion spot.

By the end of January 1925 he had scored 14 goals in 22 appearances and ended the season as the Club's leading scorer even though he left the Reds for Preston shortly after his last appearance in January.

He only stayed at Preston until the end of the season and then he had spells at Clapton Orient, Hearts, Morton, Torquay and then Exeter, before retiring in 1930.

He moved back to Scotland and died at Rosyth in 1964 in his mid-sixties.

Leading League Scorer in:
1924-1925 - 14 goals, 22 appearances

22 – CLATWORTHY RENNOX

Following the departure of William Henderson Clatworthy 'Charlie' Rennox was signed from Clapton Orient in March 1925. Rennox made his debut at home in a 2-0 victory over Portsmouth on 14 March 1925 as United pushed for promotion. He only managed four appearances that season but it was the following season when he really impressed.

Back in Division One United were defeated in two of their opening three games. Manager John Chapman clearly felt something was not quite right and he brought Rennox into the side, along with Jimmy

Clatworthy Lennox

Hanson, to improve the attack. The move must have worked as that fourth game of the season saw both players score as United achieved a 2-2 draw at Aston Villa.

Five days later Rennox netted again – a highly significant goal – as he scored United's first goal at Manchester City's Maine Road stadium. The match ended 1-1 after Rennox had taken the lead with 'a smart shot'.

The next match saw Rennox score twice as United defeated Leicester 3-2. United were now looking like a side capable of making an impression in the First Division although there were occasional high profile setbacks, like the 5-0 defeat at Anfield and the 6-1 Manchester derby defeat at Old Trafford (The Empire News reported that Rennox scored the 'one': "Two minutes from the end Rennox obtained United's only consolation in the midst of a goalmouth scrimmage. It was a game that will be long remembered at Old Trafford."), but overall United impressed game after game. Rennox was one of the season's biggest stars and fans loved him. Well known for his heading abilities and the strength of his play Rennox was outstanding as the Reds ended 1925-26 ninth. He was United's leading scorer.

Surprisingly, the following season was not as great for Rennox. Managerial changes may have impacted his selection during 1926-27 and he ended that campaign after scoring seven goals in 22 appearances. The following July he was transferred to Grimsby Town but, surprisingly, he never appeared in his new side's first team.

Leading League Scorer in: 1925-1926 - 17 goals, 34 appearances

23 – JIMMY HANSON

Mancunian Jimmy

Hanson arrived at Old Trafford in May 1924 after spells with a variety of local sides, including Stalybridge Celtic and Manchester North End. He had been well-known in the region from an early age and had appeared in the Manchester Boys side from the age of 12. He had also played for England schoolboys. In December 1922 a reader of the Manchester Football News even recommended the Reds take a look at him, which they did in 1923-24.

Jimmy Hanson

At that time the United management gave him a couple of trials. The first saw him net a hat-trick against Accrington Stanley in a Mid-Week XI game and then he was drafted into the Central League against Huddersfield Town. It wasn't a surprise when at the end of that season he was signed on professional terms.

He made his first team debut at home to Hull City in November 1924 – he scored in the 2-0 victory – and he played in the following couple of games and scored in each. Despite his goal a game record he was dropped as regular centre-forward William Henderson returned to the side after a three game absence.

The following season Hanson re-appeared in the first team, making 24 League appearances and scoring five, but he still wasn't a permanent fixture in the side. In fact that didn't come until the latter stages of the 1926-27 season.

In 1927-28 he scored ten goals in 30 games and followed this with 19 goals (6 from the penalty spot) during the 1928-29 season. Inevitably, he topped United's scoring chart that season and he was also the Club's only ever-present as the Reds ended the season 12th in Division One.

1929-30 was Hanson's benefit season

and the player had scored five goals in 17 games before tragedy struck in his 18th League game of the campaign. On Christmas Day at home to Birmingham City he suffered a broken fibia after only fifteen minutes play. The injury ended his career.

Away from football he focused on his family's trade and became a monumental stonemason.

Leading League Scorer in: 1928-1929 - 19 goals, 42 appearances

24 – HENRY 'HARRY' ROWLEY

Staffordshire born Harry Rowley joined the Reds from Shrewsbury Town in May 1928 for a fee of £100 and made his debut the following October as United won 2-1 at Huddersfield Town. He kept his place for the following seven games but had only managed one goal (in a 5-1 defeat at Sunderland) during that spell.

Rowley returned to the side on New Year's Day and scored as the Reds drew 2-2 with Aston Villa. He impressed and by the season's end he had made 25 League appearances and scored five goals, but it was the 1929-30 season that saw him at his best. Although United were struggling, inside left Rowley was a consistent and reliable figure throughout the season. He ended the season on 12 goals from 40 games.

Sadly, the Reds were relegated at the end of the following season and Rowley, after scoring seven goals in 29 games, was viewed as one of the Club's most saleable assets. Rowley was sold, alongside Billy Dale, to Manchester City with Bill Ridding making the opposite journey as part of the deal.

At Maine Road Rowley only managed 18

League games before being loaned to Oldham where he impressed once more (scoring 14 goals in 70 League games). United re-signed him for £1,375 in December 1934.

During his time away from Old Trafford the Reds had struggled and come close to both going out of business and being relegated to Division Three. Rowley's return came during a more positive season and his eight goals from 24 League appearances helped United to a fifth place finish in Division Two.

The following season saw United challenge for promotion from the start and Rowley netted a career best 19 from 37 appearances, though he was not top scorer (that honour belonged to George Mutch).

United struggled in Division One and were relegated in 1937. That summer Rowley moved on again. This time he joined Burton Town as player-manager and then he joined Gillingham during the 1938 close season (a few months after they had failed to gain re-election to the Third Division South).

By the time war broke out Rowley was almost 35 and, inevitably, like so many other players he was unable to resurrect his career once full time football resumed after the war.

Harry Rowley

Rowley died on 19th December 1985 a month short of his 81st birthday.

Leading League Scorer in:

1929-1930 - 12 goals, 40 appearances*

*Note: * Rowley's goalscoring ratio in 1929-30 was better than Spence who scored 12 League goals in 42 games that season.*

The approach to Old Trafford in the late Fifties. Although the overall scene is recognisable today, almost everything in the image has been redeveloped.

The Football Season Daily Reminder

October

1st October 1988

United drew 2-2 at Tottenham thanks to goals from Hughes and McClair.

2nd October 1971

George Best and Alan Gowling both scored as Sheffield United were defeated 2-0 in front of an Old Trafford crowd of 51,735.

3rd October 1981

A Sammy McIlroy hat-trick helped United to a 5-0 Old Trafford victory over Wolves before 46,837.

4th October 1930

A devastating Manchester derby – City won 4-1 – caused United's relegation worries to worsen. It was the Reds' ninth straight defeat of the season the Athletic News claimed: "City obviously grew sympathetic and declined to rub it in." Inevitably, United were relegated at the season's end.

5th October 1977

United played a home European tie at Plymouth.

The Reds had drawn 1-1 at St. Etienne, France in the first leg, however crowd trouble disrupted the match. The Reds were initially thrown out of the competition, but ultimately the punishment was reduced and United were re-instated so long as their home game was played 200 miles from Old Trafford. Home Park, Plymouth was chosen and the game ended 2-0 to United. The match was also beamed back to Old Trafford.

6th October 1982

Peter Beardsley played his one and only first team game for United when he wore the number ten shirt in the 2-0 League Cup victory over Bournemouth. He didn't last the full

Manchester United Football Club Limited
Old Trafford, Manchester

CLOSED CIRCUIT TELEVISION
LIVE FROM PLYMOUTH

EUROPEAN CUP WINNERS CUP
FIRST ROUND—SECOND LEG

UNITED
v.
ST. ETIENNE

WEDNESDAY, 5th OCTOBER, 1977
7-30 p.m.

ADMISSION
80p

ninety minutes – he was substituted with Norman Whiteside his replacement.

7th October 1970

A solitary goal from Bobby Charlton saw United through to the fourth round of the League Cup after victory over Portsmouth. The game was watched by 32,068 at Old Trafford.

8th October 1969

Best, Burns and Kidd combined to give United a 3-0 victory at Southampton in Division One.

9th October 1974

Arthur Albiston made his debut against Manchester City in the third round of the League Cup at Old Trafford. The Reds won the tie 1-0 with a goal from Gerry Daly. The official attendance was 55,159. At the time United were a Second Division side and City a First.

10th October 1959

Arsenal were defeated 4-2 by United with goals from Charlton, Quixall, Viollet and an own goal.

11th October 1937

Bobby Charlton was born at Ashington, Northumberland.

12th October 1988

A McClair hat-trick and goals from Robson and Bruce meant the Reds defeated Rotherham 5-0 before 20,597 at Old Trafford in the League Cup 2nd round 2nd leg tie.

13th October 1979

Mancunian Wes Brown was born.

14th October 1978

United drew 2-2 at Aston Villa with goals from Macari & McIlroy.

15th October 1983

Ron Atkinson's United defeated his former side West Bromwich Albion 3-0 (Albiston, Graham & Whiteside) before 42,221 at Old Trafford.

16th October 1926

Two goals from Spence helped United to a 3-0 victory at Bury in Division One in front of 22,728 at Gigg Lane.

17th October 1956

A crowd of 75,598 witnessed United's 3-2 victory over Borussia

UNITED'S "GOLDEN ERA" AT MAINE ROAD

It may be a £75,000 profit for 3 seasons

BY TOM JACKSON

POST-WAR football has brought a financial boom to Manchester United. Final returns from their "golden era" at Maine Road, when they hired City's ground for senior matches, will probably reveal an aggregate profit of £75,000 on the last three seasons.

United's balance-sheet for 1948-49—their closing spell at Maine Road—will soon be issued to shareholders. It is believed to show all-time records in attendances, gate receipts, and profit on the season's working.

THE SCALE

THIS is how their profits have soared since normal League and Cup soccer was resumed after the war—season 1946-7 £13,393, 1947-8 £22,329, with last season's margin likely to be in the region of £40,000.

Attendances at remodelled Old Trafford are limited to below 50,000, and, therefore, United may not be able to show such handsome dividends at the end of the current season.

But already they have one source of satisfaction — bigger gates at Central League games. So far they have averaged 3,550 at Old Trafford and twice exceeded the 5,000 mark.

From a cash angle this means the difference between £44, which represented their takings at one reserve game last season, and £224, their highest so far.

When City used Old Trafford for Central League fixtures takings on one occasion were only £4 15s., barely enough to cover the transport of playing kit to the ground!

MEETS THE BLUES

CUMMINGS
Burnley's centre half against City at Turf Moor on Saturday.

SOCCER
MANCHESTER CITY (v. Burnley), away. Saturday: Powell; Phillips, Westwood; Walsh, Fagan, Emptage; Oakes, Myers, Turnbull, Clarke.
SOUTHPORT (v. Oldham), home. Saturday: Birkett; Bradshaw, Boyle; Hitchen, Bellas, Hacking; Rothwell, Dainty, Walsh, Wyles, Maddison.

RUGBY LEAGUE
ROCHDALE HORNETS (v. Swinton), away. Saturday: McGilvray; Nicholson, Winstanley, Butler, Williams; Jones, Wilde; Wagstaff, Croft, Groom, Thorning, Fearnley, Tucker.

es to town

rsenal ?

B MAY BE DECIDED UPON ESTER CITY 22-YEAR-OLD LUB DIRECTOR HAVE TAKEN

date of the next meeting depends on how long these investigations take."

IN the office of Mr. Wilfred Wild, the City secretary, a bag of mail is gradually expanding and developing into a second and third bag—full of applications for tickets for next month's England-Ireland international at Maine Road.

But by the time the English and the Irish F.A.s and the League clubs and the season-ticket holders have been

AMATEUR BOXING

Dortmund in the European Cup at Maine Road. This remains the Reds' highest home attendance in European competition.

18th October 2008

Despite being goalless at half time United defeated West Bromwich Albion 4-0 in the Premier League meeting at Old Trafford. The goals were scored by Rooney (56), Ronaldo (69), Berbatov (71) and Nani (90).

19th October 1892

Full back James Brown was involved in an accidental collision with Darwen's Joe Aspden in a Lancashire Combination reserve game. Aspden was injured and taken to Darwen's 'dressing tent'. Sadly four

says later Aspden died as a result of the collision. James Brown gave evidence at the inquest: "I am a factory operative and reside at Rose Villa, Stanley Street, Newton Heath. I was playing in the Newton Heath team at Darwen on Saturday week. I was at left full-back. The right wing pair were coming down the field and the outside placed the ball over the half-back's head. I went to meet it, slipped and missed the ball, and struck one of their players [Aspden] in the stomach." A verdict of accidental death was reached.

20th October 1949

The Manchester Evening News carried the story of United's record-breaking profits during their stay at City's Maine Road stadium. They claimed the Reds had made £75,000 profit from their final three seasons at the ground and could claim new records in attendances, gate receipts and profits.

21st October 1981

Nemanja Vidic was born in Uzice. At the time of his birth the town was known as Titovo Užice (named after Yugoslavian President Tito) and was in Yugoslavia. The city suffered significantly from war in the 1990s – including several bombings during 1999. Today it forms part of Serbia.

22nd October 1980

£1.25m signing from Nottingham Forest Garry Birtles made his debut. The Reds beat Stoke 2-1 at the Victoria Ground with goals from Joe Jordan and Lou Macari.

23rd October 1982

The Manchester derby ended honours even after a brace from Frank Stapleton ensured a 2-2 draw before 57,334 at Old Trafford.

24th October 1985

Wayne Rooney was born in Liverpool. Four years earlier United defeated Liverpool 2-1 at Anfield with goals from Albiston and Moran.

25th October 1985

The Mirror newspaper reported that Ron Atkinson's United were suffering an injury crisis. The Reds had started the season with a 13 game unbeaten run and the view was that the following day's game at Chelsea would prove to be a struggle because of selection issues. Fans need not have worried as Atkinson's side beat the Pensioners 2-1 with goals from Hughes and Olsen.

26th October 1986

The Manchester derby was televised live for the first time. Mick McCarthy netted for Jimmy Frizzell's

THE MIRROR, Friday, October 25,

RON'S BUYING TIME
..but United won't rush to buy men

By BOB RUSSELL

RON ATKINSON is buying time to protect Manchester United's unbeaten League record at Chelsea tomorrow.

United's injury crisis eased yesterday when Gordon Strachan and John Gidman were given the go-ahead to resume full training on Monday.

But manager Atkinson still faces the immediate problem of putting a team together for the trip to Stamford Bridge.

He's hoping that Remi Moses may be sufficiently recovered from his recurring ankle trouble to fill in for injured skipper Bryan Robson. Moses broke down in last Saturday's 1—1 home draw with Liverpool.

At the moment though United, in their manager's words, are "hoping to be able to buy time until Strachan and Gidman are available."

Atkinson concedes his squad is down to the bones but insists he has no immediate plans to splash out into the transfer market.

Versatile reserve Clayton Blackmore is also struggling and Robson is at least a fortnight away

from full recovery from a hamstring strain.

So Atkinson will continue with wingers Peter Barnes and Jesper Olsen at Chelsea if Moses fails a late fitness test.

Chelsea are unbeaten at home.

■ Striker Jim Tolmie became Manchester City's latest casualty when he injured a knee in a collision with team-mate Jim Melrose during training yesterday.

Assistant manager Jimmy Frizzell said: "The fear is that it could be damaged ligaments and that might mean Jim is a couple of weeks out of action."

■ Everton's England midfielder Peter Reid, out six weeks with an Achilles tendon injury, suffered a setback in training yesterday and sees a specialist today.

POINTING THE WAY . . . Ron Atkinson's Manchester United are setting a hot pace in their bid to take the League championship from Everton. But Ron couldn't **Picture: Albert Cooper** stop Goodison boss Howard Kendall from winning the Manager of the Year award from the Northern branch of the Football Writers' Association in Manchester last night. Kendall proudly displayed the Canon League trophy—and no doubt fancies Atkinson's FA Cup, too!

Giants wake up

By HOWARD BOOTH: Leeds..6, Wigan..28

WIGAN'S Central Park giants emerged from attempts—to give Wigan a lead they never sur-

PLAYBOY

TOP DOG

SUMMARY

side as the relegation-bound Blues managed a 1-1 draw at Maine Road. Shortly after this match United dismissed Ron Atkinson.

27th October 2007

After Nani opened the scoring in the third minute the Reds defeated Middlesbrough 4-1 at Old Trafford. The other goals came from Rooney (33) and Tevez (55 & 85).

28th October 1989

A brace from Brian McClair ensured a 2-1 victory at home to Southampton before 37,122.

29th October 1970

Edwin Van Der Sar was born in Voorhout, Netherlands.

30th October 1886

Newton Heath drew 2-2 at Fleetwood Rangers in the FA Cup, however the tie was awarded to Fleetwood when the Heathens refused to play extra time.

31st October 1981

Goals from Birtles (above, in action against City) and Moses ensured a 2-1 victory at home to Notts County in Division One. Ron Atkinson's Reds attracted a crowd of 45,928.

Plug

In 1977 a spin off comic from the Beano was produced called Plug. It followed the story of 'Percival Proudfoot Plugsley', the Bash Street Kids character Plug, and included lots of new characters. It also included features such as the one illustrated here.

This page (opposite) is from issue forty and profiled United. 'Merlin' Hill was, of course, Gordon Hill who scored 51 goals in 133 League and cup appearances.

Plug also featured a team of insects called Antchester United managed by Matt Bugsy. All of the players' names were puns on real footballers (although there was one genuine name – Mike Summerbee!) with Brian Greenfly, Mantis Buchan & George Beastie being based on United stars. The best pun was that of 'Gnat' Lofthouse.

United's Profit Comparison

In between Christmas and New Year 1912 the Reds issued their financial report and accounts for the period including the 1911-12 season.

The accounts were surprisingly late – the Athletic News reported that this may have been because of investigations by the FA or may have been because the figures were 'colossal' in their opinion.

The actual details provide an interesting comparison with United's modern day plight.

In 1911-12 League matches brought in receipts of £9,370 and Cup ties brought in a further £7,060. Once reserve and other minor competitions were taken into consideration, the total gate receipts for 1911-12 were £16,877 with United's share (once appropriate figures had been passed on to opposition clubs) standing at £13,954.

There was also a further £223 from season ticket sales.

Other income from player transactions, prize money and food/drink sales brought in an around £2,000.

In October 2010 it was reported that the Reds had income of £100m from match day operations, £81m from commercial deals and £105m from media activity.

In terms of expenditure the Reds paid £4,938 in players' wages and a further £1,400 on interest charges in 1911-12. Staff costs equalled £131.69m claimed a report in 2010 while other operating costs stood at £53.9m.

Due to the large 1912 profit of approximately £10,000, it was decided to pay shareholders the maximum dividend allowed of 5 per cent.

United's club debt, as reported in October 2010, stood at £521.7m although it was reported that the Club had an operating profit of £100.79m.

The Affairs of Manchester United.

Surely rather belated, the first annual meeting of the shareholders of the Manchester United Football Club will be held this (Monday) evening at the offices. The balance-sheet to be submitted is for the season 1911-12. This shows that the total receipts from League matches were £9,370 and that Cup-ties brought in a revenue of £7,060. The total gate receipts were £16,877, and the net, after paying the shares of Cup-ties to other clubs, £13,954 7s. 9d.—a sum which is supplemented by £223 for season tickets. In round figures the complete revenue for last season amounted to about £16,000, while the total expenses amounted to £13,526 11s. 8d. It is interesting to note that £4,938 was paid to players in the form of wages, and debenture interest absorbed £1,400.

It is passing strange that this balance-sheet should make its appearance nine months after the close of the last campaign. Evidently the figures are colossal. Possibly the F.A. supervision has also caused some delay. We understand that the directors proposed to pay the full dividend of five per cent.

We hear that the takings of Manchester City and Manchester United are in excess of last year. Indeed, it would not be surprising if Manchester City present the best balance-sheet in their history next summer, provided the team gains its power and has normal luck in ties. The League receipts of the club are at least £3,000 in excess of previous campaign.

Southern Trial Game.

An interesting amateur trial game will be held on Wednesday at the Stamford ground (lent by the directors of the West Ham Football Club), between London and the Southern Counties, the latter being selected from the counties of the Southern Counties'

The Athletic News
AND CYCLISTS' JOURNAL.
MONDAY, DECEMBER 30, 1912.

AN INCIDENT IN THE BATTLE OF MANCHESTER.

UNITED'S LEADING SCORERS

Our story of all the players who have topped the seasonal League goalscoring charts for the Reds through to the start of the 2011-12 season moves on to 1930-31.

THE PROFILES (PART THREE)

25 – TOMMY REID

Born at Motherwell on 15th August 1905, Reid originally made his name playing for Clydebank in 1925-26. Liverpool paid £1,000 for his signature that season and he went on to score 31 goals in 51 League games for the Merseysiders.

At the start of February 1929 Reid joined United and made his debut in the 3-2 defeat at home to West Ham on 2nd February. Although the result went against the Reds Reid had actually scored on his debut. It was enough to ensure he kept his place for the remaining 16 games. During that period he netted a total of 14 League goals – including seven goals in four games – but the following season saw him manage only 13 appearances. The Reds struggled without him and ended the season 17th in Division One.

Injury affected him again in 1930-31 but this time he managed to appear in 30 of the 42 League games and scored 17 goals – the season's best. Despite his goals, United were relegated.

Reid kept contributing in Division Two and scored 17 goals once more in his 25 League appearances.

In 1932-33 Reid netted ten goals in eleven appearances by Christmas, however his United career was nearing its end and the following month he was loaned to Oldham Athletic. Whether it was United's parlous financial state at the time or a desire to help near neighbours Oldham isn't clear but Reid's arrival at Boundary Park seemed to be more in Oldham's favour than United's. At Oldham Reid immediately impressed and the Latics' supporters' club raised the £400 needed to make his move permanent.

After two years at Oldham Reid moved to Barrow, then had a spell at Rhyl Athletic in 1938.

Reid passed away at Prescot on Merseyside in 1972.

Leading League Scorer in:
1930-1931 - 17 goals, 30 appearances

26 – BILL RIDDING

Heswall-born Bill Ridding had a bright start in the game. At his first professional club, Tranmere Rovers, he became noted for his goalscoring exploits and in March 1930 Manchester City signed him for £3,000.

Ridding made his City debut on 19th April 1930 and made nine appearances, scoring four, before United signed him on 23rd December 1931. The transfer fee was an interesting one – United gave the Blues Harry Rowley and Billy Dale while Ridding and a fee of around £2,000 came to Old Trafford (occasionally this is incorrectly recorded as a fee paid to City).

His first season with United brought three goals from 14 appearances and then in 1932-33 he scored 11 in 23 appearances as he topped United's scoring charts. Unfortunately, he suffered with cartilage trouble and only managed five appearances in 1933-34.

These were difficult days for the player as injury seemed to dog his every move. In a bid to get fit he took a job as a bus

Bill Ridding

conductor claiming that the regular climbing of the bus stairs would be good exercise for his knee! He also focused on physiotherapy.

He left United for Northampton Town on 2nd August 1934 but injury continued to affect his career. Further spells at Tranmere (August 1935) and Oldham (October 1935) brought little joy for him personally and he was forced to retire that season through on-going cartilage issues.

He remained with Oldham for several seasons as a coach and trainer, before moving to Bolton as trainer in August 1946. He later became Bolton's manager before resigning in 1968.

His final sporting years saw him take on the role of physio to Lancashire CCC. He died in Bolton on 20th September 1981.

Leading League Scorer in:
1932-1933 - 11 goals, 23 appearances

27 – NEIL DEWAR

Neil Dewar arrived at Old Trafford in February 1933 at the age of 24 for a fee of £5,000. His earlier career had seen him play for Third Lanark in Scotland and it was reported, at the time of his arrival, that he had netted 23 times in 28 appearances during 1932-33 and 35 in 36 games the previous season.

Viewed as a knowledgeable player at the time he was well-known for his dribbling abilities.

In 1933-34 he was an ever-present for the first 21 League games of the season and scored eight goals, but was transferred to Sheffield Wednesday in December of that season (Wednesday's George Nevin and Jack Ball made the opposite journey).

At Sheffield Scottish international Dewar hit the headlines after it was reported that he had eloped with the daughter

Neil Dewar

of a United director, Councillor AE Thomson. Thomson ultimately resigned from the Old Trafford board as a result of the publicity, while Dewar and his girlfriend married at a registry office.

In 1937 he returned to Third Lanark for a club record £1,800 and remained with them until 1940. He continued to play amateur football in Argyllshire until 1947.

Dewar died on 10th January 1982. His son Neil Dewar junior played for Altrincham and Stalybridge Celtic in the 1960s.

Leading League Scorer in:
1933-1934 - 8 goals, 21 appearances

28 – GEORGE MUTCH

For two seasons Aberdeen-born George Mutch topped United's League goalscoring charts and it is fair to say that his goals were a significant factor in the Reds' 1936 Second Division title success.

Mutch arrived at Old Trafford in the 1934 close season for a fee of £800 and made his debut a month short of his 22nd birthday in the opening game of the 1934-35 season against Bradford City. The game ended in a 2-0 victory but it wasn't until his fourth game that he netted his first goal. In that match, at home to Barnsley, Mutch netted a hat-trick as United won 4-1 but the key aspect of that feat was that all three goals came in a thrilling five minute

spell when it seemed Mutch could attack at will.

Once he found his goalscoring touch Mutch seemed unstoppable, and he ended the 1934-35 Second Division campaign as top scorer with 18 goals from 40 appearances. His goals helped the Reds to a fifth place finish, but the following season Mutch was an ever-present as United won the Second Division title. He broke the twenty goal a season barrier and was, of course, top scorer again.

The following season was not as successful for the player. Injury limited his appearances – he started 28 League games and scored seven – but not his appetite for the game. United missed Mutch's goals and were relegated at the end of the season.

Inevitably, First Division clubs were interested in the talented forward and in September 1937 Mutch was transferred to Preston North End for £5,000. It was a successful move and Mutch helped his new club finish third in Division One and win the 1938 FA Cup. In fact the 1938 final became known for the activities of the player in the final minutes of the game.

WILLS'S CIGARETTES

G. MUTCH (MANCHESTER UNITED)

With the tie goalless and in the final 30 seconds of extra time (a draw would have brought a replay in those days) Mutch was brought down in the penalty area by Huddersfield's captain Alf Young. He received treatment for some considerable time before he was able to take the penalty. He hit the ball with power and it entered the net after hitting the underside of the crossbar and rebounding off the goal line.

Inevitably, World War Two affected his career but when full-time national football resumed after the war Mutch signed for Bury (October 1946). A spell at Southport followed before in 1950 he returned to his native Aberdeen and opened a grocery business. He passed away in March 2001 at the age of 88.

It is worth noting that during 1937-38 he made his Scottish international debut and, possibly, would have made further appearances had war not intervened.

Leading League Scorer in:
1934-1935 - 18 goals, 40 appearances
1935-1936 – 21 goals, 42 appearances

29 – TOMMY BAMFORD

Born at Port Talbot on 2nd September 1905, Tommy Bamford joined United in October 1934 from Wrexham. That month the Reds had visited Wrexham to play in a benefit game for the Gresford Colliery Disaster and it seems likely the player had been spotted that day and that possibly discussions took place on various transfers between the sides – as well as Bamford United signed Billy Bryant while James Rice made the opposite move.

Bamford was already well-known for his goalscoring exploits and had netted 174 goals in 204 League appearances for the Welsh club. In 1933-34 he was the Third Division North's second highest scorer with 44 League goals – still to this day a record for Wrexham.

At United, Bamford made his debut a memorable one as he scored the only goal of the game at Newcastle on 20th October 1934. He ended that season with a very good goal to game ratio – he scored nine goals in 19 League appearances. The following season he scored seven goals in the first seven games as United focused on promotion and, by the season's end, he had netted 16 goals in 27 games as the Second Division title was won.

In Division One Bamford continued in fine form – netting 14 in 29 games to be the season's highest scorer - but eight of these came in the first seven matches and he was replaced by Rowley at times. He returned to the team for the final four matches as the Reds looked to avoid relegation. Bamford helped enormously – he scored four goals in the first three games following his return but while the Reds were undefeated they had dropped two crucial points. In the final game of the season the Reds suffered a 1-0 defeat at West Bromwich Albion and United were relegated with two points less than 'safe' Bolton and Leeds.

Back in Division Two Bamford topped United's charts again with 14 goals from 23 appearances but injury had limited his chances. The following summer, despite helping United to promotion, he was transferred to Swansea Town.

Bamford passed away at Wrexham in December 1967 but is remembered today for many goalscoring exploit, particularly those at Wrexham in 1934.

Leading League Scorer in:
1936-1937 - 14 goals, 29 appearances
1937-1938 – 14 goals, 23 appearances

30 – JIMMY HANLON

Manchester born Jimmy Hanlon joined the Reds on amateur forms in November 1934, turning professional a year later. As with most youngsters coming through the ranks during this period, Hanlon had to wait some time for his first team chance but when it came he seized the opportunity.

On 26th November 1938 he made his debut at home to Huddersfield Town before a Division One crowd of 23,164 and found the net as the game ended in a 1-1 draw. It was an important point as United were at the foot of the table and tipped for relegation. Clearly Hanlon must have impressed and he retained his place as centre-forward for the rest of the season.

Hanlon was one of the Reds' more consistent players and his goals – 12 in 27 appearances – helped United move away from the relegation zone and on to a 14th place finish.

Although it may seem like hyperbole, it should be stressed that Hanlon's goals preserved United's First Division status at a time when relegation could have seriously killed off any hope that the Reds would ever become a major side. The 1930s

CHURCHMAN'S CIGARETTES

J. J. HANLON (MANCHESTER UNITED)

were a difficult decade for United but by preserving their Division One status in the final season before the war meant that post-war the Reds were able to compete at the highest level. Had the Reds been relegated the situation in 1945 would have been much more severe – imagine what would have happened to a Second Division club whose home had been severely damaged in the war.

For Hanlon the war years were tough. He became a sergeant in the Durham Light Infantry but was captured by the Italians in Crete. He became a prisoner of war for three years.

In peacetime Hanlon resurrected his football career and he scored seven goals in 27 appearances during the 1946-47 season when the Reds finished as runners-up to Arsenal – he had scored twice as the Reds beat Arsenal 5-2 at Maine Road in September. Unfortunately, Hanlon was no longer United's first choice as the season ended

and in 1948-49 he appeared in one League game – a 3-1 victory over Aston Villa on 25th September – before being transferred to Second Division Bury. Further spells at Northwich Victoria and Rhyl followed and in 1953 he helped the North Wales club to Welsh FA Cup success.

Hanlon died in January 2002 at the age of 84.

Leading League Scorer in:
1938-1939 - 12 goals, 27 appearances

31 - JACK ROWLEY

Wolverhampton born Jack Rowley was from a well-known footballing family. His father had been a goalkeeper with Walsall, while his younger brother Arthur went on to be a popular goalscorer with Leicester and Shrewsbury.

Pre-war Rowley had first been spotted by Wolves, but it was with Bournemouth & Boscombe Athletic that he made his first professional appearances. At Bournemouth the sixteen year old scored ten goals in his first eleven games and it was no surprise when the big clubs travelled to the south coast on scouting trips.

In October 1937 – Rowley celebrated his 17th birthday that month – he signed for United (£3,000) and made his debut on 23rd October 1937. After the match he discussed with Walter Crickmer his role and asked if he could play in the reserve team as he felt he wasn't quite ready for Second Division football. Crickmer agreed to the request and Rowley gained experience in the reserves for a few games. Six weeks after his debut he returned to

Jack Rowley

the side for the 4th December visit of Swansea Town and his decision to play in the reserves had clearly paid off as he scored four goals in the 5-1 victory over the Welsh side.

Rowley four in great Maine-road victory

MANCHESTER UNITED 6   CHARLTON ATHLETIC 2

FOUR goals (including a hat-trick) by ROWLEY, following goals by Morris and Pearson, gave Manchester United a 6—2 victory over the Cup-holders, Charlton Athletic, at Maine-road to-day. Ahead 4—1 at half-time United dominated the game and only on rare occasions did Charlton threaten the Manchester goal.

Their goals came in the follow-   [which VAUGHAN had merely

Rowley remained a key member of the team for the rest of the season, scoring nine goals in 29 appearances as the Reds achieved promotion on goal average.

During World War Two Rowley guested for Tottenham (winning the League South title in 1943-44), Distillery, and Wolves (winning a War Cup winners' medal).

Once peacetime football resumed Rowley was a key member of Matt Busby's attack and was outstanding as the Reds challenged for the League title in 1946-47. Nicknamed 'The Gunner' Rowley scored 26 goals in 37 games that season – at that point a United record – and the following season he scored 23 in 39 appearances as the Reds challenged again for the title. Those goals included United's equaliser in the record-breaking 1-1 draw with Arsenal at Maine Road on 17th January 1948 – record-breaking because that match attracted a record United home attendance and the League's record crowd of 83,260 (though still not the highest competitive crowd at the ground).

That season Rowley also scored twice in the 4-2 victory over Blackpool in the FA Cup final – this cup win ended a long drought of 37 years without a major trophy success. United celebrated wildly and Rowley's name was established as one of the Club's biggest heroes.

In the years that followed 'The Gunner' continued to deliver – in 1948-49 he was top scorer again as the Reds finished as runners up once more – and he also delivered in international football. In November 1949 he scored four against Ireland at Maine Road in a match whose significance is often overlooked. That game is often quoted as part of the British Home International

Tournament which it was, but it had another significance as the first World Cup qualifying match ever played in England. The Rowley goals should therefore be viewed as of much more significance than usually considered. Altogether he managed six full England internationals.

In 1951-52 Rowley netted an astounding 30 goals in 40 League games as Busby's United finally won the League. The Reds won the title by four points and Rowley's goals had brought so many valuable points throughout that season. His seasonal total had, of course, eclipsed his own United goalscoring record. He had set the tone for the entire season when he netted hat-tricks in the opening two games.

Although he appeared less often in 1952-53 he still managed to score 11 in 26 League games and followed this with 12 in 36 in 1953-54. He scored seven in 22 League games during his final season, 1954-55, but left the Reds in February 1955 to become Plymouth's player-manager.

Rowley's managerial career saw him move on to Oldham in 1960, Ajax in 1963, Wrexham in 1966, Bradford in 1967 and back to Oldham in 1968.

After his football career came to an end he ran a newsagents in Shaw, Oldham. He died in June 1998 at the age of 77.

Rowley should always be remembered as one of United's major stars. Without him, the Reds may never have achieved their first successes under Matt Busby.

Leading League Scorer in:
1946-1947 - 26 goals, 37 appearances
1947-1948 - 23 goals, 39 appearances
1948-1949 - 20 goals, 39 appearances
1949-1950 - 20 goals, 39 appearances
1951-1952 - 30 goals, 40 appearances

32 – STAN PEARSON

Born in Salford on 11th January 1919, Stan Pearson arrived at Old Trafford via the Adelphi Lads' club. Known to be a fan since the 1925-26 season when the Reds reached the FA Cup semi-final, he joined United as an amateur in December 1935 and signed professional forms in May 1937.

In November 1937 he made his debut at Chesterfield in Division Two as the Reds won an incredible game 7-1. He was only 18 and went on to make 11 League appearances that season.

The following year Pearson appeared in nine League games but when the 1939-40 season commenced he appeared in all three of the opening matches. It looked as if he had become a permanent fixture, however war intervened and the League campaign was brought to a halt. These games were later expunged from the records and Pearson's career took a different direction as he, like so many others, enlisted in the armed forces.

When League football returned in 1946 Pearson was a vital member of Matt Busby's side. An ever-present in 1946-47 he netted 19 League goals and the following season

scored 18 in 40. He was, of course, one of the scorers when the Reds beat Blackpool in the 1948 FA Cup Final – the first trophy success of Busby's reign and the first major honour since 1911. Pearson and the other players were major stars and feted for their part in bringing significant success to the Reds.

In 1948 Pearson also made his England debut – he went on to score five goals in eight internationals.

A consistent player and goalscorer, Pearson finally topped the United goalscoring charts in 1950-51 with 18 goals in 39 games as the Reds finished second. The following season he netted 22 in 41 games and it is fair to say that his contribution – and that of Rowley of course - had a major impact as United won the League title after a forty year absence.

In 1952-53 Pearson topped the Reds' goalscoring charts for a second time, but United were in a transitional period as those players who had served the Club well during the war years and immediately after were starting to be replaced by younger players from United's excellent youth system. Ultimately, Pearson was a victim

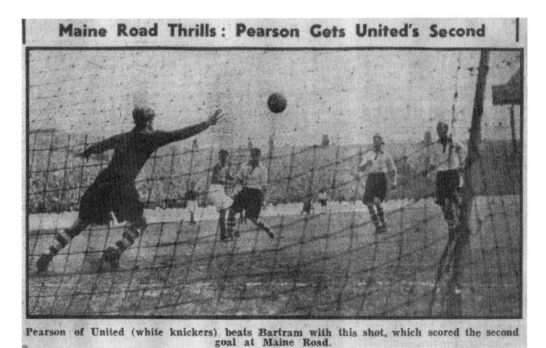

Maine Road Thrills : Pearson Gets United's Second

Pearson of United (white knickers) beats Bartram with this shot, which scored the second goal at Maine Road.

Goal! Pearson scores Manchester United's first goal at Maine-road this afternoon.

of this transformation himself as Jackie Blanchflower made his way into the first team.

After making 11 appearances in 1953-54 (and 312 League appearances in total, plus the 3 expunged games), Pearson moved to Bury in February 1954. Later he played for and managed Chester before becoming a newsagent in Prestbury.

He died in Alderley Edge on 20th February 1997, a month after his 78th birthday.

Leading League Scorer in:
1950-1951 - 18 goals, 39 appearances
1952-1953 - 16 goals, 39 appearances

33 – TOMMY TAYLOR

A powerful header of the ball, Tommy Taylor was a tremendous and popular player from the moment he joined the Reds from Barnsley in March 1953. Signed for a fee of £29,999 because Matt Busby did not want to burden him with the tag of being a £30,000 player – although this is a pittance in comparison with modern day fees at the time this would have been perceived as a big deal. According to legend Matt Busby gave the extra pound to a tea-lady!

Taylor made his League debut in the 5-2 victory over Preston on 7th March 1953 and scored twice. It was a great start and in the ten games that followed he netted a further five goals.

In 1953-54 – Taylor's first full season – he scored 22 goals in 35 League appearances

and topped United's scoring charts as the Reds challenged for the title. They finished that campaign fourth but everyone could feel the momentum that was building and Taylor was at the heart of that. He went on to top the scoring charts for three successive seasons including the 1955-56 title winning campaign.

As well as his exploits in the League of course, Taylor scored United's only goal in the 1957 FA Cup final and was a significant member of the 1956-57 European Cup side that reached the semi-final. He netted eight goals in eight games including a hat-trick in the first home game and a goal in the very first European tie at Anderlecht – a trademark header in the second half.

By this time of course Taylor was an England international and had already appeared for his country in the 1954 World Cup finals. He seemed a certainty for the 1958 World Cup and a permanent fixture in United's attack for years to come when tragedy struck.

Taylor was a victim of the Munich Air Disaster and was only 26 when he lost his life. By that time he had appeared in 19 England internationals and scored 16 goals. He had also appeared in 166 League games for the Reds, scoring 112 goals. In Europe Taylor had netted 11 goals in 14 appearances.

At the time of his death Taylor was joint top scorer for 1957-58 with 16 goals from 25 appearances.

The grandson of a former Barnsley player,

Taylor was one of United's greatest stars. Munich robbed both United and England of a highly talented player and one who seemed destined to win many, many honours for club and country.

Leading League Scorer in:

1953-1954 - 22 goals, 35 appearances
1954-1955 - 20 goals, 30 appearances*
1955-1956 - 25 goals, 33 appearances

*Note: * Taylor's goalscoring ratio in 1954-55 was better than Dennis Viollet who scored 20 League goals in 34 games that season. Also some sources credit Taylor with an additional goal, but usually this is quoted as own goal by Scoular in the Newcastle game of 23rd October 1954.*

34 – LIAM 'BILLY' WHELAN

Dublin born Liam Whelan was an inside forward who first appeared for the Reds in the two-legged 1953 FA Youth Cup final against Wolves. Whelan scored in both games as United won 9-3 on aggregate and it was a great introduction for the player.

Renowned for his dribbling, Whelan made his debut in the 2-0 victory at Preston North End on 26th March 1955. He appeared in a further six League games that season with his first goal coming in his second game - a thrilling 5-0 win over Sheffield United on 2nd April watched by 21,158 at Old Trafford.

The following season Whelan appeared in 13 League games, including a run of ten consecutive games in January to March 1956. United won the title that season and Whelan also collected a medal for his part in the Club's Central League title success that year.

It was the 1956-57 season when Whelan topped the charts and established a permanent place in United's first team. First choice from the opening game, Whelan had a fantastic run in September and October when he scored a goal a game for eight

Tommy Taylor

Liam Whelan

Billy Whelan scoring the second goal against Manchester City in September 1956.

consecutive matches. Those goals helped United set the pace in the title race and by the end of the campaign Whelan had netted 26 goals in 39 League games and was, without doubt, one of the most significant players of the season. He was, of course, a member of the side that reached the European Cup semi-final and the FA Cup final that season.

1957-58 started well for the player with a hat-trick in the opening victory over Leicester City and a further 9 goals in the 19 League games that followed, however the emerging Bobby Charlton had replaced him at inside-right before the end of 1957. Whelan remained a vital member of the squad and it seemed as if he would ultimately regain his place as the campaign progressed and the pressures of competing for three major competitions took their toll. Sadly, while travelling as a squad member, Whelan was a victim of the Munich Air Disaster.

Whelan's last first team game was against Chelsea in Division One on 14th December

1957 and ten days before that he appeared in his last European match.

At the time of his death Whelan was 22 and had much to offer the game of football.

Leading League Scorer in:
1956-1957 - 26 goals, 39 appearances

35 – DENNIS VIOLLET

Mancunian Dennis Viollet lived close to Maine Road and came from a family of City supporters, however despite the great Blues 'keeper Frank Swift pushing the youngster's case to City's scouts it was Swift's good friend Matt Busby who actually gave Viollet his break.

Viollet had a trial for United at the age of 14 – the Reds were still playing at Maine Road at this point. A few months later, May 1948, the Manchester Evening Chronicle's Alf Clarke reported on an England-Ireland schoolboy international. Viollet scored for England that day and Clarke described his contribution: "England's victory over Ireland was a match rich in first class, constructive football, with each goal a gem, with a surfeit of sound and spectacular forward play by England which Ireland could not equal.

"The craftsman who paved the way for Ireland's 4-0 defeat was Viollet, whose display at inside-left must have made the many Football League scouts who were present really envious. Viollet was simply methodical in all that he did. He was unselfish, rarely wasted a pass and his spoon feeding of Longden, enabled the Rotherham outside-left to have a most successful game."

Viollet became a professional for United at the age of 17 and two years later, in April 1953, he made his debut in the 2-1 victory at Newcastle United. The following week he scored his first League goal in the 2-2 draw with West Bromwich Albion at Old Trafford before 31,380.

Although he wasn't United's first choice number ten when the 1953-54 season commenced – that was still Stan Pearson – Viollet did make the position his own by the end of the campaign. That season he scored 11 goals in 29 League games.

The following season, 1954-55, Viollet scored twenty goals in 34 League games and was joint top scorer with Tommy Taylor, although Taylor had appeared in fewer matches. The two men shared the honour again in 1957-58, although the Munich Air Disaster had, of course, made comparisons meaningless and impossible. Viollet survived the crash – although inevitably it impacted every moment of the rest of his life and at one point it looked as if injuries he had sustained would end his playing career. He was one of only four players who

Dennis Viollet

appeared in the final match before the crash (at Red Star Belgrade) and the first European game following it (the semi-final V AC Milan). He scored an emotional goal against Milan as the Reds won 2-1 but the return ended in a 4-0 defeat.

Viollet managed two League appearances in 1957-58 after Munich and also appeared in the 1958 FA Cup Final, but it was the following season when his career should be viewed as returning. That season he scored 21 goals in 37 League appearances and then in 1959-60 he netted an incredible 32 goals in 36 League games – a new United record.

Jack Rowley's 30 goal record set in 1952 was passed in the 5-0 victory over Fulham on 26th March 1960 when Viollet netted twice to take his total to 31. In the next match (V Sheffield Wednesday) Viollet scored his 32nd League goal.

In 1960-61 Viollet scored 15 goals in 24 League appearances and followed this with seven in 13 in 1961-62. In January 1962 he was transferred to Stoke in a shock £25,000 move.

At the Victoria Ground the former United star won the Second Division title and appeared in the League Cup final. He made over 200 League and Cup appearances for Stoke before moving to the USA to play in Baltimore.

A spell as player-manager at Linfield followed, as did coaching spells at Preston and Crewe. In 1978 he returned to the States as a coach and in the 1990s he was in charge of the Jacksonville University Dolphins until 1995 and had spells at Richmond Kickers and Jacksonville Cyclones.

Bobby Charlton

On 6th March 1999 he died of cancer aged 65. An annual competition, the Dennis Viollet Cup, was arranged and is competed for by Jacksonville University and the University of North Florida.

Leading League Scorer in:
1957-1958 - 16 goals, 22 appearances*
1959-1960 - 32 goals, 36 appearances

*Note: * Viollet's goalscoring ratio in 1957-58 was better than Tommy Taylor who scored 16 League goals in 25 games that season.*

36 – BOBBY CHARLTON

One of the most written about of all the Club's star players, Bobby Charlton is well known worldwide for his contribution to the United cause and to England.

The nephew of the great Newcastle centre-forward Jackie Milburn, Charlton had a true footballer's upbringing in the north-east. Born in Ashington, Charlton joined United after earning England Schoolboy honours.

He appeared in United's thrilling FA Youth Cup finals of 1954, 1955 and 1956 before making his first team debut on 6th October 1956 when he scored twice as Charlton Athletic were defeated 4-2 at Old Trafford.

Due to the quality of United's squad at the time, Charlton was unable to retain his place, however by the season's end he had scored ten goals in 14 appearances. Not bad for someone who wasn't guaranteed a place.

The following season, 1957-58, Charlton made occasional appearances before replacing Liam 'Billy' Whelan in the number eight shirt shortly before Christmas – a position he made his own until the Munich Air Disaster.

After Munich Charlton played at outside-left as the Club tried to create a new side. Charlton was one of the Reds' most consistent players and, inevitably because of what had happened at Munich, one of the focal points for the media and the public. In the first full season after the disaster he topped United's goalscoring charts with 29 goals in 38 League games as

United astounded the football world with a second placed finish – considering all the Club had gone through this was an amazing achievement.

Although the years that followed were not as successful in the League, Charlton was a reassuring presence. In 1960-61 he topped United's charts once more, and then in 1963 he was a member of the side that won the FA Cup. Often the significance of this success is not considered, but winning the FA Cup actually meant that only five years after the disaster Busby had created a side capable of national success. It also meant United had qualified for Europe again and, on 15th October 1963, Charlton scored (V Willem II) his first European goal since that fateful game in Belgrade in 1958.

As the 1960s progressed Charlton was a regular for England and was, of course, a member of the team that won the World Cup in 1966. He was also voted Football Writers' Footballer of the Year and won the European equivalent that year. Twelve months earlier he had helped United to the League title.

In 1966-67 Charlton scored 12 goals and was an ever-present as the Reds won the title again, and then in 1968 he was, of course, a member of the side that won the European Cup at Wembley. Inevitably, this was a highly emotional night for him, coming a decade after the disaster.

As football moved into the 1970s United began to change. Matt Busby had retired, though he remained at Old Trafford, and the side began to struggle to some extent. Nevertheless Charlton remained a key figure and in 1972-73 he topped the Club's goalscoring charts for the last time. The record was not a great one – six goals in 35 games – but that says more about United's attacking options at the time than it does about Charlton.

In April 1973 a crowd of over 44,184 at Stamford Bridge witnessed his final League game for United. In the close season he became Preston's manager, but resigned in August 1975.

He had a spell as a player with Waterford in 1976 and a director at Wigan Athletic (including a brief spell as caretaker-manager). He also set up a world-renowned football school and became a director of United.

In 1994 he became the first footballer since Stanley Matthews to be knighted for his services as an ambassador to football (of course Matt Busby and Alf Ramsey, his managers at United and England, had also been knighted for their managerial achievements). He was also part of Manchester's bidding team for the Olympics during the 1990s.

Charlton, to many fans worldwide, remains the public face of Manchester United. In August 2011 he was one of the guests assisting with the 2011-12 Champions League draw for UEFA.

Leading League Scorer in:
1958-1959 - 29 goals, 38 appearances
1960-1961 - 21 goals, 39 appearances
1972-1973 - 6 goals, 36 appearances

Bobby Charlton

Beckham's Future?

In 1994 Garth Dykes wrote "The United Alphabet", a book published by ACL Colour Print & Polar Publishing. In that book Dykes included a profile of United player David Beckham. At the time the youngster had only appeared as a substitute in a League Cup tie and so Dykes' assessment of the player was not based on achievement, simply on potential.

His comments make interesting reading.

Knowing what we know now, it seems Beckham more than delivered on that potential.

BECKHAM, David Robert Joseph

Role : Midfield 1992-
5' 11" 10st.7lbs.
b. Leytonstone, 2nd May 1975

CAREER : Essex Schoolboys/UNITED trainee July 1991, pro. Jan 1993.

Debut v Brighton & Hove Albion (a) (sub)
FLC 2 leg 1, 23.9.92

David Beckham

England Youth international David Beckham's first senior appearance came twenty minutes from the end of the drawn Football League Cup tie at Brighton, when he came on as substitute for Andrei Kanchelskis. A member of United's highly successful FA Youth Cup team, he collected a winners' medal in 1992 (when he scored in the away leg at Crystal Palace) and a runners-up medal in 1993. Beckham is comfortable in possession and, for his years, shows remarkable vision and creativity from the middle of the field. One of many fine younger players waiting on the wings, he is expected to exert increasing pressure on the senior squad in the not too distant future.

Appearances :
FLC: 0(1) app. 0 gls.
Total: *0(1) app. 0 gls.*

Wage Demands

When forward Adam Carson joined Newton Heath in the summer of 1892 the club was preparing for its first season in the Football League. Carson was signed from Glasgow Thistle and the Scottish media were upset with the methods being undertaken by 'English agents' to secure Scottish stars.

The Scottish Sport newspaper reported that Carson had joined Newton Heath on extravagant terms: "£10 down and £3 per week in the playing season, £2 per week off season."

It is worth noting that the maximum wage in 1901 was set at £4 a week, so Carson's 1892 salary can be said to have been significant, especially as the Heathens had not yet kicked a ball in the Football League.

Despite the expense, Carson only managed 13 appearances in the League for the Heathens, though he did score three goals in those matches. He moved across east Manchester and joined near-neighbours Ardwick on 15th March 1893.

After seven games (and another three goals!) Carson moved to Liverpool, but was unable to find his way into their League side.

The Football Season
Daily Reminder
November

1st November 1936

Half-back Eddie Colman (below) was born in Salford. He made his United first team debut shortly after his 19th birthday in 1955. By the time of his debut Colman had already helped the Reds to three consecutive FA Youth Cup successes.

2nd November 1983

Frank Stapleton (right) scored twice as United defeated Spartak Varna in the ECWC second round second leg. The Reds won the tie 4-1 on aggregate. Fifty four years earlier, future United manager Matt Busby made his debut for Manchester

City in their 3-1 defeat of Middlesbrough.

3rd November 1983

Ron Atkinson's United defeated Port Vale 1-0 in the 2nd round of the League Cup at Vale Park. Frank Stapleton was the scorer.

4th November 1986

United were defeated 4-1

Delaney dazzles the Derby defence

By ALF CLARKE

MANCHESTER UNITED 4   DERBY COUNTY 1

FIGHTING back with splendid spirit after a "gift" goal, Manchester United trounced Derby County 4—1 at Maine-road. United played grand football and by sheer skill and artistry made the County look a very disappointing side.

Derby's goal came through **CARTER**, but soon **PEARSON** scored two for United and these were followed by goals by **MITEN** and **ROWLEY**.

at Southampton in the League Cup. This was the last match before Alex Ferguson was appointed manager.

5th November 1949

The Reds defeated Huddersfield Town 6-0 in the League with goals from Pearson (2), Rowley (2), Delaney & Mitten.

6th November 1986

Alex Ferguson was appointed manager.

7th November 1978

Rio Ferdinand (below) was born in Peckham, London.

8th November 1947

Jack Rowley scored all four United goals as the Reds drew 4-4 at home to Huddersfield Town before 59,772 at Maine Road.

9th November 1946

United beat Derby 4-1 in the first post war League season (above). Reports claimed the attendance

reached over 60,000 with some fans sat between the Maine Road touchline and the terraces, but the official attendance was later submitted as 57,340.

10th November 1982

A goalless League Cup tie at Bradford City was followed up with a 4-1 United victory in the

ENGLAND

Reserve
BROOME
Aston Villa

Reserve
TAYLOR
Bolton Wanderers

1

WOODLEY
Chelsea
Photo: M/c. Evening News

2

SPROSTON
Manchester City
Photo: M/c. Evening News

3

HAPGOOD
Arsenal
Photo: M/c. Evening News

4

WILLINGHAM
Huddersfield Town
Photo: M/c. Evening News

5

CULLIS
Wolverhampton
Photo: M/c. Evening News

6

MERCER
Everton
Photo: Daily Express

7
MATTHEWS
Stoke City
Photo: M/c. Evening News

8

HALL
Tottenham Hotspur
Photo: M/c. Evening News

9
LAWTON
Everton
Photo: M/c. Evening News

10
STEPHENSON
Leeds United
Photo: Albert Wilkes and Son

11
SMITH
Millwall
Photo: M/c. Evening News

English Linesman: **L. DALE**, SHEFFIELD
Red Stripe

Referee: **P. CRAIGMYLE**, SCOTLAND

Irish Linesman: **S. THOMPSON**, BELFAST
Blue Stripe

replay. Ultimately the Reds progressed to their first League Cup final this season.

11th November 1938

Old Trafford staged the England-Ireland international. This was a remarkable game that ended 7-0 to England. Willie Hall scored a record-breaking hat-trick in four minutes (36-40 mins) and went on to score five goals in total.

12th November 1910

For the first time all season United failed to score. The League game with Notts County ended in a disappointing 0-0 during a season which saw the Reds

UNITED SEEKING ADDITIONAL RESERVE POWER

BY THE CAPTAIN

MANCHESTER UNITED may soon be adding to their playing strength. Their chief aim is to consolidate reserve strength. The team have so far escaped serious injuries to key men, but difficulties might arise if Rowley or Charlie Mitten, who have not missed a senior match, were suddenly ruled out for first-team duty.

Manager Busby recently prospected in Ireland while his "scouts" are out in force every week looking for promising players as part of a set policy to build up reserve strength.

Rowley, Pearson, and Aston joined the England party at Southport to-day in readiness for Wednesday's Maine Road international.

Lancashire face tiring journeys

BY JOHN KAY

LANCASHIRE'S cricketers are to undertake some long

---

win their second League title. Fifty nine years later the Reds played out a goalless League Cup tie at Derby County. They won the replay 1-0 with Brian Kidd the only scorer.

13th November 1965

A great United performance brought victory at Filbert Street as Leicester City were defeated 5-0 with goals from Herd (2), Best, Charlton & Connelly.

14th November 1949

The Manchester Evening News reported that United were looking at recruiting more reserves. Manager Matt Busby had recently been on a scouting trip to Ireland (above).

15th November 1958

Hyde-born Warren Bradley made his debut in the 6-3 defeat at Bolton. Bradley was a school teacher and brought into United as a part-time professional as the Reds tried to recover from the Munich disaster. He stayed at the Club for almost four years and later became a key member of the former players' association.

16th November 1974

Paul Scholes was born in Salford. On the same date in 1938 Old Trafford staged the England-Ireland international.

17th November 1956

United defeated Leeds 3-2

RESULTS,

DIVISION I

ARSENAL ... 3		BOLTON W. 0				
H.-T.: 2—0		Att. 35,000				
BIRM'GHAM. *		CHARLTON.. *				
H.-T.: 1—1		Att. 35,000				
BURNLEY .. 3		WOLVES 0				
H.-T.: 1—0		Att. 27,000				
CARDIFF C.. *		SUNDER'LD.. *				
H.-T.: 0—0		Att. 20,000				
CHELSEA .. 4		LUTON T. .. 1				
H.-T.: 2—0		Att. 36,000				
M/C UTD. .. *		LEEDS U. .. 2				
H.-T.: 1—1		Att. 52,131				
NEWCASTLE *		EVERTON.. *				
H.-T.: 0—0		Att. 40,000				
PORTSM'TH. 0		BLACKPOOL 0				
H.-T.: 0—0		Att. 24,000				
PRESTON .. 3		ASTON V. .. 3				
H.-T.: 2—0		Att. 20,000				
SHEFF'LD W. *		TOTTENH'M *				
H.-T.: 0—0		Att. 28,000				
W. BROM. .. 1		M/C CITY .. 1				
H.-T.: 0—0						

* FOR RESULT SEE STOP PRESS

	P.	W.	D.	L.	F.	A.	Pts.
M/C UNITED	17	12	3	2	42	25	27
*TOTTENHAM ..	16	12	1	3	48	22	25
BLACKPOOL ..	17	9	4	4	42	29	22
LEEDS UTD. ..	18	9	4	5	33	26	22
BURNLEY	18	7	7	4	27	19	21
WEST BROM. A.	17	7	6	4	25	21	20
BOLTON WAND..	18	7	6	5	25	24	20
WOLVES	17	8	3	6	42	31	19
PRESTON N.E. ..	18	7	5	6	35	39	19
*ARSENAL	18	9	1	8	38	35	19
*BIRMINGHAM ..	16	7	4	5	32	25	18
ASTON VILLA	16	6	5	5	27	33	17
LUTON TOWN ..	17	5	6	6	29	27	16
CHELSEA	17	5	6	6	26	28	16
M/C CITY	18	5	4	9	27	36	14
*CARDIFF CITY..	16	4	5	7	23	33	13
*EVERTON	17	5	3	9	25	37	13
*SHEFFIELD W...	17	5	2	10	35	41	12
PORTSMOUTH ..	17	3	6	8	30	39	12
*NEWCASTLE ..	17	4	4	8	18	35	12
*SUNDERLAND ..	16	3	2	11	31	42	8
*CHARLTON ATH.	17	3	2	12	21	43	8

MIDLAND LEAGUE

NOTTS FOR. R. 2	DONCASTER R. 3	
LINCOLN C.	BRADFORD C.	

UNITED'S RALLY

THE Manchester "Derby" at Maine-road was a match of real sensations. It will be a long time before a game like it is seen again, writes Alf. Clarke. Never have United fought with such determination as on this occasion and never will they win a more sensational victory.

On paper it looked a good thing for Manchester City, and it was shaping that way with City two goals in the lead a quarter of an hour after the re-start, Smith having scored both City goals from left-wing corner kicks after the interval.

But United's dogged determination earned them equality and then victory in the last two minutes.

with goals from Whelan (2) and Charlton. The victory ensured a two point lead, after 17 games, at the top of the table. Spurs were second with a game in hand. The Reds went on to win the title.

18th November 1944

Goals from Morris (2) and Mycock gave United a 3-2 victory over landlords City at Maine Road before 20,764 in the wartime 'Football League North'.

19th November 1988

Alex Ferguson's United drew 2-2 at Southampton. This was the fourth of five consecutive score draws for the Reds in the League.

20th November 1880

The first reported football game played by Newton Heath was staged on this day against Bolton's second team.

21st November 1953

United beat Blackpool 4-1 in Division One. Tommy Taylor scored a hat-trick.

22nd November 1980

Two goals from Joe Jordan helped United to a 4-1 Division One victory over Brighton.

23rd November 1929

A Harry Rowley goal was enough to ensure victory over Burnley in front of an Old Trafford crowd of 9,060 in Division One. Despite being a top flight side these were difficult days for the Reds. United's next home game – a derby with Bolton – was watched by only 5,656.

24th November 1951

Gorton-born Roger Byrne made his United debut in a goalless League game at Liverpool before 42,378. He became an ever-present for the rest of the season as he helped the Reds to the 1951-52 League Championship – the Club's first title since 1911.

25th November 1978

Jimmy Greenhoff scored his eighth goal of the season as the Reds defeated Chelsea 1-0 before 28,162 at Stamford Bridge.

26th November 1966

David Herd scored four as United defeated Sunderland 5-0 at Old Trafford. The other goal was netted by Denis Law.

27th November 2007

Despite conceding a goal in the 21st minute, United Overcame Sporting Lisbon in the Champions League group stage. Tevez scored the equaliser in the 61st minute with Ronaldo making it 2-1 in the final minute at Old Trafford. Despite a 1-1 draw with Roma United qualified for the latter stages by heading their group.

28th November 1981

Goals from Birtles and Stapleton ensured a 2-0 victory at home to Brighton.

29th November 1973

Ryan Giggs was born in Cardiff.

30th November 1963

A Denis Law brace gave United a 2-1 victory at Sheffield United in Division One.

Progressive Attendance Record

The following provides the progression of United's record attendances. These are for Manchester United first team home games regardless of venue.

North Road

11,000	V Ardwick (Manchester City, FA Cup), 3 October 1891
12,000	V Blackburn Rovers, 5 November 1892
15,000	V Sunderland, 4 March 1893

Bank Street

18,000	V Blackburn Rovers (FA Cup), 10 February 1894
20,000	V Derby County (FA Cup), 15 February 1896
25,000	V Small Heath (Birmingham City), 15 November 1902
40,000	V Manchester City, 25 December 1902
45,000	V Bolton Wanderers, 22 September 1906

Old Trafford

50,000	V Liverpool, 19 February 1910*
60,000	V Manchester City, 17 September 1910
65,101	V Aston Villa (FA Cup), 4 February 1911
70,504	V Aston Villa, 27 December 1920**

Maine Road

83,260	V Arsenal, 17 January 1948

NOTE: * The Manchester Courier claimed the attendance for the opening game at Old Trafford was 50,000 including a 'fair number who got in without paying'. Presumably there were approximately 5,000 who got in without paying as most sources claim the attendance as 45,000.

**This remained United's highest League crowd at Old Trafford until 9th April 2006 when 70,908 watched the 2-0 victory over Arsenal in the Premier League. The Reds highest attendance at the stadium is 76,098, set for the visit of Blackburn on 31st March 2007. The Old Trafford record attendance stands at 76,962 for Wolverhampton Wanderers V Grimsby Town on 25th March 1939.

Old Trafford during construction in 1909 (top) and shortly after completion in 1910 (middle). Right: United fans in 1948.

Top: **Fans at Old Trafford's opening game on 19 February 1910. Note the umbrella proclaiming Rocca's Brigade. Louis Rocca was an influential figure for many years at United.**

Bottom: **Old Trafford in 2004. Compare with the 1910 image on page 97.**

LEAGUE LEADING GOALSCORERS - BEST RATIO

We've listed over 120 years' worth of great United goalscorers, but which seasonal leader actually has the best goals to game ratio?

The following takes each seasonal record scorer and identifies the twenty players with the best goals to game ratios. The all-time best is Bob Donaldson with a ratio of 1.318 goals per game during the 1891-92 season, however Donaldson's record was achieved in the Alliance League. If we ignore that competition the League leader is Denis Law who, in 1963-64 possessed a record of a goal per game for all the matches he played.

Significantly, the next highest player is actually a modern day star, Cristiano Ronaldo.

Right: **Bob Donaldson**

	Year	Division	No. of Goals	No. of Appearances	Average goals per game	Player
1	1892	Alliance	29	22	1.318	Donaldson
2	1964	One	30	30	1.000	Law
3	2008	Premier	31	34	0.912	Ronaldo
4	1906	Two	30	33	0.909	Picken
5	1960	One	32	36	0.889	Viollet
6	1896	Two	16	19	0.842	Cassidy
7	1908	One	25	30	0.833	Turnbull (Sandy)
8	2010	Premier	26	32	0.813	Rooney
9	1965	One	28	36	0.778	Law
10	1909	One	17	22	0.773	Turnbull (Jimmy)
11	1959	One	29	38	0.763	Charlton
12	1956	One	25	33	0.758	Taylor
13	1952	One	30	40	0.750	Rowley (Jack)
14	2003	Premier	25	34	0.735	Van Nistelrooy
15	1898	Two	22	30	0.733	Boyd

	Year	Division	No. of Goals	No. of Appearances	Average goals per game	Player
16	1958	One	16	22	0.727	Viollet
17	2002	Premier	23	32	0.719	Van Nistelrooy
18	1947	One	26	37	0.703	Rowley (Jack)
19	1968	One	28	41	0.683	Best
20=	1955	One	20	30	0.667	Taylor
20=	1957	One	26	39	0.667	Whelan

Denis Law

UNITED'S EUROPEAN CUP WINNERS' CUP RECORD

After winning the FA Cup in 1990, the Reds qualified for the European Cup Winners' Cup (ECWC). At the time the ECWC was viewed by UEFA as their second most significant tournament behind the European Cup and ahead of the UEFA Cup. It had been formed in 1960.

Alex Ferguson guided United to success in the competition with a memorable victory over Barcelona in the final. This was the Reds' first – and only – success in the competition despite a proud record in domestic competition which led to qualification. Of course, in seasons where United also qualified for the European Cup or Champions League then the ECWC place would be passed on to the other FA Cup finalists.

The following table shows each of United's ECWC campaigns.

Season	Reason For Qualification	Round Reached	Manager
1963-64	FA Cup winners	Quarter-final	Matt Busby
1977-78	FA Cup winners	Second round	Dave Sexton
1983-84	FA Cup winners	Semi-final	Ron Atkinson
1985-86	*United qualified as FA Cup winners, however English clubs were banned from competing following the Heysel Disaster*		
1990-91	FA Cup winners	Winners	Alex Ferguson
1991-92	ECWC winners	Second round	Alex Ferguson
1994-95	*FA Cup winners, however United competed in the Champions League due to League position*		
1996-97	*FA Cup winners, however United competed in the Champions League due to League position*		

The final season of the ECWC came in 1998-99 as European football was restructured.

By that time United had competed in the tournament during five seasons. Only Tottenham Hotspur, the first English winners, had played in more ECWC campaigns (they had played in six).

By the end of 1999 the English record in the ECWC was:

Winners: Tottenham (1963), West Ham (1965), Manchester City (1970), Chelsea (1971 & 1998), Everton (1985), United (1991) and Arsenal (1994). It is worth noting that Aberdeen won the competition in 1983 when Alex Ferguson was their manager.

Finalists: Liverpool (1966), Leeds (1973), West Ham (1976) and Arsenal (1980 & 1995).

When the competition ended there had been 32 separate winners. The only sides to win the trophy more than once (with the number of times each has been ECWC runners-up in brackets) were:

**MANCHESTER UNITED
FC BARCELONA
MAY 15 - 1991** KICK-OFF 20.15
STADION FEIJENOORD ROTTERDAM

Barcelona 4 (2)
Anderlecht 2 (2)
AC Milan 2 (1)
Chelsea 2 (0)
Dynamo Kyiv 2 (0)

Some claim that the trophy was permanently given to Barcelona when it was abolished in 1999 as a mark of their record as the most successful side in the competition. However when the City Of Manchester Stadium staged the UEFA Cup final in 2008, UEFA allowed City to display the original trophy, alongside the UEFA Cup (and the European Cup presented to Liverpool to mark their fifth success) in a special exhibition at Eastlands. UEFA claimed the ECWC had been stored at their headquarters in Switzerland.

THE MANCHESTER UNITED COLLECTORS' CLUB

Manchester United, is a name as recognisable to many throughout the world as that of McDonald's or Coca Cola. For the thousands of regular match going supporters and for those attending games spasmodically, there is much more to the following of their favourite football club than the ninety minutes action out on the pitch. Their dedication to their red shirted heroes from Manchester M16 stretches far beyond the journeys up and down motorways, and the hours spent in some non-descript airport.

The hundreds, no thousands of pounds spent on match tickets, travel and refreshments are often matched, perhaps not exactly pound for pound, by many of those same supporters who collect programmes and memorabilia connected with Manchester United Football Club.

Today, the market surrounding football memorabilia is enormous, with that connected with United at the pinnacle. Some of those items are relatively easy and inexpensive to obtain, while others are extremely rare with a price tag which would shock many. All, however, have been keenly collected regardless of cost.

None of the items contained within the pages of this or any other book focusing on the Reds carry a price tag, of course, as prices paid are purely down to the individual concerned. More often than not the price paid also depends on how much a collector requires a certain item. To be honest, an item is simply worth as much as the next person is willing to pay for it.

For collectors of United memorabilia there is the 'United Review Collectors Club', which is run by Dumfries based supporter/collector Iain McCartney. McCartney is well-known to United fans. He has written countless acclaimed books and articles on United, including biographies of Duncan Edwards and Roger Byrne; a history of Old Trafford and 'Forgotten Fixtures', which covered every first team friendly from 1946 – 2009.

We've asked Iain, a key figure behind the 'Collectors Club' for over twenty years, to look back on his time running the organisation while also focusing on the countless items available to the collector or enthusiast.

The 'United Review Collectors Club', which I believe was the first of its kind, was formed way back in 1981 by Kevin Burthem, Alan Bradshaw and Roy Cavanagh, from Warrington, Urmston and Worsley respectively. The trio of keen collectors used to meet on a regular basis for a couple of pints and a chat about everything United, and after a few discussions decided to form a club for like-minded fanatics.

Alan was the first editor, producing forty issues of the newsletter. He was followed by Kevin, who produced a further twelve issues, before I took over the reins twenty years ago.

THE OFFICIAL PROGRAMME

The ONLY OFFICIAL ORGAN of Manchester City, Newton Heath, Broughton Rangers, & Salford Clubs

No. 2.   SATURDAY, SEPTEMBER 10th.   ONE PENNY.

ENTERED AT STATIONERS HALL.

TO FOOTBALL PATRONS!

The **Official Football Programme**

IS THE ONLY LIST ALLOWED TO BE SOLD ON THE GROUNDS OF THE MANCHESTER CITY, NEWTON HEATH, SALFORD, and BROUGHTON RANGERS,

The "PROGRAMME" is also sold in the approaches to the Grounds, and can be had from all Newsagents.

Be sure and ask for the **Official Programme.**

Amusements.

COMEDY THEATRE—To-Night. THE PRIVATE SECRETARY. Popular prices: 2s. 6d., 1s., 9d., and 6d. Monday, Sept. 12th, THE MOODY-MANNERS OPERA COMPANY.

THEATRE ROYAL. TO-NIGHT AT 7-30. TWO LITTLE VAGABONDS.

PRINCE'S THEATRE. TO-NIGHT at 7-30. A GREEK SLAVE, by Mr. GEO. EDWARDS' CO.

FREE TRADE HALL. 2-30 AND 7-30. HAMILTON'S HISPANO-AMERICAN WAR AND GREAT EXCURSIONS. VARIETY TROUPE.

ZOOLOGICAL GARDENS, BELLE VUE. OPEN EVERY DAY FROM 10 A.M. The Grand Spectacle of the STORMING OF DARGAI. Admission: Firework Days until 4 p.m., 6d. each; after 4 p.m. 1s. each.

NEW BRIGHTON TOWER,
(The Highest Structure in England)
GRAND THEATRE OF VARIETIES.
Admission Free. Seats Extra. Four Permanent Bands. 30 Acres of Gardens. Old English Fair. Ascents to Top of Tower, 6d. ILLUMINATIONS. Eleven Thousand Electric Lamps. **MAGNIFICENT BALL ROOM.**
Ferry Steamers and Mersey Tunnel Railway provide quick and constant service from Liverpool. **Entrance to Gardens, 6d.**

Bedford Park Athletic Grounds

ROCK FERRY,

Adjoining L. & N. W., G. W., and Mersey Tunnel Joint Station.

THESE GROUNDS ARE AVAILABLE FOR ALL CLASSES OF

SPORTS—CYCLING, RUNNING, COURSING, PIGEON SHOOTING, TRAINING, &c.

ALSO THE GROUNDS OF THE

ROCK FERRY FOOTBALL CLUB.

FOR TERMS APPLY—

Mr. LUKE LEES, Proprietor,

Bedford Hotel, Rock Ferry.

In the early days of the 'Club', the newsletters covered mainly programmes from pre-war to date, while it was, as it is today, an outlet for collectors to advertise their wants and sales, enabling collections to be improved. But since taking over the running of the 'Club' - which has seen membership cover not simply the length and breadth of the UK, but from every corner of the globe - collecting football memorabilia has diversified from more or less programmes only, to anything and everything connected with Manchester United. This is something that has been embraced by the 'Collectors Club' newsletters since I took over.

The popularity in collecting football related memorabilia in its many formats is best illustrated by the auction houses scattered around the country. Not so long ago they would not entertain such items, but today are quick to grasp as much as they possibly can, augmented by the increasing number of former players who have decided to realise the value of their medals and other odds and ends.

With such a wide range of members, from the young novice collector to the top United collectors in the country/world, it has been something of a challenge to maintain a standard approach within the pages of the newsletter. There's a need to feature items that appeal to everyone, keeping a balance between programmes and everything else, and also pre-war and more modern items.

Thankfully, members are happy to contribute from time to time, with details of items that they have recently picked up or allowing access to their collections. A few years ago, one collector promised to do some scans of the pre-World War One programmes that he had, but kept forgetting and apologising when we met that he hadn't done so. In the end, he said that as he kept forgetting he would bring me the folder that they were in and I could take them away, do what I wanted with them and bring them back whenever I was finished! True to his word, he turned up with a folder of around a dozen United aways, all pre-1920 and said simply there you are and walked off.

The general content of the newsletter has not simply been a collection of articles on various collectable items, but through its pages I have also tried to inform members of special items that they might not have heard about and can be picked up from various sources. I have also tried to keep them, or at least those who are interested, up to date with some of the many books that are available with the regular and popular 'United Bookshelf', occasionally offering special publishers deals.

Anything connected with the football club falls under the collecting umbrella, offering an additional avenue to venture down, enabling me to feature items on Old Trafford, United Sports Days, former players, bank cards and countless other items.

I think it is fair to say that since taking over the 'Club', I have covered as wide a range of

Newton Heath Notes.

Act 1.

IF they had so arranged it the Newton Heath officials could not have found a better team than Chorley to test the abilities of their eleven. It was plain to be seen that the Juniors, if we may call them such, intended to obtain a victory, and in failing to do so they experienced exceedingly hard lines. They were much the better team, and showed the weak points of the Heathens to a nicety. The latter team played the usual friendly game, but some of them found it out to their cost, and were probably surprised when they found themselves left off the team. "Curly" Jones was the only one of the new comers that did anything like, and he really played a "class" game. The forwards put no devil into their play, and the way some of them shaped would have disgraced a school-boy. Cairns did well at times, but both Brooks and "Chorley" Jones did little of any good. Being the opening game was an excuse, and we have hopes of their turning out good men. Cartwright rambled about a good deal, but it was probably with a view to help Morgan. You are discharged, Walter, this time, but don't do it again.

Act 2.

When they came to serious business, however, the Heathens played a very different kind of game. Of course alterations had been made in the forwards, and the ever-popular Fred was standing by the side of the very happy Harry. It was evident from the start that they meant business, and although Old Sol was looking straight into their faces, and a powerful wind tried to smash up their combination, they stuck to their guns, and Private Cassidy hit the target before the interval. The second half saw the Heathens in good trim, attack and defence both being good. Goal number two was not long in coming, and although the Gainsborough men tried hard they failed to get a solitary point. Thus the Heathens booked their first League points. It was a brilliant win, and proves that the locals are a very good lot. If the team is kept together success is assured.

A "GRATE FITE."

The game at Clayton last Saturday proved a battle royal. Right from the start both teams went at it hammer and tongs, with the result that play was fast and furious. There was very little in the teams, but the winners were entitled to their honours. In the closing stages much feeling was imparted into the game and the referee had a warm time of it. If Saturday's form is kept up the attendance at Combination fixtures will improve considerably.

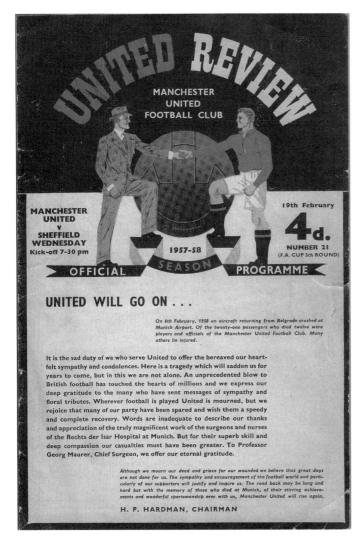

UNITED WILL GO ON . . .

On 6th February, 1958 an aircraft returning from Belgrade crashed at Munich Airport. Of the twenty-one passengers who died twelve were players and officials of the Manchester United Football Club. Many others lie injured.

It is the sad duty of we who serve United to offer the bereaved our heart-felt sympathy and condolences. Here is a tragedy which will sadden us for years to come, but in this we are not alone. An unprecedented blow to British football has touched the hearts of millions and we express our deep gratitude to the many who have sent messages of sympathy and floral tributes. Wherever football is played United is mourned, but we rejoice that many of our party have been spared and wish them a speedy and complete recovery. Words are inadequate to describe our thanks and appreciation of the truly magnificent work of the surgeons and nurses of the Rechts der Isar Hospital at Munich. But for their superb skill and deep compassion our casualties must have been greater. To Professor Georg Maurer, Chief Surgeon, we offer our eternal gratitude.

Although we mourn our dead and grieve for our wounded we believe that great days are not done for us. The sympathy and encouragement of the football world and parti-cularly of our supporters will justify and inspire us. The road back may be long and hard but with the memory of those who died at Munich, of their stirring achieve-ments and wonderful sportsmanship ever with us, Manchester United will rise again.

H. P. HARDMAN, CHAIRMAN

memorabilia as I possibly could, with even Newton Heath items finding their way onto the pages, with an article in my 100th newsletter covering a visit to the Colindale Newspaper Library in London, where there is a collection of Heathens programmes from 1898 -1901.

The programme in those distant days was "The Official Programme – The Official Organ of the Manchester City, Newton Heath, Broughton Rangers and Salford Club" and was published by – Mersey Athletic Publishing Company, 41 Arcade Chambers, St Mary's Gate, Manchester.

Underneath, was a statement which read – "To Football Patrons! The Official Football Programme is the only list allowed to be sold on the grounds of the Manchester City, Newton Heath, Salford and Broughton Rangers.

The twelve page programme was also sold on the approaches to the grounds, where the boy sellers would wear official badges, and could also be had from all newsagents.

Over the years, I have also been able to include exclusive interviews on collecting topics with the likes of Sir Alex Ferguson, Martin Edwards and George Graham, as well as Roy Calmels, the man behind 'Sports Programmes', United programme dealer Keith Ennion and various editors of the 'United Review'.

One two occasions, the newsletter has taken on something of a different format, with Volume 14 issue number two dedicated to Sir Matt Busby following his death, with his career in football told through various programmes and items of memorabilia. Volume 26 number one took on a similar format following the death of George Best. This issue, or at least some of them, were actually printed in full colour for the first and only time.

The only reason some of them were, was due to the printer giving me a price to do it in colour, then half way through the print run, deciding that he had made a mistake and it would be more than double. Needless to say a different printer was found for subsequent issues.

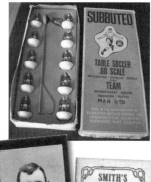

Due to United's success, there is perhaps a wider range of programmes and memorabilia out there to collect. However, this also has a diverse effect, with the popularity of the club also forcing the prices up, making anything with Manchester United on it more expensive to buy than that of any other club.

But why do people collect?

Some purely for pleasure, perhaps from a historical point of view, others as an investment – a pension plan. The financial side is certainly something that creeps into the equation, particularly in more recent times with increasing every day living costs putting pressure on many to sell and as they are not getting any younger, and with no one to leave their collection to, or no-one with any interest in it, decide that perhaps it is time to cash in and enjoy some benefits from the sum it brings.

It is sadly something that faces every collector, but until that unfortunate day arrives, there is much pleasure to be gained from collecting United related memorabilia. The programmes cover the games played (or in some cases failed to take place), while a collection of match reports and cuttings (my own Achilles heel) create a complete history of the football club that nothing else can match.

Pre-war cigarette cards, postcards and their post-war cousin, the trade cards, help build up a photographic history of the players who pulled on the famous red (or whatever colour the modern day player happens to be wearing).

Match tickets, especially for the travelling Red, bring back the memories of trips to far off countries and tales of countless motorway service stations, railway stations, as well as reflecting the rising cost of following your team.

Menus capture the celebrations following yet another success, while for those who can afford it, there is the possibility of owning a medal from such a triumph or a jersey worn by a player who took part in a particular game.

There are so many collecting arms and they need not all be expensive, but they all guarantee to bring hours of enjoyment, countless friendships and give you a small bit-part in the history of Manchester United Football Club.

If you are a collector of United memorabilia or are interested in finding out more about the "United Review Collectors Club" then contact Iain McCartney. Please write to (including a SAE): The United Review Collectors Club, 7 Cartha Road, Lochvale, Dumfries, DG1 4JB.

The Football Season Daily Reminder
December

1st December 1906

The first Manchester derby in Division One was played at City's Hyde Road ground (see image on page 110). Although United (as Newton Heath) had joined the First Division in 1892 the Blues had joined Division Two. In 1894 the Heathens were relegated while City were promoted in 1899, meaning there was no opportunity for the two sides to meet in the top flight until the Reds were promoted in 1906.

2nd December 1944

United defeated Crewe 4-1 in the Football League North. Wartime football was played on a regional basis between traditional Football League sides from all divisions with two championships per season. The Reds ended the First Championship that year in thirtieth place. Twenty-two years earlier United defeated Rotherham 3-0 in Division Two (left) before an Old Trafford crowd of 13,500.

3rd December 1988

Goals from Milne, McClair and Hughes ensured a 3-0 Division One victory over Charlton in front of an Old Trafford crowd of 31,173.

4th December 1957

Despite a second leg 1-0 defeat at Dukla Prague, United progressed to the European Cup quarter-final. The first leg had ended 3-0 at Old Trafford.

5th December 1987

Goalkeeper Chris Turner returned to the side for his first game of the season (Gary Walsh had appeared in the previous 16 League games). The Reds won 2-0 at Queen's Park Rangers.

MANCHESTER'S GREAT FOOTBALL DAY: SCENES AT

6th December 1952

A crowd of 27,617 witnessed the 3-2 defeat of Middlesbrough at Old Trafford. The game marked the debuts of David Pegg and John Doherty.

7th December 1972

Secretary Les Olive, acting on behalf of the Club, sent a letter to all First and Second Division clubs informing them that the Reds would like to receive offers for George Best. On the same date in 2002 Scholes (opposite) and Veron both scored as United defeated Arsenal 2-0 in the Premier League at Old Trafford. Attendance 67,650.

Telegraphic Address: "STADIUM" Manchester
Telephone: 061-872 1861/2

MANCHESTER UNITED Football Club Ltd
OLD TRAFFORD, MANCHESTER, M16 0RA

Manager:
F. O'FARRELL.

Secretary:
L. OLIVE.

LO/IP
7th December, 1972

The Secretary
First and Second Division Clubs

Dear Sir,

We wish to inform you that we are prepared to receive offers for the transfer of registration of the following player:-

	Age	Position
G. Best	26	Forward

This does not give you permission to approach the player and all enquiries should be made to our Manager, Mr. F. O'Farrell.

Yours faithfully,

L. Olive

Secretary

8th December 2009

A Michael Owen hat-trick (44th, 83rd and 90th minutes) ensured a United victory at Wolfsburg in Group B of the Champions League. Wolfsburg had equalised in the 56th minute with a goal from future City player Edin Dzeko.

9th December 1976

The day after a friendly between United and a South Wales XI at Cardiff, it was revealed that the match had raised almost £8,000 for Newport County. The previous night's game had ended in a 1-0 defeat however.

10th December 1963

Tottenham Hotspur were defeated 4-1 (4-3 on aggregate) in the European Cup Winners' Cup second round. Spurs had won the competition the previous season when they became the first English side to win a European competition. This tie was the first time United had faced an English side in Europe.

11th December 1954

Colin Webster scored a hat-trick in the 4-2 victory over Burnley at Turf Moor in Division One.

12th December 1992

£1.2m signing Eric Cantona made his debut at home to Norwich following his transfer from Leeds.

13th December 1986

For the second game in succession United drew 3-3. The first was at home to Spurs (7th December, attendance 35,957) and the second was at Aston Villa. Amazingly the goalscorers were the same in both matches – Davenport (2) and Whiteside.

14th December 1985

Blackmore, Hughes and Strachan provided the goals as United defeated Aston Villa 3-1 at Villa Park in Division One.

15th December 2009

A thirtieth minute Rooney penalty set the Reds up for a 3-0 victory at home to Wolves. Vidic (43) and Valencia (66) completed the scoring in front of a crowd of 73,709.

Ireland Came To See Match, Scored Goal

MANCHESTER U. 1, WREXHAM 0

A GALLANT Manchester United defence—a very gallant defence indeed—earned them both points against Wrexham, at Maine-road. It was an unexpected result—more so because of United's misfortune before the game. Neither Woodcock nor Bowden (Arsenal) put in an appearance, and Hession, from the "A" team and Ireland (Reading), who happened to turn up at the ground to see the game, filled the vacancies.

Neither was a success, though Ireland got the all-important goal after 30 minutes. For most of the time United battled with only three cylinders functioning in the attack —Mycock (the best of the line), Bryant and Chadwick, and this was made more apparent after the interval when the trio moved into the inside forward berths and became a real menace. In fact, Bryant, at centre-forward, should have scored with practically the last kick.

Crompton, who figured in goal in the absence of Breedon, injured, saved his side repeatedly, and he had splendid support from Roach and Roughton.

Wrexham looked like sweeping all before them, for Dix had two splendid drives in the opening minutes which might have found the net. But he joined in the general deterioration of the Wrexham attack eventually.

Tudor did well at centre half-back and Jefferson was a good right back.

16th December 1944

United beat Wrexham 1-0 in the wartime 'Football League North' with a goal from a Reading player called Sid Ireland. Amazingly, the player had arrived at United's temporary home Maine Road to watch the game, ended up playing and scored the only goal of the game. Fifty-four years later Andy Cole scored as United drew 1-1 with Chelsea at Old Trafford.

17th December 1966

A David Herd hat-trick helped the Reds to a 4-3 win at West Bromwich Albion. Denis Law also scored.

Crompton, the Manchester United goalkeeper, watches a shot from Westwood, Bolton Wanderers, flash past the far upright.

18th December 1921

Future goalkeeper Jack Crompton was born in Newton Heath. Due to World War Two Crompton's League opportunities did not come until he made his United debut in August 1946. Over the following decade he made 211 first team appearances and appeared in the 1948 FA Cup final success.

19th December 1987

After his £825,000 transfer from Norwich Steve Bruce made his debut in the 2-1 Division One victory at Portsmouth. Six years earlier wintry weather put paid to the Stoke City V United Division One game. The match eventually took place on 23rd January 1982 with United winning 3-0 with goals from Birtles, Coppell and Stapleton.

20th December 1958

With help from an own goal by Chelsea's Scott, the Reds won 3-2 at Stamford Bridge.

21st December 1957

Albert Scanlon was amongst the scorers as United beat Leicester City 4-0 in front of an Old Trafford crowd of 41,631.

22nd December 1984

John Gidman, Bryan Robson and Gordon Strachan scored as Ron Atkinson's United defeated Ipswich Town 3-0 at Old Trafford, attendance 35,168.

John Gidman
MANCHESTER UNITED

23rd December 1975

A Lou Macari goal ensured a point at Everton for Tommy Docherty's side. The Doc's Reds had been promoted the previous season and were to end this season third in Division One.

24th December 1960

Chelsea were defeated 2-1 at Stamford Bridge and were beaten again in the next game. On Boxing Day the United-Chelsea game ended 6-0.

25th December 1957

United defeated Luton 3-0 in their last League game on Christmas Day. The game, played at Old Trafford, was watched by 39,444.

26th December 1946

Stan Pearson scored the only goal of the Boxing Day Division One game with Bolton (above) at Maine Road, watched by 57,186. The goal came in the second minute after the Wanderers goalkeeper had cleared off the line. After that there was little to separate the sides and, according to one newspaper, United goalkeeper Jack Crompton was the game's star.

27th December 1977

Leicester were defeated 3-1 at Old Trafford. It was Andy Ritchie's second League game for the Reds and followed a 6-2 victory at Everton the previous day.

28th December 1974

Playing their first League derby with Oldham since February 1935 United suffered a shock 1-0 defeat at Boundary Park. It was only the Reds' fourth defeat of the season at this point. On the same date in 1912 United beat City 2-0 in the Manchester derby with Enoch West scoring both goals.

29th December 1979

A crowd of 54,295 witnessed United's 3-0 defeat of Arsenal in Division One. Dave Sexton's Reds ended the season second – it was their highest finish since 1968.

30th December 1978

United's game at home to West Bromwich Albion was Granada TV's featured match on their Kick Off programme. Sadly, Gerald Sinstadt introduced an

interesting game but a 5-3 United defeat to Ron Atkinson's side.

31st December 1910

Defender Mick Hamill signed from Glasgow Celtic. Hamill (below) was actually a forward at the time he signed but was converted to wing half by manager Ernest Mangnall. He went on to make 59 appearances and scored two goals but left the Reds in the 1914 close season apparently as a result of a dispute over an alleged promised benefit. Hamill, believed to have been born on the Falls Road in Belfast, stayed in Ireland playing for Belfast Celtic until 1920 when Mangnall re-signed the player. This time however he joined Mangnall at Manchester City. After spells in the USA he returned to Belfast in 1926.

Hamill's death was tragic – he was found in the Laggan Canal in July 1943. Some reports suggest his death was as a result of his alleged involvement with the Republican movement.

When is a record not a record?

Almost every United fan knows that the Reds hold the record attendance for a League game. Most know it was for a match with Arsenal in 1947-48 and that the game was actually played at Maine Road, not Old Trafford, due to the wartime bombing of United's ground.

What seems to confuse most fans though is the actual attendance of this game. The figure most often reported is 81,962, however other figures (often 82,500 & 83,260) are also quoted. So what was the actual attendance and why is there confusion?

When the game was played on 17th January 1948 is was fairly obvious that this was a highly significant attendance – newspapers commented that 'thousands were outside the ground when the game started' – and in the days that followed much was made of the size of the gate. It was described as a record for a League game.

Prior to the match the League record stood at 82,905 for Chelsea's home game with Arsenal in October 1935, and so if the United-Arsenal match was a record then the crowd had to be in excess of that figure. This means that anyone quoting 81,962, or indeed the less often quoted 82,500, could not be right if they also claim that the attendance is a record for a League game.

Today, 81,962 appears often, but the figure does not accurately reflect the attendance and the significance of the fixture to the Reds. The more appropriate figure for this game is actually 83,260.

83,260 is a record for the Football League and research during the last decade has confirmed that this is the most likely attendance of all for this game. Research material made available for a variety of books, especially "Football Through The Turnstiles" by Brian Tabner, has verified that the attendance was reported to the Football League as 83,260. Other books, most notably "Manchester: A Football History" and "The Football Grounds of Great Britain", have backed up that figure.

So, where did the different attendance figures come from?

It seems that 81,962 was the total number of people who paid specifically to see this game. At the time of the match United did have some season ticket holders but these were not included in the 81,962 figure. This was a common procedure at the time and, as the venue staging the game was actually owned by Manchester City, it was up to City's secretary to record the actual attendance. Wilf Wild, the City secretary, is believed to have calculated that the actual attendance when United season ticket holders were added to the figure came to 83,260. It is believed that Wild submitted this figure to the competing clubs (United and Arsenal) and then to the Football League.

As three of the most comprehensive books analysing football grounds, attendances and Manchester football all agree that the attendance is 83,260, and two of them claim to have utilised actual official Football League statistics, then it appears clear that this figure should be recognised as the actual attendance. It also justifies the belief amongst virtually the entire football community that the United-Arsenal game attracted the Football League's record crowd.

If 83,260 is not accepted as the true attendance of this match, and 81,962 is, then United do not hold the record League attendance and Chelsea do. It's as simple as that.

Interestingly, Chelsea don't claim their game as the record.

The United-Arsenal match itself attracted such a large attendance because both United and Arsenal stood a realistic chance of winning the League. The Gunners were leading the race for the Championship with Burnley, Preston and United close behind. Matt Busby was building a real footballing side.

Arsenal had just been knocked out of the FA Cup and it was felt that United would test Arsenal like no other League side had managed all season. This became a game

all Mancunians wanted to see and queues formed some time before turnstiles were due to open.

Thirty minutes before play it started to rain, and at times during the match it rained heavily. At the time Maine Road's vast Kippax terracing was not roofed, meaning most spectators became drenched.

The game itself started with United captain Johnny Carey winning the toss. The opposing captain was the future City and England manager Joe Mercer.

From the start United attacked with Morris putting Arsenal under great pressure on a couple of occasions. The Reds came close a few times with most newspapers focusing on either the chances that came United's way or the great work made by Arsenal's defence. The Manchester Evening Chronicle reported: "A four man United forward movement saw the ball interpassed cleverly among Rowley, Pearson, Morris, and Mitten

United's temporary home from 1941-1949, Maine Road.

before the left winger, with a curling shot, drove the ball outside at the angle of the upright and crossbar.

"Pearson, with a quick header was also not far off the mark a moment later, and this was thrilling spectacular football, with the great crowd shouting themselves hoarse."

Arsenal took control for a while but United had the better of the early play. Then came the first goal. Journalist Tom Jackson reported: "United continued to force the run of the play, but there was always danger in these quick Arsenal raids. This was emphasised in the 18th minute when Arsenal sprang one of their surprises by taking the lead with a goal from Lewis.

"United's defence, I thought, was slow in clearing a corner kick from McPherson, and though Aston tried to hook the ball away from the goalmouth, he planted it straight to Roper, who quickly transferred for Lewis to put in a short low shot from close range."

The goal seemed to focus United minds a little and they attacked in style. Jackson: "There was one remarkable spell with Swindin performing acrobatic saves from a series of headers and shots rained at him by the over eager home attack."

After 27 minutes United were level: "It was cut and thrust football all the way between two eager teams, and Swindin, who had given a great display, was unlucky to be beaten after 27 minutes by a shot from Rowley which hit a defender's legs and skidded into the corner of the net. The move followed a throw in on the left, Rowley hitting a low shot from twenty yards range which struck Mercer to be diverted on the greasy surface past the 'keeper."

The game remained frenetic throughout but ended 1-1.

After the game, a United director went over to Arsenal's manager Tom Whittaker in the Maine Road board-room and declared: "What a dream team we'd have, if we could field your defence and our forward line." Whittaker smiled and responded: "But our forwards are part of our defence, and our defence is part of our attack!"

Arsenal remained League leaders and a few months later they won the title on 59 points with Busby's United second on 52 points.

Johnny Carey heads the ball during the record breaking United-Arsenal game. Note the United flag flying proudly over Maine Road's Popular Side.

UNITED QUOTES

"That one single challenge decided the match, because you can never replace a goalkeeper. Jackie Blanchflower, who took over in goal, was magnificent but couldn't prevent us losing 2-1. Really that was a season when we should have won the double."

Matt Busby commenting on the injury to goalkeeper Ray Wood in the 1957 FA Cup final.

***

"I watched the game from the sidelines, still on crutches after the air disaster and I feel doubly sad to see the lads go down to Bolton Wanderers 2-0 after everything they had achieved."

Matt Busby's view of the 1958 FA Cup final.

***

"It made no difference to me. Money was never my God. I was just happy to be doing the thing that I loved best... playing football."

George Best explaining during the 1980s that money had not been his motivation.

***

"Georgie went off on one of his runs, after he'd gathered a long kick up field from Alex Stepney. As usual with George, he kept me in suspense until the last possible moment, before he slid the ball home. Winning that trophy was wonderful for me and also for the Club and our supporters. I felt we had achieved my life's ambition."

Matt Busby talking about George Best's goal in United's 1968 European Cup final victory at Wembley Stadium.

***

"If you think that Bobby Charlton was a contemporary of Duncan's, and turned out to be probably our finest ever international, it makes you realise how good Duncan was, when you realise he was streets ahead of any player, including Bobby, when we were at United. Duncan could play anywhere."

Wilf McGuinness explaining in the early 1980s how great a player Duncan Edwards was.

"The only time you can comment on the game constructively is when you won."

Tommy Docherty answering critics who felt his criticism of the referee after United had defeated Bristol City 2-1 at Old Trafford on 19th January 1977 was a bit excessive.

***

"Unprecedented measures to beat soccer violence are introduced, with positive action against the notorious hooligans of Manchester United."

The Daily Mail (6th April 1977) reported that the Sports Minister Denis Howell had told the Commons that United's fans were to be banned from standing at away grounds. Bristol City had already banned fans from the 7th May meeting. Manager Tommy Docherty was not happy, he felt the authorities should go further – a few days earlier he had called for hooligans to be birched!

***

"The friendly rivalry and the uninhibited enjoyment of the northerners provide a fascinating contrast for any student of humanity. The Mancunians are born and bred in a county which will always be the first home of professional football."

Journalist Geoffrey Green (1911-1990) commenting on the passion Mancunians experienced for football.

***

"He is the best player in the world by absolutely miles. He is streets ahead of Messi, streets ahead of Kaka – and, you never know, he may come back."

Sir Alex Ferguson commenting on Cristiano Ronaldo after the player's move to Real Madrid, Summer 2009.

***

"The great thing is we are bouncing into the final. We can look forward to it."

Sir Alex Ferguson's feelings after winning the 2007-08 title as he looked forward to the 2008 Champions League Final.

***

"I think this has got the makings of our best team ever. I think we deserved to win the game. In the first half we were frustrated and we should have been three up, but they scored right on half time. They got a lucky break there and I thought Chelsea were the better side in the second half."

Sir Alex Ferguson's view of the 2008 Champions League Final.

***

"I want more nights like this again but I don't think you can beat '99. Penalties can be a lottery. It's how close the teams have been all season."

Ryan Giggs' view of the 2008 Champions League Final.

***

THE BEST PERFORMING TITLE WINNERS?

Now that United have eclipsed all other clubs and have recorded the most League title wins, it seems fair to try and identify which of those seasons was actually the most successful purely in terms of League performance.

Obviously, United's treble and double winning seasons brought more trophies than simply the League title, but ignoring multiple successes "The Big Book Of United" has tried to identify the greatest title winners.

If we focus purely on points margin, then the biggest winning margin came in 1999-2000. That season 18 points separated the Reds from second placed Arsenal. The next best winning margins stand at: 11 (1955-56), 10 (1992-93 & 2000-01), 9 (1907-08 & 2010-11), 8 (1956-57 & 1993-94). However, the number of points for a win changed in 1981 from two to three, and so all winning margins before that date cannot be directly compared to more recent seasons.

A fairer comparison may be to convert the winning margin into how many victories this represents. This would mean that a nine point margin in 2010-11 would equate to three wins,

1951-52 title winners. *Back (l to r):* **Busby, Blanchflower, Aston, Allen, Chilton, Gibson, Cockburn & Curry (trainer).** *Front:* **Pearson, Rowley, Carey, Downie & McShane**

but the same margin in 1907-08 would equate to 4.5 wins. Although 1999-2000 remains the best, this calculation creates a different view of the winning margin.

What is clear though is the fact that teams from the nineties, fifties and 1907-08 appear near the top of these tables proving that at least three generations of the Reds have been significantly better than their nearest rivals.

The following represents the best twelve seasons:

Season	Played	Points	Winning Margin	No. of Wins Represented by Margin	Runners-up
1999-00	38	91	18	6	Arsenal
1955-56	42	60	11	5.5	Blackpool
1907-08	38	52	9	4.5	Aston Villa
1956-57	42	64	8	4	Tottenham Hotspur
1992-93	42	84	10	3.33	Aston Villa
2000-01	38	80	10	3.33	Arsenal
2010-11	38	80	9	3	Chelsea
1993-94	42	92	8	2.67	Blackburn Rovers
1996-97	38	75	7	2.33	Newcastle United
2006-07	38	89	6	2	Chelsea
1951-52	42	57	4	2	Tottenham Hotspur
1966-67	42	60	4	2	Nottm Forest

Another way of trying to identify the best season would be to calculate the number of points per game. By doing this 1999-2000 again comes out on top, but is followed by several recent seasons:

Season	Played	Points per game ratio
1999-00	38	2.394737
2008-09	38	2.368421
2006-07	38	2.342105
2007-08	38	2.289474
1993-94	42	2.190476
2002-03	38	2.184211
1995-96	38	2.157895
2000-01	38	2.105263
2010-11	38	2.105263
1998-99	38	2.078947

Of course, points per game is unfair on those seasons when 2 points were awarded for a victory. If a calculation is made assuming the same points (three) were awarded for wins throughout these title winning years, then the table varies a little with the 1956-57 season appearing as the fifth best.

Season	Played	Points per game ratio assuming all were 3 points for a win
1999-00	38	2.394737
2008-09	38	2.368421
2006-07	38	2.342105
2007-08	38	2.289474
1956-57	42	2.190476
1993-94	42	2.190476
2002-03	38	2.184211
1995-96	38	2.157895
2000-01	38	2.105263
2010-11	38	2.105263
1998-99	38	2.078947
1964-65	42	2.071429
1955-56	42	2.02381
1966-67	42	2
1992-93	42	2
1907-08	38	1.973684
1996-97	38	1.973684
1910-11	38	1.947368
1951-52	42	1.904762

Ultimately, fans will have their own view of United's greatest title winning season, but it's clear that based on points, whichever way you look at it, the 1999-2000 season stands ahead of the rest.

UNITED TIMELINE

The purpose of *The Big Book Of United* is to provide features on United's history rather than a detailed history of the Reds. However, it's important to understand the development of the Club through time, and so over the following pages *The Big Book Of United* provides snapshot material on the Club's history.

We start with activities that led to the formation of the side that ultimately became United.

1877

■ Liverpudlian Fredrick Attock appointed Carriage & Wagon Superintendent at the Newton Heath engine shed of the Lancashire & Yorkshire Railway (LYR) Company. He remained in the role until his health began to fail in 1895.

1878

■ Members of the LYR Carriage and Wagon department based at Newton Heath came up with the idea of forming a sporting organisation. It was formed by the Dining Room Committee. By 1882 Fredrick Attock was recorded as the Club's president.

1880

■ Newton Heath LYR Cricket & Football Club is known to have played a competitive fixture. The first reported game (though there could have been earlier matches) took place on 20th November 1880 at the Pikes Lane ground Bolton when Bolton Wanderers second team beat the Heathens 6-0. Some sources claim the Heathens wore green and gold.

1881

■ Newton Heath faced West Gorton (later Manchester City) for the first time in November at North Road. The Heathens won 3-0 before a crowd recorded as 3,000. The return match the following March ended 2-1 to West Gorton before 5,000 at Kirkmanshulme Cricket Ground.

1882

■ A fixture list recorded the Club's name as "Newton Heath (LYR) Cricket and Football Club. It also highlighted that Fredrick Attock was the Club's president and another Liverpudlian Thomas Gorst was vice president.

1885

■ Newton Heath appeared in the inaugural Manchester Cup final. They were defeated 3-0 by Hurst from Ashton-under-Lyne.

1886

■ The second Manchester Cup final ended in a 2-1 victory by Newton Heath over Manchester FC. The Heathens entered the FA Cup for the first time, drawing 2-2 at

Fleetwood but the tie was awarded to their opponents when Newton Heath refused to play extra time.

1887

■ Newton Heath appeared in their third successive final but the game ended in a 2-1 defeat to West Manchester. The Gorton Reporter reported its surprise at the defeat: "Newton Heath have lost the Manchester Cup! The final tie for the 'much coveted trophy' came off at Whalley Range on Saturday before 6,000 spectators."

1888

■ Denton were defeated 7-1 as Newton Heath won the Manchester Cup. They also joined a newly formed competition called The Football Combination. The Combination was set up as a response by clubs who were not invited to join the newly organised Football League. Despite a widely held view, Newton Heath did not apply to join the Football League in 1888 (and therefore did not receive the 'one vote' that is often incorrectly claimed).

1889

■ The Football Combination collapsed due to the varying level of commitment by its members. Newton Heath had played 11 games, losing only twice, and were viewed as having the best record at the time of the Combination's collapse.

■ Newton Heath won the Manchester Cup with a 7-0 victory over Hooley Hill. They applied to join the Football League, but came ninth with one vote (four sides were elected/re-elected).

1890

■ Newton Heath won the Manchester Cup once more with a 5-2 victory over Royton. They also finished 8th in the

newly formed Alliance League. The Alliance was viewed by many as an unofficial Second Division of the Football League.

■ The Heathens tried to join the League again but were rejected once more.

1891

The emerging Ardwick (Manchester City) defeated Newton Heath 1-0 in the Manchester Cup final. The Heathens had set a record however by appearing in all seven of the opening Manchester Cup Finals.

■ Newton Heath finished ninth in the Alliance and applied to join the Football League again, as did Ardwick. Both Manchester sides were rejected in favour of Stoke and Darwen. Surprisingly, the Heathens received no votes while Ardwick at their first attempt managed four votes.

1892

■ Newton Heath finished second in the Alliance League. The Football League was extended with a two club increase to the First Division and the formation of the Second Division. Newton Heath applied to join the enlarged First Division and were accepted with 6 votes (The Heathens gained one more vote than rejected Sheffield United). It is believed the Manchester clubs agreed not to stand for election to the same division as this may have split the vote - local rivals Ardwick chose not to apply for the top division but were accepted into the new Second Division instead.

1893

■ At the end of their first League season the Heathens finished bottom of Division One, five points behind nearest rivals Accrington (who resigned as a result of their lowly finish). Newton Heath and fellow

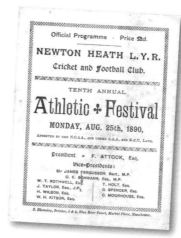

Official Programme · Price 2d.

NEWTON HEATH L.Y.R.
Cricket and Football Club.

TENTH ANNUAL

Athletic ✦ Festival

MONDAY, AUG. 25th, 1890,

APPROVED BY THE N.C.A.A. AND UNDER A.A.A. AND N.C.U. LAWS.

President = F. ATTOCK, Esq.

Vice-Presidents:
Sir JAMES FERGUSSON, Bart., M.P.
C. E. SCHWANN, Esq., M.P.
W. T. ROTHWELL, Esq.   T. HOLT, Esq.
J. TAYLOR, Esq., J.P.,   G. SPENCER, Esq.
H. WILSON, Esq.   C. MOORHOUSE, Esq.
W. H. KITSON, Esq.

S. Blomeley, Printer, 2 & 4, Blue Boar Court, Market Place, Manchester.

strugglers Notts County had to compete in end of season Test Matches with the leading sides in Division Two to determine whether they would be relegated. Newton Heath were successful and retained their Division One place.

■ The Heathens moved to a new home – Bank Street, Clayton (often referred to at the time as Bank Lane).

1894

■ For the second successive year the Heathens ended the season bottom of Division One (as with 1893 they were nine points from safety). This time defeat at Blackburn to Second Division Liverpool caused the Manchester side to be relegated.

■ Newton Heath were stopped from changing their name to Manchester Football Club after discussions between the FA and the RFU blocked them.

1895

■ The Heathens were third in Division Two but failed in the promotion deciding Test Match to Stoke City, played at Cobridge, Burslem (Port Vale). On 9th March they defeated Walsall Town Swifts 14-0 but the visitors appealed against the state of the Bank Street ground and the weather. The game was replayed, with the Heathens winning 9-0 a few weeks later.

1896

■ Newton Heath finished sixth in Division Two. It had been a mixed season with a few shock defeats following impressive victories.

1897

■ The Heathens were second in Division Two but missed promotion via the Test Match system. They played eight games in the FA Cup – winning five and only losing one – but still only reached the third round (although this was the quarter-final) after playing in three of the qualifying rounds.

1898

■ The Heathens finished fourth in Division Two, missing out on the final year of the Test Matches.

1899

■ The Heathens finished fourth in the Second Division for the second successive year.

1900

■ The first game of the new century was a friendly with Manchester City at Hyde Road. The Heathens were defeated 2-1 before a crowd of 7,000 on New Year's Day. The first League game of the Twentieth Century ended with the same scoreline but this time the opponents were Bolton Wanderers. Newton Heath finished the season fourth in Division Two once again.

1901

■ Under new manager James West the Heathens ended the 1900-01 Division Two campaign in tenth place.

1902

■ The Club reformed as Manchester United with the new name being formally agreed at a meeting on 24th April 1902. Reports from the period are unclear who specifically came up with the idea. Louis Rocca would later claim it was his suggestion, but reports from the time imply it may not have been him. Some suggest Dentonian James Brown came up with the name. Despite many myths developed over the years which talk of names like Manchester Central (there are valid reasons why this name is unlikely ever to have been proposed) and Manchester Celtic, the only other name recorded as being suggested at the meeting was a compromise aimed at including Newton Heath within the title.

F. J. West .... 117 .... 20 37
Dr. Lee .... 116 .... 16 100

Newton Heath F.C.

CLUB'S NAME TO BE CHANGED TO MANCHESTER UNITED.

An important public meeting in connection with the Newton Football Club was held in the New Islington Public Hall, Ancoats, Manchester, on Thursday evening. The chief business was to consider the future of the club. The hall was packed, and Mr. J. Brown, who occupied the chair, said it was intended that Dr. Bishop should have presided, but in a letter from that gentleman he stated his business in Parliament prevented him from attending. He, however, expressed himself willing to assist them in placing the old club in the position it once occupied. He hoped, also, the Manchester public would help in giving to Manchester what Manchester should never be without — a first-class First League team.—(Applause.) Mr. Brown reverted to the fact that he, personally, together with Harry Stafford and three others had thought that a thousand pounds would be necessary to lift the club out of the mire. They had offered to find that money, and if the money were to be lost they were quite content to lose it in the interests of the cause.—(Applause.) Further, he wanted them to understand that if the venture was a success the five

proposition has been made by one of the leading clubs, but it is doubtful whether it will come to anything:

The proposal to change the name of the Newton Heath club to Manchester United will not be received with favour in certain quarters, but there is no doubt it is a step in the right direction. Visiting teams and their supporters have many times been led astray by the name of the club, and have journeyed either by car or train to Newton Heath only to find that they were miles away from the home of the club. A mistake of this kind not very long ago put a team in a very awkward position. They reached the old ground in North Road, and then found it a difficult matter to procure conveyances to take them across to Clayton. The result was that the players reached the ground within five minutes of the fixed time for starting the game. We should imagine that the League clubs generally will support the change.

During the past season Darwen, one of the oldest Association clubs in the county, have made a plucky effort to keep their head above water, and by cultivating young players and working economically they have proved successful. They have gone through the season without sustaining defeat in the Lancashire League, and this has been done notwithstanding that they have been without Gate and M'Ivor, who, before the opening of the season, threw in their lot with Blackburn Rovers. Dewhurst, the Rovers' centre-forward, was brought out by Darwen, who have, owing to financial reasons, been unable to keep other good players. If they part with any men during the playing season they can command transfer fees for them; while if they wait until after the curtain is rung down this month end, they will run the risk of losing them without obtaining any monetary advantage. Realising this a few days ago, they communicated with a number of League clubs inviting offers for the transfer of certain players whom they were unable to retain, and as a result Newcastle United, Sheffield United, and Aston Villa bid against each other for Dawson, the outside left. The best offer came from the Sheffielders, and Darwen have had a windfall of over £100 by the deal. The Blackburn Rovers, who had Dawson's League signature, have also had to be arranged with.

1903

■ The first season as United ended with the Reds fifth in Division Two. Ernest Mangnall was appointed manager. It was to prove to be one of the most significant managerial appointments ever and ultimately transformed United into a major side.

1904

■ Mangnall's Reds missed promotion by a point to Woolwich Arsenal.

1905

■ Charlie Roberts (right) became United's first England international when he appeared in England's 1-1 draw with Ireland at Ayresome Park on 25th February 1905.

■ United ended the season third in Division Two again.

1906

■ Promotion was achieved with United finishing second to Bristol City in 1905-06.

■ The first Division One Manchester derby took place on 1st December 1906 at City's Hyde Road.

1907

■ United made heroes of Billy Meredith, Herbert Burgess, Sandy Turnbull, and Jimmy Bannister after the former City players had been forced out of Hyde Road. They were transferred to the Reds in December 1906 and made their debuts on New Year's Day 1907. Most Mancunians, including those of a Blue persuasion, were happy as it was seen as a good way to ensure the players remained in the city. It also helped United, Manchester's poor relations at the time, establish themselves as a force. Within four years Meredith & Co. had helped the Reds win their first honours – two Championships & the F.A. Cup.

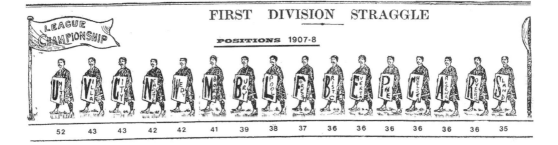

FIRST DIVISION STRAGGLE

POSITIONS 1907-8

52 43 43 42 42 41 39 38 37 36 36 36 36 36 36 35

1908

■ United won the Football League for the first time. The Reds finished nine points ahead of their nearest rivals Aston Villa and Manchester City.

■ The Reds also won the first ever Charity Shield.

1909

■ The final week of the 1908-09 season was very interesting for United fans. Not only did the Reds win the FA Cup for the first time (by beating Bristol City 1-0) but they also helped to relegate Manchester City. The Blues were relegated at the end of 1908-9 on goal average. Bradford City were the team that survived after they defeated Cup winners United 1-0 on the final day of the season (five days after the Cup final).

1910

■ Old Trafford opened with a 4-3 defeat by Liverpool on 19th February. Part of the old Bank Street ground collapsed shortly after the move.

1911

■ Mangnall guided the Reds to their third major trophy in four seasons as United won the First Division title by a point from Aston Villa.

1912

■ United ended the 1911-12 season thirteenth but at the start of the following season the Club was devastated when manager Ernest Mangnall – the man responsible for bringing United their first successes and for the move to Old Trafford - announced he was

Above: **Old Trafford as it looked in 1912.**

Below: **Scenes from the 1912 Old Trafford derby match.**

leaving the Reds. Worst still, he was joining Manchester City. His final game in charge was the Old Trafford derby, played after he announced he was leaving. The Blues won 1-0 and the Umpire newspaper reported: "United speeded their manager rejoicing with 2 points to his new club."

1913

■ New manager JJ Bentley guided the Reds to a fourth placed finish.

1914

■ The 1913-14 season ended with United 14th in Division One. War broke out shortly into the 1914-15 season but the decision was taken by the authorities to continue with the League programme.

1915

■ United experienced a season of struggle which ended with the Reds 18th – one point above the relegation zone – but controversy reigned. The meeting with Liverpool in

April, which ended with a surprise 2-0 victory, was viewed suspiciously as a fixed match.

■ The League was suspended and between 1915 until 1919 regional football was organised instead.

1916

■ United competed in the Lancashire Section of the wartime Football League – which comprised of all the Lancastrian teams of the period plus Stoke - and the Subsidiary Tournament (southern section) which followed. The southern section comprised of United, City, Oldham, Everton, Liverpool, and Stockport, with the other Lancastrian teams featuring in another section.

■ In dispute with United, Billy Meredith returned to Manchester City during the war years.

1917

■ In May Sandy Turnbull, cup winner in 1909, was killed while serving in the trenches. At the time of his death he was a member of the 8th battalion of the East Surrey Regiment. His death is recorded on the Memorial in the Faubourg-d'Amiens Cemetery at Arras, France.

1918

■ The end of the war came too late for the Football League to resume, but a final season of regional football was performed.

1919

■ The first Football League match following the war ended 1-1 at Derby County on 30th August 1919. United's first victory came at Sheffield Wednesday on 8th September when the Reds won 3-1 with goals from Meehan, Spence and Woodcock.

1920

■ According to the Sporting Chronicle a record Old Trafford United League crowd was set at 72,000. Other sources claimed the attendance for United V Aston Villa as 70,504. Often the more specific attendance

MASCOT FOR ENGLISH CUP-HOLDERS.

Since the Australian Rugby team set the fashion among footballers with their mascot kangaroo, clubs in this country have been presented with tokens of luck. The latest to receive a mascot are the Manchester United F.C., who have been presented with a goat by The Bensons, the music-hall artistes. Charlie Roberts, the United captain, is accepting the gift from Mr. Benson on the stage of the Ardwick Empire, Manchester. *Daily Sketch photograph.*

Opposite: United in 1913-14. Back: Hodge, Gipps, Knowles, Beale, Stacey, Hamill, Whalley. Front: Meredith, Woodcock, Anderson, West & Wall.

Above: In September 1909 the Daily Sketch reported that United had been presented with a goat as the Club's new mascot by the music hall artists The Bensons.

Below right: Joe Spence scored in United's first league game following World War One, August 1919.

United 1920-21. Back: Spence, Forster, Greenwood, Moore, Mew, Silcock, Meehan & Partridge.
Front: Harrison, Miller, Leonard, Sapsford & Hopkin.

United 1922-23. Back: Barson, Hilditch, Ballen (trainer), Mew, Silcock, Grimwood & McBain.
Front: Lochhead, Wood, Moore, Spence, Williams & Thomas

figures were based on actual number of people who paid to attend that game and did not include season ticket holders. Typically United would have had between 100 and 2,000 season ticket holders during the inter-war period. Whatever the ultimate attendance it would be approximately 80 years before Old Trafford held a greater League crowd.

1921

■ In November John Chapman replaced John Robson, who had left the previous month, as United manager.

1922

■ A difficult 1921-22 season ended with United relegated to Division Two.

1923

■ Frank Mann signed for the Reds and appeared in the final ten League games of the 1922-23 season.

1924

■ The opening months of the 1924-25 season saw United defeated only once in 18 League games. That form helped set the Reds up for promotion.

1925

■ Following promotion United's first home League game ended in a 3-0 victory over Aston Villa in front of 41,717 fans.

1926

■ United reach the FA Cup semi-final for only the second time in their history after defeating Fulham 2-1 in the quarter-final. They lost the all-Manchester semi-final 3-0 to City at Bramall Lane.

1927

■ After the suspension of John Chapman and brief reign of player-manager Clarrie

Hilditch Herbert Bamlett was formally appointed the new manager.

1928

■ A season of struggle was salvaged with impressive victories in United's final three games. A 6-1 home win over Liverpool before 30,625 at Old Trafford ensured the Reds ended 1927-28 above the relegation zone in 18th place.

1929

■ Tom Reid signed for United from Liverpool and netted 14 goals in 17 League appearances during the final months of the 1928-29 season. That record helped the Reds finish 12th in Division One.

1930

■ Supporter dissatisfaction led to a negative atmosphere surrounding Old Trafford. Boycotts were threatened and attendances dropped as the Reds ended the season 17th.

1931

■ Attendances plummeted – three 1931 League crowds were below 4,000! - further as supporter dissatisfaction and on the pitch struggles grew. Across Manchester a new side Manchester Central FC were hoping to replace the Reds as Manchester's second team, prompting City and United to work together to kill off the threat to the Reds.

1932

■ Playing in Division Two since the start of the 1931-32 season, United's woes continued. Financial problems added to the playing struggles. Successful businessman James Gibson became chairman and his astute leadership was to save the Club.

1933

■ Despite Gibson's financial acumen the side continued to struggle and the 1933-34 season opens with two Division Two defeats.

1934

■ Victory over Millwall in the final match of the season ensured United avoided relegation to Division Three.

1935

■ Eleven games into the 1935-36 Second Division season United had gathered 16 points out of a possible 22. It might not seem such an achievement in comparison with modern seasons but it did mean that the Reds' fight back had begun.

1936

■ United won the Second Division title.

1937

■ After one season in the top flight the Reds were relegated.

United's saviour James Gibson.

Three major Old Trafford sporting venues around 1930 - United (top), Lancashire CCC (bottom) and the White City Stadium shortly after its redevelopment for greyhound racing. (right).

W. G. ROUGHTON views the tree that grew in MANCHESTER UNITED'S blitzed grandstand.

After being bombed in 1941 parts of Old Trafford became overgrown until the opportunity came to start the rebuilding work after the war.

1938

■ Promotion was achieved with United in second place while local rivals City were relegated from Division One. Although they had no idea at the time, this would prove to be a very significant season to earn promotion. The following season would be the last in peacetime football for several years and the difference in League status between the two sides would mean that post-war the Reds would have the advantage and prestige over City for the first time, or at least the first time since the day Mangnall moved to City in 1912.

1939

■ The outbreak of war brought a suspension of the Football League. Regional competitions were set up with United initially competing in the Western Division during 1939-40.

1940

■ The Reds ended the first wartime season 4th in the Western Division.

1941

■ Old Trafford suffered bomb damage with the main areas affected being the Main Stand and the pitch.

1942

■ United finished first in the Football League Northern Section (Second Championship) in 1941-42.

1943

■ Like most sides, United utilised the guest system during the war. This allowed players on the books of over clubs to play for other sides in individual matches. Often players would appear for sides close to their military base. Irishman Billy Walsh – a Manchester City player – appeared for United in the final two games of the 1942-43 season (both against Liverpool). Several City and United players would appear for their normal rivals during this period including United's Harry McShane.

1944

■ Shortly before Christmas United finished 30th in the Football League North (First Championship) of the 1944-45 season.

1945

■ Former City and Liverpool star Matt Busby became United's manager.

Secrets of MANCHESTER UNITED

GRAND NEW FOOTBALL SERIES

By LOUIS ROCCA

Fifty-five years with Manchester United and now the club's chief scout, Louis Rocca reveals "behind the scenes" stories of the famous "Reds."

To-day's instalment—

Compares the Play of BILLY MEREDITH AND STANLEY MATTHEWS

Exclusively in the

Evening Chronicle

1946

■ The first peacetime League season kicked off with a 2-1 United win at Maine Road to Grimsby Town before 41,025.

1947

■ United finished second in the first post-war League season.

1948

■ Blackpool were defeated in United's first FA Cup success since 1909. This brought to an end a period of 37 years without major trophy success (United won the League in 1911). Average attendances reached an all-time high of 54,890 – a figure not bettered until 1967-68.

1949

■ United returned to Old Trafford.

1950

■ The Reds finished their first season back at Old Trafford fourth. Surprisingly, attendances had actually dropped by over

Top: **United and Derby fans at the 1948 FA Cup semi-final.**

Above: **Johnny Carey is lifted by Charlie Mitten and Jack Crompton after the 1948 FA Cup success.**

The 1952 League Champions celebrate - (l to r) Cockburn, Aston, Berry, McNulty, Byrne, Allen and Carey. Assistant trainer Bill Inglis pours the champagne.

5,000 following their return home. The 1948-49 average had been 48,808 while the next season crowds averaged 43,232.

1951

■ Roger Byrne made his League debut in a goalless game at Liverpool on 24th November 1951.

1952

■ United won their third League title with a thrilling 6-1 victory over Arsenal on the final day of the season.

1953

■ Tommy Taylor signed for £29,999 – Matt Busby did not want to burden him with a £30,000 price tag. United beat arch-rivals

Fans apparently locked out of United's 4-0 FA Cup victory over Leeds on 27 January 1951.

The 1955-56 title success (left) is celebrated at City's 1956 FA Cup final success (below).

Bottom: Tommy Taylor (crouching) scores United's only goal of the 1957 FA Cup final against Aston Villa.

Wolves 9-3 on aggregate in the FA Youth Cup final.

1954

■ After one League appearance in 1952-53 Duncan Edwards became an established member of the side from his second appearance (31/10/53) onwards. He made 24 League appearances in 1953-54. Jack Rowley scored the first United goal of the 1954-55 campaign, but this was to be the last season for the veteran of the 1948 FA Cup winning team.

1955

■ United won the FA Youth Cup for the third successive season. They were captained by

Eddie 'snake-hips' Colman and the following November he made his League debut.

1956

■ League champions United became the first English side to accept the invitation to appear in the European Cup. Bobby Charlton made his debut in October 1956.

1957

■ United narrowly missed out on the double. After winning the League, the Reds were defeated 2-1 by Aston Villa in the FA Cup final. Harry Gregg arrived from Doncaster for a record goalkeeper's fee of £23,000.

1958

■ The Munich Air Disaster. The post-Munich side reached the FA Cup final.

1959

■ Despite the horrendous losses and injuries sustained at Munich, United managed to challenge for the League title the following season. The Reds finished second, six points behind champions Wolves.

1960

■ The first game of the 1960s ended in a shock 7-3 defeat at Newcastle on 2nd January before 57,200. Although it is widely assumed otherwise, United competed in the first season of the League Cup.

1961

■ The season ended with a seventh placed finish. David Herd arrived in the close season for a fee of £40,000 from Arsenal. Herd's father Alec had played with Matt Busby at Manchester City in the thirties.

1962

■ Former Huddersfield and Manchester City star Denis Law signed from Torino. It was a British record fee of £115,000.

1963

■ United beat Leicester City 3-1 in the FA Cup final. The success ensured a positive end to an otherwise poor season – the Reds finished 19th on 34 points.

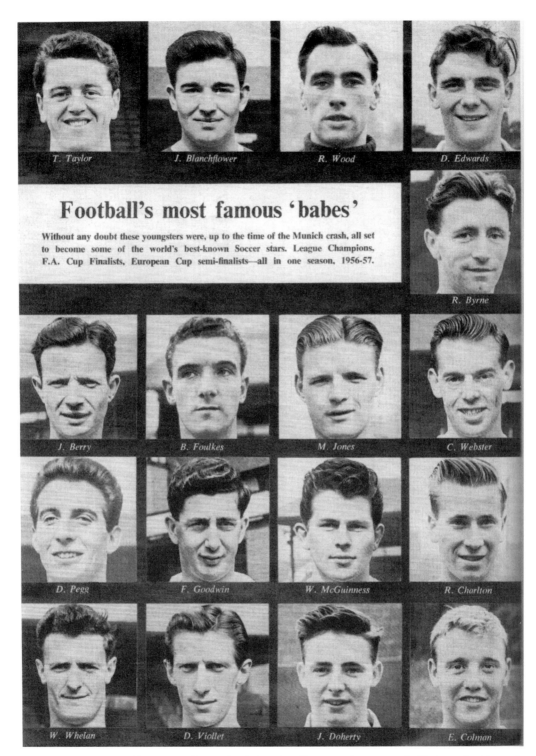

Football's most famous 'babes'

Without any doubt these youngsters were, up to the time of the Munich crash, all set to become some of the world's best-known Soccer stars. League Champions, F.A. Cup Finalists, European Cup semi-finalists—all in one season, 1956-57.

T. Taylor | J. Blanchflower | R. Wood | D. Edwards | R. Byrne | J. Berry | B. Foulkes | M. Jones | C. Webster | D. Pegg | F. Goodwin | W. McGuinness | R. Charlton | W. Whelan | D. Viollet | J. Doherty | E. Colman

Opposite: **1958 - United leave Manchester for Belgrade. The return journey ended in tragedy. Many of the 'Busby Babes' (above) lost their lives in the disaster.**

A post Munich United for 1958-59. Back: Charlton, Scanlon, Carolan, Gregg, Goodwin & Cope. Front: McGuinness, Viollet, Foulkes, Quixall & Morgans.

United in 1962-63: Back: Law, Brennan & Foulkes. Standing: Dalton (physio), Setters, Gaskell, Gregg, Crerand & Crompton (trainer). Sitting: Dunne, Quixall, Cantwell (captain), Herd & Stiles. Front: Giles & Charlton.

David Herd, Denis Law & Maurice Setters celebrate the 1963 FA Cup success over Leicester City.

1964

■ United's first European campaign since Munich saw the Reds reach the quarter-finals of the European Cup Winners' Cup, losing 6-4 on aggregate to Sporting Lisbon.

1965

■ The Reds won the League title and reached the semi-final of the FA Cup. They also reached the semi-final of the Inter Cities Fairs' Cup where they lost a replay 2-1 after

drawing 3-3 on aggregate with Ferencvaros. This was United's only season in the competition that was subsequently replaced by the UEFA Cup.

1966

■ Partizan Belgrade beat United 2-1 on aggregate in the European Cup quarter-final. Goalkeeper Alex Stepney signed from Chelsea for £55,000. England won the World Cup with Nobby Stiles and Bobby Charlton appearing in the final.

MANCHESTER

WORLD CUP 1966

Wembley 1968. *Top:* **John Aston.** *Centre:* **Brian Kidd scoring.** *Bottom:* **George Best.**

1967

■ United won the League title for a seventh time. The following season Brian Kidd made his debut.

1968

■ Matt Busby's quest to win the European Cup ended with victory over Benfica at Wembley. The Reds also finished second in the League and attracted a new record average attendance of 57,552 – due to ground capacity changes this remained their best until 1999-2000.

1969

■ The Reds reached the semi-final of the European Cup, but were defeated 2-1 on aggregate by AC Milan. Manager Matt Busby retired and was replaced with Wilf McGuinness in time for the 1969-70 season.

1970

■ McGuinness' Reds ended the 1969-70 season eighth in Division One. George Best scored six goals as Northampton Town were defeated 8-2 in the FA Cup fifth round. United went on to finish third in the FA Cup – that season a third place play off took place between the losing semi-finalists.

Ten years ago – 6th February, 1958 – there was Munich. No signal this, to maudlin reminiscence or the hurtful probing of time-healed wounds.

Yet it is a special time. A decade is a convention in the life-span; a marker on the endless tides of time; so in this week ten years on from Munich it would be unseemly not to remember.

In remembering there can be no total escape from a lingering sadness – but it is not my wish to engender melancholy here. Rather would I draw on the rich storehouse of unclouded memory for recall of the golden days when those whose time was short were writing their imperishable chapter of Manchester United history.

Such is the fleeting passage of time that already there is a generation of young Old Trafford devotees among us who know them only as legends – names in the folklore of football to be uttered with uncomprehending awe.

There is not space here for detailed enlightenment of the individual talents of those who died at Munich – but each one, in his own way, is inextricably interwoven in the fabric of success spun during Matt Busby's brilliant Old Trafford reign.

But some measure of their total meaning to Manchester United can be indicated here. The players among them inherited an awesome task. Most were little more than school-boys – the Busby Babes – when on to their shoulders passed the burden of sustaining the greatness achieved by Johnny Carey and his men.

Where Carey's men left off – they had to carry on. How brilliantly they bore the load. Blending with the more mature ones they confirmed and consolidated the club name as a by-word in Europe for all that was best in football.

At home they were fast becoming an irresistible force, as illustrated by their winning of the League championship twice in the two years immediately preceding Munich.

Each one, to a greater or lesser degree, was a star in his own right – yet their power lay in collective strength. Flamboyance was scorned in the cause of the greater good for the greater number – a discipline which came as much from within as without.

MUNICH*
Ten years afterwards
by Arthur Walmsley
(Sports writer for the Sun)

What Olympian heights would they have scaled had fate allowed them their full span? There lies a whole realm of fascinating speculation. Those of us who saw them flowering would put no limit on their potential. At home they were already undisputed masters – only the time that was denied prevented them extending that dominance to Europe and the world.

But United then, as now, were more than a team on the field. They were a team right through from the backroom – and here again Munich took its toll.

For those "backroom boys" were not just men doing a job – but loyal servants dedicated to a cause. The cause was "Manchester United" and they, as much as any player, played their own parts in building the mystique which now surrounds the club's name wherever Soccer is played.

So with the ten-year cushion between Munich and emotion we can remember them not in sorrow but in appreciation for their services to football and their club.

Let us remember then, players Geoff Bent, Roger Byrne, Eddie Coleman, Duncan Edwards, Mark Jones, David Pegg, Tommy Taylor and Billy Whelan; secretary Walter Crickmer; trainer Tom Curry and coach Bert Whalley; and United Review writers Alf Clarke and Tom Jackson.

Indeed, those who knew and saw them will never forget.

---

*This article was originally written for the programme dated February 10th - the United v. City match - unhappily postponed. Such is the importance of the tenth anniversary of Munich that we are glad to reprint this fine tribute by Arthur Walmsley.

1968 - The Munich disaster is remembered in the United Review.

1971

■ After Matt Busby returned as manager, Frank O'Farrell was formally appointed for the start of the 1971-72 season. The new season opened with United playing home games at Anfield (V Arsenal) and the Victoria Ground, Stoke (V West Bromwich Albion). The attendance at Anfield was 27,649 and 23146 at Stoke. The FA had forced United to play those games away from Old Trafford due to crowd disturbances the previous season.

1972

■ Frank O'Farrell was sacked on 16th December after an embarrassing 5-0 defeat at Crystal Palace. He was replaced by Tommy Docherty.

1973

■ United ended the season 18th in Division One after Docherty's surgery had ensured the Reds escaped the drop zone.

1974

■ Docherty's United were relegated in 21st place on the last day of the season.

1975

■ The Reds won the Second Division title. They also attracted an average attendance of around 48,000 – an increase on their previous Division One campaign.

1976

■ Southampton beat United in the FA Cup final. 1975-76 had been a great season however as the Reds also sustained a title challenge for much of the year. Ultimately, Docherty's United finished third.

1977

■ In February Jimmy Greenhoff scored a hat trick as United beat Newcastle 3-1 at Old Trafford. It was the first United League hat trick since November 1974. United won the FA Cup, but manager Tommy Docherty

Stewart Houston chasing the ball during the 1976 FA Cup final.

Kevin Moran is consoled by Everton's Peter Reid as he leaves the field, Wembley 1985.

was dismissed following revelations of an affair with Mary Brown, the wife of the Club physio. The two later married.

1978

■ The Reds finished tenth in Division One at the end of Dave Sexton's first season as manager. The new manager had signed two powerful stars from Leeds United – Joe Jordan and Gordon McQueen.

1979

■ A thrilling FA Cup final ended in a 3-2 Arsenal victory over United. Ray Wilkins had joined the Reds from Chelsea for a fee of £850,000.

1980

■ A Granada TV World In Action programme investigated chairman Louis Edwards' meat business and share dealing at United. Four weeks after the investigation Edwards died following a heart-attack.

1981

■ Dave Sexton was replaced by Ron

Atkinson as United manager in April. Frank Stapleton, John Gidman and Remi Moses were signed, but their arrivals were soon eclipsed by the record-breaking £1.5m signing of Bryan Robson.

1982

■ The Reds finished third in Division One. Sixteen year old star Norman Whiteside appeared in the World Cup finals in Spain.

1983

■ Brighton were defeated 4-0 in the FA Cup final replay but United lost 2-1 in the League Cup final to Liverpool.

1984

■ The Reds reached the ECWC semi-final but were defeated 3-2 on aggregate by Juventus.

1985

■ United beat Everton in the FA Cup final. Kevin Moran became the first player sent off in a FA Cup final.

1986

■ Despite a fourth placed finish and decent domestic cup runs in 1985-86, plus of course two FA Cup successes, Ron Atkinson was dismissed and replaced with Alex Ferguson. Influential captain Bryan Robson had been injured for a significant part of the 1985-86 season.

1987

■ Ferguson's first season ended with the Reds eleventh in Division One.

1988

■ United finished second in the title race.

1989

■ Michael Knighton negotiated to take over United and celebrated by demonstrating his ball skills on the Old Trafford pitch before the United-Arsenal game at the start of the season.

1990

■ United defeated Crystal Palace in the FA Cup to bring Alex Ferguson his first major English honour. Les Sealey, Denis Irwin and Neil Webb arrived.

1991

■ FA Cup holders United won the ECWC by beating Barcelona in Rotterdam. They also won the Super Cup and appeared in the League Cup final. Ryan Giggs made his United first team debut.

1992

■ League football was restructured. A new Premier League replaced the First Division as the Country's top competitive league. United won the League Cup for the first time when they defeated Nottingham Forest 1-0 before 76,810 at Wembley.

OFFICIAL MATCHDAY MAGAZINE £1

F.A. CUP

SEMI-FINAL

HI-TEC

REPLAY

Wednesday,
11th April, 1990
Kick-off: 7.45 p.m.
at Maine Road,
Manchester.

OLDHAM ATHLETIC v **MANCHESTER UNITED**

Bryan Robson and former Red Andy Ritchie during the 1990 FA Cup semi-final.

1993

■ United became the first Premier League title winners, with a ten point advantage over Aston Villa. This was their first full League title since 1967.

1994

■ The Reds won the Premier League by eight points over high-spending Blackburn Rovers, and the FA Cup. At Wembley, United easily defeated Chelsea 4-0 with goals from Cantona (2), Hughes and McClair. Ferguson's side were also League Cup finalists, losing 3-1 to Aston Villa.

1995

■ Blackburn won the title by a point with United in second place. The final match of the season had seen the Reds draw 1-1 at West Ham – another goal would have brought the title. United were also FA Cup finalists, losing 1-0 to Everton. United broke the British transfer record when they signed Andy Cole from Newcastle for a fee of around £7m.

1996

■ The Reds won the Premier League - four points ahead of Newcastle - and the FA Cup. Eric Cantona scored the only goal of the Cup Final against Liverpool at Wembley Stadium before 79,007.

1997

■ The Reds won the Premier League with a seven point advantage over three clubs – Newcastle United, Arsenal and Liverpool. Newcastle, who started the season managed by Kevin Keegan but ended it with Kenny Dalglish, finished second on goal difference.

1998

■ United and Arsenal fought for the 1997-98 Premier League title with the London side having the upper hand as the season neared its end. Successive draws to Liverpool and Newcastle in April, meant the Reds had needed Arsene Wenger's side to drop points in the final games. Even though United won their final three matches, the Gunners held on. Arsenal won the Premier League on 78 points with United one point behind. The year saw Jaap Stam (£10.75m) and Dwight Yorke (£12.6m) sign.

1999

■ The Reds won the Premier League, the FA Cup and the Champions League. They also won the Inter-Continental Cup. Alex Ferguson was knighted.

2000

■ The Reds won the Premier League with a winning margin of 18 points over Arsenal. United signed Fabien Barthez for £7.8m from Monaco.

2001

■ The Reds easily won the Premier League again despite losing their final three League games and taking only four points in the final five matches. The winning margin was ten points over nearest rivals Arsenal. Ruud van Nistelrooy was signed for £19m and Argentinian midfielder Juan Sebastian Veron arrived for a British record £28.1m.

2002

■ United finished third – their lowest position since the birth of the Premier League – ten points behind champions Arsenal and three points behind runners-up Liverpool. The Reds beat the British transfer record they already held when they signed Rio Ferdinand from Leeds for a reported £30m.

2003

■ The Reds won the Premier League and appeared in the League Cup final. They also won the Charity Shield at the start of the 2003-04 season when they defeated

Beckham's departure in 2003.

Arsenal 4-3 on penalties after a 1-1 draw. Cristiano Ronaldo was bought from Sporting Lisbon for £12.24m.

2004

■ United defeated Millwall 3-0 in the FA Cup final with goals from Van Nistelrooy (2) and Ronaldo before a crowd of 71,350 in Cardiff. The year saw Louis Saha (£12.825m), Alan Smith (£7m) and Wayne Rooney (£27m) sign.

2005

■ The Reds were FA Cup finalists, losing 5-4 on penalties after a goalless draw with Arsenal in Cardiff. The 2005-06 season opened with a 3-0 victory over Debreceni at Old Trafford on 9th August 2005. This was a Champions League qualifier and was watched by 51,701, with goals from Ronaldo, Rooney and Van Nistelrooy. The Reds also won the second leg 3-0 but went out in the phase one group stage after defeats by Lille Metropole and Benfica.

2006

■ United won the League Cup for the second time in their history. They defeated Wigan Athletic 4-0 at the Millennium Stadium in Cardiff. Michael Carrick was signed for £18.6m and Nemanja Vidic (right) for £7m.

2007

■ The Reds won the Premier League, and were Champions League semi-finalists and

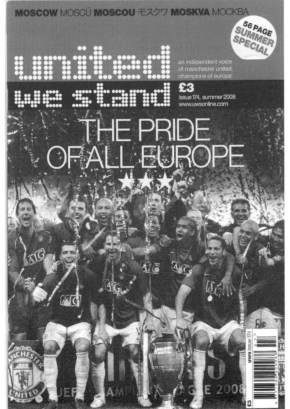

Above: **United's squad as described in the October 2007 Dynamo Kiev programme.**

FA Cup runners-up, losing 1-0 to Chelsea. United defeated Chelsea 3-0 on penalties in the Charity Shield after a 1-1 draw. In July Nani was signed for a reported £12m from Sporting Lisbon and Anderson came from Porto for £18m. The previous month Owen Hargreaves arrived for £17m from Bayern Munich.

2008

■ An amazing 2007-08 season ended with the Reds successful in the Premier League and the Champions League. They also won the FIFA World Club Cup. The Champions League final was an all-English affair in Moscow and saw United defeat Chelsea 6-5 on penalties after a tense 1-1 draw. Dimitar Berbatov arrived from Tottenham Hotspur on transfer deadline day for £30.75m.

2009

■ The Reds won the Premier League and the League Cup, but were runners-up to Barcelona in the Champions League. In the League Cup they defeated Spurs 4-1 on penalties after a goalless game. Antonio Valencia signed for around £15.25m from Wigan, but Cristiano Ronaldo was sold for a reported £80m to Real Madrid.

2010

■ United won the League Cup and were runners-up in the Premier League. The Reds also defeated Chelsea 3-1 in the traditional curtain-raiser the Community Shield with goals from Berbatov, Hernandez and Valencia. Chris Smalling was signed for £10m from Fulham.

2011

■ The Reds became the first side to win a total of nineteen League titles when they overtook Liverpool's record in 2010-11. United also appeared in the Champions

League final against Barcelona at Wembley.

■ United defeated City 3-2 with a goal from Nani four minutes into added time in the Community Shield at Wembley before 77,169.

Old Trafford in 2008.

TICKET PRICES

The admission price to sit in K Stand for the FA Cup tie with Queen's Park Rangers on 29 January 1977 was £1.20 for an adult ticket. The Reds won the tie with Lou Macari scoring the only goal. Attendance 57,422

Two shillings and sixpence (12½p in today's money) would be enough to buy a ticket for the European Cup quarter-final with Red Star Belgrade at Old Trafford in January 1958. The true value of the ticket today, considering average earnings and inflation, would be approximately £6.

A ticket to stand at the 1983 League Cup final against Liverpool could be bought for £4.

£2.60 would buy a terracing ticket for the Old Trafford derby of March 1986. The game ended in a 2-2 draw before 51,274. In February 1990 £3.50 bought a similar ticket for the 1-1 drawn Manchester derby watched by 40,274.

CHELSEA
FOOTBALL & ATHLETIC CO. LTD.

STAND	ROW	SEAT
H	Q	27

WEDNESDAY **OCTOBER** 2nd 1963
Football League, Div. I.
KICK-OFF 7.30 p.m.
CHELSEA v.
MANCHESTER UNITED

This portion to be
retained
PRICE 6/-

Secretary

CHELSEA
FOOTBALL & ATHLETIC CO. LTD.

STAND	ROW	SEAT
NEW	13	77

Football League, Div. I.
CHELSEA v.
MANCHESTER UNITED
Wednesday **SEPT.** 30th 1964
KICK-OFF 7.30 p.m.

PRICE **7/6**
This portion
to be retained

Secretary

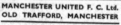

MANCHESTER UNITED F.C. Ltd.
OLD TRAFFORD, MANCHESTER

**PADDOCK
OLD TRAFFORD**

FOOTBALL LEAGUE CUP
QUARTER FINAL

UNITED
v.
EVERTON

No. 2268

WEDNESDAY 1st DEC., 1976
Kick-off 7-30 p.m.

Admission 80p

L. Olive
Secretary.

Issued subject to the Rules, Regulations and
Bye-Laws of the Football Association.
No Ticket exchanged nor money refunded.
This portion to be Retained

As a capacity attendance is
expected, it is strongly
recommended that patrons
ENTER THE GROUND
not less than 30 minutes
before kick-off.

THE EMPIRE STADIUM, WEMBLEY
The Football Association
**Challenge Cup
Competition**
Final Tie
SAT. MAY 12, 1979
KICK-OFF 3 p.m.
YOU ARE ADVISED TO TAKE UP
YOUR POSITION BY 2.30 p.m.

No ticket genuine unless it carries
a Lion's Head watermark below

TURNSTILES **A**
ENTRANCE
33

ROW
14
SEAT
134

1. This ticket is not transferable.
2. This counterfoil must be retained
   for at least 6 months.

CHAIRMAN
WEMBLEY STADIUM LTD.

OUTH TERRACE SEAT
£8.00

BE RETAINED   SEE PLAN AND CONDITIONS ON BACK

**MANCHESTER UNITED
FOOTBALL CLUB plc**
SPONSORED BY
SHARP ELECTRONICS (U.K.) LTD.

RUMBELOWS CUP - 3RD ROUND
UNITED v LIVERPOOL

WED 31 OCT 1990 KO 08:00 EVENING

B STAND

STAND	ROW	SEAT
B3	B ;	63

ADULT MEMBER   Price 7.50
STRS 3&4
TO BE RETAINED

**HEREFORD UNITED
FOOTBALL CLUB**
(1939) LTD.

ADMISSION THROUGH
TURNSTILE 3, 4, 5 & 6
BLACKFRIARS TERRACE

F.A. CUP—4th ROUND

Hereford United
v
MANCHESTER UNITED

Sunday, 28th January, 1990
K.O. 1.00 P.M.

This Ticket is valid on above date
or date when match is played.

£5

PRINT PLUS, 12a Widemarsh Street, Hereford. Telephone 272233.

It would cost £8 to watch United's Premier League meeting with Chelsea on 17 April 1993 in the uncovered West Stand lower tier. A similar fixture in October 1963 between the sides at Stamford Bridge would cost six shillings to sit under cover. The 1963 game ended in a 1-1 draw before 45,351, while the 1993 match saw the Reds win 3-0 four games from the end of their 1992-93 Premier League winning season.

A junior Stretford End ticket for United's 1-1 draw with Liverpool in Division One on 19 October 1985 cost £1.20, while an adult ticket for the same game (in the United Road Paddock) cost £2.60. Eight years earlier an adult ticket for a similar position at the Scoreboard End cost a bargain 80p.

A seat ticket to watch Chelsea V United at Stamford Bridge on Wednesday 30 September 1964 cost seven shillings and sixpence. It would have been well worth it as United won 2-0 with goals from Best and Law. The attendance was 60,769.

When United faced Everton in the fourth round of the League Cup in 1993 Reds fans had to pay £11 to sit in Goodison's Park End. A crowd of 34,052 saw Giggs and Hughes score as United progressed to the fifth round. That season United reached the final.

It would have cost £1.50 to stand in the East Enclosure when Gordon Hill netted twice against Derby County in the FA Cup semi-final at Hillsborough in 1976.

A League Cup quarter final ticket for United V Everton in December 1976 cost 80p to stand in the Paddock at Old Trafford. Attendance 57,738. To stand in the Paddock in 1959 would have cost 3s 6d (17½p).

An FA Cup final seat ticket for the 14th row at either end of Wembley Stadium in 1979 cost £8. United faced Arsenal in a memorable final. 21 years earlier three shillings and sixpence brought a terracing ticket for the West Stand as United faced Bolton in the final.

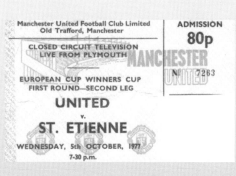

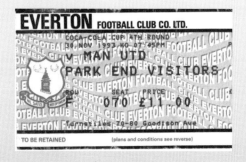

United Kits

Many people assume United have always played in a predominantly red shirt, certainly since the name change in 1902. However, this is not accurate. Red has usually been the dominant colour, but other colours have been worn. Alongside this the question of whether 1902 was the start of the Club's use of red has been raised from time to time. Green and gold are widely believed to be the original colours of Newton Heath, but how long were they used for, and did red ever play a part in the Heathens' match wear?

To try and identify some hard facts The Big Book Of United has asked Kit enthusiast Tim Ashmore to provide a commentary on United's kits over the years. Ashton-u-Lyne born Tim is one of the key figures behind the excellent website Unitedkits.com. He provides a few answers that may surprise readers.

Charlie Moore wearing the first choice red V shirt of 1925-26.

According to popular knowledge, Newton Heath L&YR's first colours were green and gold. People inevitably bring to mind an image of the players taking to the pitch at North Road and Bank Street in halved jerseys with lace-up collars in those famous colours, only for them to adopt their current red, white and black upon the change of name to Manchester United in 1902.

In reality, it has proven impossible to find any evidence of the colours of the club's earliest kits. The Lancashire and Yorkshire Railway's livery was dark green with ornate polished brasswork at the time of the club's founding, so there may be some basis in truth to the legend. However, the first contemporary reference we have found mentioning the colour of the shirts was from a Bolton newspaper report in September 1889, which included a description of Newton Heath playing in "their familiar red and white costumes".

In 1892 the Athletic News annual recorded the Heathens colours as "red & white quarters". The term "quarters" has proven a contentious issue with football historians, some describing them as being in the same style as Blackburn Rovers traditional home shirts - with two differently coloured panels on the front and two on the back – while others liken them to harlequin style shirts - with four panels on the front and four on the back. All of the surviving photographs of the team prior to 1894 show the players wearing jerseys in the Blackburn style, however"

For a couple of seasons in the mid-1890s, the club's colours were indeed recorded in the Athletic News as green and gold, although during this time they wore striped or solid green shirts with gold trim.

In 1896, the Heathens switched to plain white shirts and blue - photographs from the time suggest them to be a very dark navy blue - shorts and socks, and they would retain these colours until 1902. Change colours from the Newton Heath era are largely unknown. However, from the earliest days of football, clubs generally kept a set of plain white shirts in case of a clash. Furthermore, with money being tight in later years, they probably would have retained previous seasons' jerseys for a change option should they be needed.

For the club's first season as Manchester United, a new kit consisting of red shirts, white shorts and black socks was adopted. Change shirts of white and blue stripes were also used. These colours were retained with little change for most of the following twenty years. Exceptions were the plain white change shirts used from 1905 to 1910 and the 1909 FA Cup final shirt, which was white with a red diamond or "v" over the shoulders, and a red rose of Lancashire crest presented to the Club by the music hall entertainer George Robey.

In 1922, John Chapman moved from Airdrieonians to manage United and it seems he brought his old club's colours with him. Very similar to the aforementioned 1909 FA Cup final shirts, although with a button-up collar and thicker diamond, they became United's home colours until 1927. During this time the traditional colours were retained as change kit.

When Herbert Bamlett became manager, the red shirts reverted back to being the Club's home colours with simple white ones used for clashes. In 1932, during United's wilderness years, new change kit, described as maroon and white hoops in official documents, was worn. Due to a number of victories and good performances whilst wearing it, the shirt came to be regarded as "lucky" by supporters and, for a few months at the end of the 1933/34 season, it was briefly adopted as the first choice kit. We'll never know whether it played any part in helping United avoid relegation to the third division when they wore it at Millwall on the final day of the season, but it's certainly an entertaining suggestion.

Wearing hoops, United 1934-35. Back: Manley, Topping, Hacking, Jones (T) & Griffiths. Middle: Cape, Mutch, Ball, Mackay, Hine & Jones (JT). Front: McLenahan & Vose.

Left: **Johnny Carey in blue (1948).** *Right:* **Roger Byrne in traditional red (1957).**

After the Second World War, United began to wear blue as their change colours and it was in such a kit, this time emblazoned with the Manchester coat of arms, that United won the FA Cup (their first honour under Matt Busby) in 1948. It is worth speculating whether the Umbro connection had been encouraged by Busby through his relationship with the Humphreys family established during his time as a player with City. The name Umbro was developed as a marketing name from Humphreys Brothers, and the Humphreys family had established strong links with City during the 1930s when Busby wore their kit.

In the mid-1950s, Busby worked with Umbro to design a range of "continental" style kits, modelled on those that Hungary had worn when they famously defeated England at Wembley in 1953.

These were the V-necked jerseys so famously associated with the Busby Babes, although they were also worn by many other English teams of that era. United reached the FA Cup final in 1957, and wore a white continental kit with red trim again with the Manchester arms featuring on the breast of the jersey.

In the aftermath of Munich in 1958, United again reached the FA Cup final, where they wore their home colours for the first time in a major final. This time around, the shirts featured an unusual crest, often thought to be a phoenix symbolising the club's rise from the ashes of tragedy. It was in reality, an emblem of the City of Manchester and the bird was an eagle, representative of Manchester's connections with ancient Rome. It is this same eagle that is part of Manchester City's club crest today.

The late 50s and early 60s saw several other small changes to the kits, such as switching

157

to white socks and long sleeves, and in 1961 the iconic, crew-necked Umbro Aztec jerseys replaced the Continentals.

Red socks were worn from 1962 to 1971, and a third kit of blue shirts and socks with white shorts was introduced for when neither the home kit nor white away was suitable to avoid a colour clash against the likes of Sunderland or Stoke. The Manchester coat of arms appeared on the jerseys worn at Wembley in 1963, and also in 1968 when United wore all blue against Benfica in the European Cup Final.

In 1971, United adopted new jerseys with a floppy collar and triangular inset. These had apparently first been worn by Aston Villa two years earlier, having been introduced by future Reds boss Tommy Docherty. A new third kit of yellow and blue replaced the old blue and white and from 1972, the club crest was embroidered on the breast of the players' shirts for the first time. For unknown reasons, a short-lived set of shirts with a polo-style collar was worn during the second half of 1974-75, United's season in the Second Division.

In 1975, United became the second English club, after Leeds United, to sign a deal with sportswear firm Admiral to supply kits and market official replicas. Players took to the pitch in countless slight variations of these shirts until 1980, but the basic home shirt had white collars and cuffs with red stripes. The away was white with three, or occasionally four, black stripes running down the left side with the crest over the top of them and were worn with black shorts with red and white flashes. Third kits were identical to the home but in blue. In 1978-79, a new crest celebrating the club's centenary was included on the shirts.

When Admiral hit financial difficulties, rivals Adidas took over as United's kit manufacturers in 1980/81. The first set of home kits saw a very simple design - a plain red shirt with the famous Adidas three-stripes running down the sleeves in white, white shorts and traditional black socks. The away kit was slightly unusual as the white shirt had black three-stripes branding running underneath the arms and down the sides, and featured a crest with a red background. Apparently, they had not considered third kits to be necessary and when United turned up at Southampton, they had to wear a set of blue Umbro third shirts from

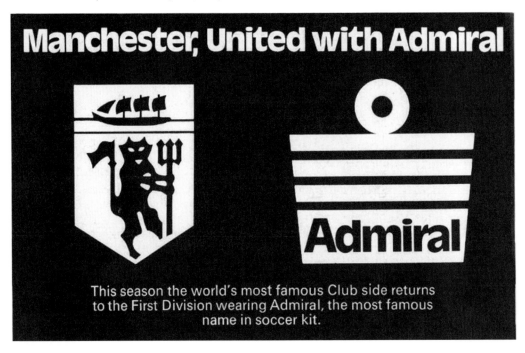

This season the world's most famous Club side returns to the First Division wearing Admiral, the most famous name in soccer kit.

1975. The following season Adidas produced their own blue third shirt in the same style as the home kit.

From 1982, United and Adidas followed a trend of releasing new kits on a two year cycle, following the likes of Liverpool, Arsenal, and Nottingham Forest. They also wore the logo of a sponsor on their shirts for the first time, that of Japanese electronics company Sharp, who at that time had a large factory located almost exactly on the site of United's birthplace in Newton Heath. New fabrics were used with a shiny look and woven pinstripes. The kits had a traditional, uniform look with V-necks. Home was traditional red, white and black, away was white with black shorts and third was all blue. Adidas stuck to this basic formula for the club's kits until 1990, when appeared an odd away kit featuring a pattern of fading "maple leaves" in blue and white. From a distance, it appeared to be light blue and could have been mistaken for something you would have expected City to be seen in. Despite this, it proved very popular amongst supporters.

In 1991, a special one-off all white kit (minus sponsors' logos to comply with regulations) was produced for United's triumph in the European Cup Winners Cup final in Rotterdam against Barcelona.

In 1992, the club reconvened its partnership with Umbro and the local manufacturer produced a set of shirts very much inspired by the past, but with a distinctly 1990s twist.

The home shirt featured a Victorian-style lace-up collar, but set off against complex patterned fabric to deter counterfeiters. The away was all blue and the shirt featured a large black club crest on a tie-dye/tiger-striped background, which also extended to the shorts. The third was green and gold - supposedly a throw-back to the Newton Heath days, but commemorating 100 years since the club's first season of League Football, when the Heathens were wearing red and white. Nevertheless, it became a classic kit and a sought-after fan favourite to this day.

Umbro were not afraid to experiment with United's colours and in 1993 they released the club's first black away kit. It was an instant success, although it is probably best remembered as being the kit Eric Cantona was wearing when he took a brief excursion into the crowd at Selhurst Park. In 1994, they added a black collar to the home shirt for the first time as well as a shadow-image of Old Trafford to the fabric. Another strip harking back to United's early days was also produced, this time a blue and white striped third kit. Again there were subtle features printed onto the shirt such as the names of hundreds of United players, and the crest from the 1968 European Cup Final.

Perhaps the most controversial moment in history of United's kits came when Umbro released a monstrous away kit in various shades and textures of grey. After four matches and no wins wearing the kit, the issue of visibility was called into question. In April 1996, United travelled to Southampton with the grey shirts paired with the white shorts from the home kit and a pair of white change socks - with the blue and white third kits in reserve.

United were 3-0 down by half time and when play resumed after the break, the players had changed into the third kits. With the third kit the match ended 3-1. It was never worn again, and Umbro issued a comparatively plain white and black kit to replace it the following season.

It was during this mid-late 90s period that United developed a reputation for introducing new kits at an alarming rate. In fact, they brought out a similar number of kits as the other teams in the Premier League at the time, but the premature replacement of the grey away and the launch of a home kit exclusively for use in European competitions gained them this notoriety.

In 2000, long-term shirt sponsors Sharp were replaced by Vodafone, and later that year it was announced that Nike would take over from Umbro as the club's kit suppliers. They founded a wholly-owned subsidiary to control Manchester United's global licensing and retail operations as part of the deal, paying United a set fee each year as part of the package. Umbro's last kits for the club were a white and black away, and a gold and black third with badges celebrating the 100th anniversary of the change from Newton Heath to Manchester United. The replica versions of these shirts were reversible with the white design on the outside and the gold on the inside.

During the Nike era, there has been much less experimentation with kit colours. A conservative choice of either white, blue or black away and third kits have so far complemented the traditional home kits.

There have been two changes in shirt sponsorship during the last few years; American insurance firm AIG took over for four years starting in 2006, before they were replaced by industry rivals Aon in 2010. A one-season only 'tribute' to the Busby Babes was released in 2006/07 and this appeared to test the water for subsequent frequent kit changes; from 2009 the club released a new home and away kit every season.

Other notable kits from Nike include a nod to that worn in the 1968 European Cup final, released just over 40 years after that event in 2008/09; a home and away shirt featuring bold chevron designs on the chest, apparently in homage to that worn in the 1909 FA Cup final (albeit in very different colours); and a one-off strip worn on the 50th anniversary of the Munich air disaster which replicated that worn by the players in 1958 almost exactly.

There was some innovation in 2011 when Nike introduced a striking away kit of bold blue and black hooped shirts with black shorts and socks.

Who knows what kits manufacturers have in store for United in future years. The one almost guaranteed aspect is that the home shirt will be some form of traditional United red.

If you are a collector of United shirts or are interested in finding out more about the Reds kits over the years take a look at unitedkits.com.

Above: Recorded as George Stacey's shirt, but kit expert Tim Ashmore believes this shirt could predate him (c.1903).

Above: A colourised image of Dick Duckworth (c.1912) and *(left)* Charlie Roberts in United's blue & white shirt from the same period.
Below: An Ogdens colour card showing United red and Frank Barson (c.1925).

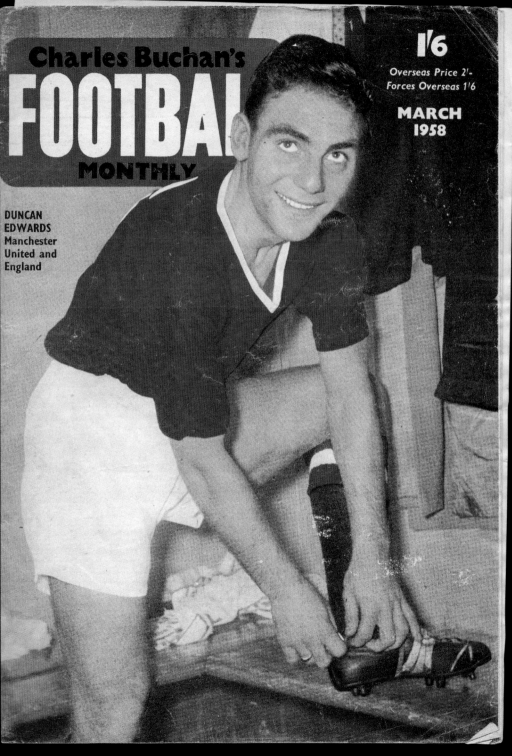

Charles Buchan's
FOOTBA
MONTHLY

1'6

Overseas Price 2'-
Forces Overseas 1'6

**MARCH
1958**

**DUNCAN
EDWARDS**
Manchester
United and
England

By the time this issue arrived in the shops Duncan Edwards had been a victim of

The Manchester coat of arms on the 1948 FA Cup shirt (above), winning captain Johnny Carey (right), the Manchester eagle badge from the 1958 final that some mistakenly believe was a phoenix (left).

A variety of shirts, including Brian Kidd's all-blue 1968 European Cup final kit, at United's museum.

Rio Ferdinand wearing the Munich
memorial kit in February 2008.
Inset: Ruud van Nistelrooy in United
red away from home (hence the
black shorts) in 2002-03.

Above: Tim Ashmore's colourised image of Newton Heath in 1892-93.
Below: The Imperial Hotel on London Road (site now occupied by Malmaison Hotel) regarded as United's HQ in the early 1900s.

John Baines Ltd and Sharpe produced promotional cards in the 1890s. These Newton Heath cards were popular and are highly collectable today.

Matt Busby celebrates United's first European Cup success in 1968.

In 2006-7 visitors on Old Trafford's stadium tour came face to face with the boss in the dressing room - or at least a photo of his head!

Below: Community artwork in Newton Heath celebrates local industry and the Reds' birth.

Visitors get the message in several languages - "Please keep off the pitch"

The First Segregated Manchester Derby?

For many the segregating of home and away supporters has always been part and parcel of football. However, there was a time when fans were allowed to mix. Naturally, they tended to congregate in specific areas, however supporters were not physically kept apart.

That all began to change with an increase in supporter misbehaviour in the Sixties, although formal segregation didn't appear until the 1970s. Perimeter fences appeared at Old Trafford following the 1974 Manchester derby pitch invasion and subsequent investigations.

This then leads to the question of when was the first segregated Manchester derby?

"The Big Book Of United" contributors have scoured the archives and have identified an announcement from 1973 that appears to answer the question. On 17 November 1973 the news was released that the following Manchester derby, scheduled for 1 December at Maine Road, would be the first to see the two sets of supporters physically separated by a barrier.

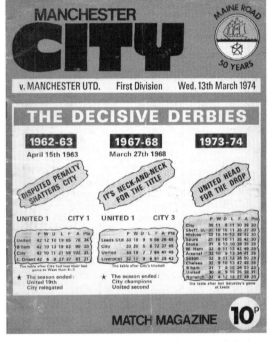

The local press carried the story:

Detailed plans have been finalised to segregate both bands of terrace fans for the forthcoming, Manchester 'derby' match at Maine Road. A temporary railing will be erected down the centre of the Kippax Street Stand, and this strategic point will be controlled by police.

Tickets for this Stand will be issued in different colours, the idea being to keep the United allo-cation separate from those bought by City followers. Each ticket will bear a turnstile number and admission to the ground will only be through the correct turnstile numbered on the ticket.

169

City fans will have entrances by turnstiles at the area towards the North Stand while United fans will be at the other end of the Kippax gaining entry through five turnstiles marked exclusively for them.

"I gather this is the first time such an attempt has been made at a derby match to split up the supporters, and it is done with the intention of keeping trouble to a minimum. The railing, which will be made of nylon ropes, will stretch from the back of the Kippax to the boundary wall at the front and be hooked to the crush barriers" explained [City] club secretary Bernard Halford.

With a 52,500 spectator capacity set on Maine Road for the match, which is on Saturday, December 1st, City will have a police force of more than 100 men on duty for the, game. Dog patrols and mounted police will also be used.

One appeal which Mr. Halford does add: "I request spectators to travel early and take up their positions 45 minutes before the kick-off. It will be a busy afternoon and if fans leave it too late the congestion will cause problems for them as well as us. We hope everyone will help."

And Kippax ticket-holders are reminded. . . "look at your turnstile number on the ticket. That, too, will save time and trouble."

Ultimately, the game did not take place as scheduled and the match was re-arranged for March 13th 1974. That game became a highly controversial derby for other reasons, most notably the sending off of United's Lou Macari and City's Mike Doyle. Both men refused to leave the field. According to referee Clive Thomas: "When taking their names I told them 'off'. They both refused to come off the field and went further away. I called them back and said: "off!" They refused and, therefore, I had no option but to pick up the ball, walk off the field of play and call off the two teams."

Eventually both sides returned to finish the game without Macari and Doyle. It ended goalless, but the newspapers recorded it as one of the worst derby games of all time. It is also believed that this ultimately became the first formally segregated Manchester derby.

UNITED'S LEADING SCORERS

Our story of all the players who have topped the seasonal League goalscoring charts for the Reds through to the start of the 2011-12 season moves on to the 1960s and some of United's most famous players.

THE PROFILES (PART FOUR)

37 – DAVID HERD

The son of Manchester City's popular Scottish international Alec, David Herd spent his formative years living in the shadow of the City stadium in one of the Blues' club houses on Maine Road. Born thirteen days before his father won the FA Cup with City, Herd started his professional football career with Stockport County. His father was based at Edgeley Park at this time, and the two players made history by becoming only the second father and son combination to appear together in a Football League game. David appeared at inside-left and Alec at inside-right for County's final League game of the 1950-51 season.

Despite showing much promise, David Herd's career took some time to develop. The main reason being that the player, like all males of his age at this time, had to perform a period of National Service. Ultimately, Herd did manage a total of fifteen appearances for Stockport by the time he moved to Arsenal for a fee variously reported as anything between £8,000 and £10,000 in 1954.

Surprisingly, Herd remained a squad member rather than a permanent first-teamer for some time at Highbury. In fact, he only managed eight games during his first couple of seasons, but this was soon to be eclipsed with an amazing record in the years that followed. In 1956-57 he scored eighteen goals in 28 games and established himself as the club's star striker by topping the Gunners' goalscoring charts for four successive seasons.

The best season of his Arsenal career came in 1960-61 when he was second to Jimmy Greaves in Division One's goalscoring charts. By that time he had also appeared in five internationals for Scotland. It was no wonder that United showed interest in the striker during the summer of 1961.

United manager Matt Busby knew the Herd family well of course. Busby had been a team mate of Herd's father at City in the thirties and with Scotland during the war, and must have known all about his qualities when he paid £35,000 to Arsenal for his signature.

Busby had actually tried to sign the young Herd several years earlier when the player was still with County, however the transfer had fallen through at a late stage, prompting Herd's transfer to Arsenal instead.

At Old Trafford, Herd soon established himself as a leading figure in the Reds transitional early sixties period. The aftermath of the Munich disaster was still impacting on United's development and, although the 1958-59 season had seen the side finish second, the years that followed saw United finish seventh twice.

Herd's first season was not a great one for the Club – they dropped to fifteenth – but the well-built forward had topped the Reds' goalscoring charts and, in truth, without his goals the League season could have been much worse.

The following year he helped Busby's side find glory for the first time since the air crash when United defeated Leicester 3-1 in the 1963 FA Cup final. He scored twice in the final – the first after 57 minutes saw him send home a powerful shot after a Charlton effort had been blocked by goalkeeper Gordon Banks, while the second came five minutes from time to guarantee victory.

That season Herd had improved on his previous season's goals tally but his nineteen goals were surpassed by Denis Law. Surprisingly, Herd was not first choice when the 1963-64 League campaign opened. The reason appears to be connected with the 1963 Charity Shield defeat by Everton. That day the Reds were shocking and were humiliated 4-0 at Goodison Park. Several players were dropped as a result, including Herd. Some chose – or were encouraged - to leave Old Trafford, but Herd stayed, determined to prove his worth once more. It didn't take him long.

His first League game of the season came on 21 September 1963. This was the season's ninth League match and Herd scored, but United were defeated 2-1 at Arsenal. Nevertheless, Herd retained his place and went on to prove to be an absolutely crucial member of that side. He netted twenty goals in thirty games – not the season's best but a significant contribution as United finished second.

Herd scored another twenty League goals in 1964-65 as Busby's side managed to win the League title for the first time since 1957. It was a tremendous achievement for the Club and for all the players, including Herd who spent most of the season as United's centre-forward in an attacking-minded side that now included George Best, alongside Charlton and Law. Law and Best were, of course, the more flamboyant personalities, and Herd's contribution was often not given the attention it deserved, but it has to be stressed that Herd was as vital a member of that side as the others.

By winning the League title Herd had matched the achievements of his father who had also won the League and the Cup while in Manchester, but the younger man ultimately eclipsed his father's achievements when he helped United to their next title in 1966-67.

On 26 November 1966 Herd scored four

goals as United defeated Sunderland 5-0, however the most significant aspect of this feat was that he had actually scored against three different goalkeepers in that match. Sunderland's 'keeper Jim Montgomery had to leave the field in the first half due to an injury and was replaced by centre-back Charlie Hurley. Later, as United's score increased, Sunderland swapped Hurley for Northern Ireland defender John Parke, but Herd's scoring continued.

Herd went on to net 16 goals that season – eight less than in 1966 when he topped United's charts for a second time – but there was a significant reason why his figure was not higher. The player had actually broken his leg while in the act of scoring a goal against Leicester on 18 March 1967. He missed the ten League games that followed.

He did return in 1967-68, but only managed six appearances and one goal in the League, plus a FA Cup appearance, before moving to Stoke in July 1968.

After two seasons at Stoke he appeared for Irish club Waterford, and had a spell as manager of Lincoln City. However, it was his time at United that ensured his name would permanently be linked with major success.

In total Herd made 201 (plus 1 as substitute) appearances in the League and netted 114 League goals for United. This was a remarkable achievement and proved Herd's significance to the Reds' cause.

Leading League Scorer in:
1961-1962 - 14 goals, 27 appearances
1965-1966 – 24 goals, 37 appearances

38 – DENIS LAW

Forever known as 'The King', Denis Law will always remain one of United's biggest football stars. A key figure behind many United successes of the sixties, Law was recognised for his amazing talent from an early age.

Born in Aberdeen in 1940, Law is often highlighted as receiving his first set of football boots on his sixteenth birthday. However, it has to be stressed that the

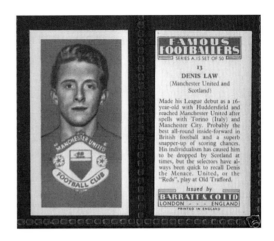

youngster was already showing great talent, with or without a pair of boots, and had actually been spotted by Huddersfield Town at this point.

Huddersfield scout Archie Beattie recommended that he attend a trial and on 3 April 1955 the West Yorkshire club signed him. On 24 December 1956 he made his debut, as a sixteen year old, against Notts County and the following year he signed professional forms for the club.

Under the tutelage of Huddersfield manager Bill Shankly, Law's career developed at a rapid rate and he made his international debut for Scotland against Wales in November 1958. He scored that day – a clearance hit his forehead before going into the net via the crossbar. It is worth highlighting that Scotland were managed by Matt Busby and Wales by Jimmy Murphy for this game. Law was 18 years and 236 days old and was heralded as the youngest Scottish international of modern times in the press.

In March 1960 Law signed for Manchester City for a League record fee of £55,000 and he immediately impressed with a goal on his debut at Leeds. He scored in his next League match and appeared in seven League games for the Blues that season.

Supporters loved his skill and older City fans compared him with the great Peter Doherty. They enjoyed his finishing of course, but they also loved his ability to tackle and hassle opponents. It took him no time at all to become established as a true blue hero.

The following season Law was City's top scorer with nineteen goals in 37 League appearances. A great record for a player who had only reached the age of 21 in February of that season. Supporters presented him with cards and keys to mark the landmark birthday, but his time at Maine Road was soon to come to a premature end as the Blues were struggling and Law was their most valuable – and sellable – asset.

Against supporter wishes the player was transferred to Torino for a fee of £100,000. It was the first time a British club had been involved in a £100,000 transfer but that hardly helped ease the blow as far as City fans were concerned. Law was their hero and without him there were real – and justified - fears for the future. Forty years later his City captain and friend Ken Barnes looked back on this period and accurately surmised: "It wasn't a great period for the club. The cup team had broken up and other players had been brought in, but we were not at the standard we'd been at just a couple of years earlier. Clearly Denis Law was a tremendous signing when he joined us in 1960 but a good player needs other good players around him to make him a great player. We weren't of the right calibre for him. After a year I guess he had to move on. During his first spell with us I did manage to teach him how to drive though!"

Law's time in Italy was also not the great success the player had hoped and, although he was clearly a very talented player, it was often difficult to play with the flair and attacking approach he excelled in. There were also some extremely worrying moments off the pitch. Most notably a car crash in February 1962. He suffered injuries but the accident almost brought the death of his team-mate Joe Baker, brother of his former City colleague Gerry.

The following close season both Joe Baker and Law left Italy for Arsenal and United respectively.

Law's arrival was the result of another record fee. This time the Reds paid £115,000 and the player had arrived at a club where his immense talents could shine. Those Mancunians of a Blue persuasion who had compared him to Doherty were now joined by Reds who admired those same qualities.

During his first season with the Reds Law netted 23 goals in 38 League appearances to top the Club's goalscoring charts. He also won the FA Cup – his first national major honour. He had netted the opening goal in the 29th minute, but it was his all-round performance that impressed the most in that match.

The following season saw Law in blistering form as he became the third player in United's history to net thirty goals or more in a League season. He also deservedly received the European Footballer of the Year award. United missed out on the title that year, but Law topped the charts again the following season (1964-65) as the Reds won the League.

Law also topped United's scoring charts in 1966-67 when the Reds won their next League title. That Championship success allowed Busby's side to challenge for the European Cup, but Law only managed to appear in three of the European fixtures that season as the Reds triumphed. Sadly, a leg injury prevented him from playing in the greatest success of the period, but he had contributed so much in the League the previous season that gave Busby's side that opportunity.

After United's European success in 1968, Law continued to be one of the Club's biggest and most important stars but success eluded the Reds. There were semi-final appearances in the European Cup, FA Cup and League Cup, but even those petered out after 1970. Law did his best to ensure United kept to their attacking values, but the Club's issues lay elsewhere.

In 1973 Law's United career came to an end when manager Tommy Docherty gave him a free transfer. He signed once more for Manchester City who, at this point were managed by Law's former colleague Johnny Hart. The following March he appeared in the League Cup final – his last domestic final – as City were defeated by Wolves.

At the end of the 1973-74 season Law back heeled the only goal of the Old Trafford derby match that many perceive to be the goal that relegated United. Factually, the goal did not matter as the Reds would have been relegated due to results elsewhere, however at the time he scored the goal neither he, nor the United fans who subsequently invaded the pitch twice, could have known specifically that the goal was an irrelevance.

Law later admitted: "I have seldom been so depressed as I was that weekend."

The player was substituted almost immediately and many have incorrectly claimed that the goal was Law's final act in his club career. Even the 2011 Community Shield match programme incorrectly claimed this as a fact. This is actually not true. Most recognise that the player took part in Scotland's 1974 World Cup campaign, but few remember that he actually competed in further first team games for the Blues. In fact Law played in two Texaco Cup games for City in August 1974 and scored his last first team goal in domestic football at Sheffield United on 6 August 1974. The Texaco Cup was regarded as a first team competitive tournament in 1974, although its importance has declined since then.

Like United, City were also in a transitional period and alongside Law, Francis Lee also made his final appearance and scored his final goal for the Blues in that season's Texaco Cup. Asa Hartford had arrived at the club and new manager Tony Book was making a number of changes. In the middle of this Law announced his retirement. The news came on 26 August 1974 and Law was photographed leaving a Manchester ground as a footballer for the last time that day.

Since 1974 Law has remained a hero to both Blues and Reds alike - an amazing feat in itself – and has performed media work. Always popular, Law was given the honour by City and UEFA of representing Manchester as the Ambassador for the 2008 UEFA Cup final staged at the City Of Manchester Stadium. He went on to perform the cup and medal presentation, as well as many other duties that promoted Manchester across Europe.

He has also been honoured with statues at Old Trafford and various other accolades. One of the most unusual for many years was the pub sign at the King's Head public house in Crown Point, Denton. For most of the late 1970s and eighties the sign depicted Law, the 'king', in a football kit.

To most fans Law will always be remembered as the King.

Leading League Scorer in:
1962-1963 - 23 goals, 38 appearances
1963-1964 – 30 goals, 30 appearances
1964-1965 – 28 goals, 36 appearances
1966-1967 – 23 goals, 36 appearances

39 – GEORGE BEST

Viewed by many as the most gifted footballer of the last sixty years, George Best was undoubtedly a remarkable talent. Although in his later life the media tended to focus on off-the-pitch activities, his health concerns and drinking habits, none of this should ever detract from what he achieved as a player, and how highly he was regarded by football fans across the world.

Best first arrived in Manchester as a 15 year old after being spotted by scout Bob Bishop in Belfast. Initially the youngster felt homesick and almost gave up on the chance to play for United, however he was persuaded to stay.

At the age of 17 he made his first team debut wearing the number seven shirt in United's seventh League game of the 1963-64 season as the Reds defeated West Bromwich Albion 1-0. It was a one-off appearance and the Irishman had to wait

for three and a half months before his next League appearance, but this time he made sure he did more than enough to keep his place. He scored as Burnley were defeated 5-1 on 28 December 1963, and went on to make a total of 17 League appearances and score four goals as United finished the season as runners-up. Best also appeared in the FA Cup run, including the semi-final defeat to West Ham and two games in the ECWC campaign.

The following season saw Best as a fully-fledged member of the first team throughout the campaign. From the start of the 1964-65 season he wore the number 11 shirt and only missed one League match as the Reds won the League title for the first time since 1957.

Best, still maturing, was already idolised by fans but this was nothing to the adulation that would follow in 1965-66 when the player was in outstanding form against Benfica in the European Cup quarter-final. Playing at Benfica's Stadium of Light Best put in a dazzling performance and netted twice in the opening twelve minutes – one a neatly flicked header, the other a run from halfway before rounding the 'keeper.

Those goals helped inspire the Reds to a thrilling 5-1 victory but, significantly, this was the first defeat Benfica had experienced at home in the competition. Pre-match United, who won the first leg 3-2, had planned to play more of a defensive game. Matt Busby later laughed: "Our plan was to be cautious, but somebody must have stuffed cotton wool in George's ears."

Reports claim a fan ran on the pitch at the end with a knife, hoping to cut off some of Best's hair as a souvenir, but this was nothing compared with the attention that

It's Christmas time for George Best and Mike Summerbee.

followed. Images of the player wearing a sombrero appeared with the tag: "El Beatle" after the Portuguese dubbed him "O Quinto Beatle" – the fifth Beatle. The image and glamour of George Best was now cemented around Europe, not simply those with an interest in English football.

Two years after the Benfica tie Best's image grew further with another memorable, perhaps the most memorable, game from the sixties – the 1968 European Cup final. Best had been an ever-present in the League when the Reds won the title in 1966-67 that enabled them to compete in the 1967-68 European Cup. He had also scored the only goal of the home leg of the semi-final against Real Madrid which, ultimately, was the goal that separated the two sides (the subsequent away leg ended 3-3). But all of this was eclipsed when Benfica were defeated 4-1 after extra time in the final at Wembley.

Best was in outstanding form in a tense final and scored in the opening period of extra time to set United up for victory. That success capped a great year for the player who also topped the Reds' and the Division One scoring charts, and was voted both the Football Writers' footballer of the year and the European player of the year. Interestingly, Bobby Charlton had come second in the European award for the second successive season, although he had won the award in 1966 with Benfica's Eusebio second.

By this time Best was at the centre of the Swinging Sixties and seemed to encapsulate a modern, care-free spirit. He had opened a boutique "Edwardia" with his friend the City star Mike Summerbee, and had even been spotted in the audience for "Top Of The Pops" dancing along to the Rolling Stones "The Last Time" in 1965. The show was recorded in Manchester at the time.

George Best became an iconic figure during this time and his fame was no longer confined to newspaper back pages. Everything Best did or said was reported on and the player was encouraged to enjoy his life. He opened nightclubs in Manchester as well. As far as the average man in the street was concerned Best had everything - fame, money, girls... He was idolised like no other footballer had ever been before.

On the pitch Best topped United's goalscoring charts for five consecutive seasons but after 1968 actual trophy success eluded the Reds. There were some great cup runs and some wonderful individual performances, including Best's own thrilling six goal feast in the 1970 FA Cup tie with Northampton, however.

Once Matt Busby retired though, the Club began to change as far as Best was concerned. Busby had acted as a wise, father-figure, prepared to offer advice to the Irishman, but once he had stepped aside Best seemed discontent. He appeared disillusioned but in 1971 admitted: "Football is the only life I know. It's brought me everything I have today. I've packed more living into nine years than most people could do in ninety."

On his lifestyle as a whole he recognised that he was a role model: "I try to keep out of trouble, because I realise I can influence some youngster in the wrong way. I had a good record for years, then I slipped. But I'm working on improving my temperament."

During this period Best often considered his future and role at United. There was talk of retirement and he even walked out on the Club for a while. On 7 December 1972 United sent a letter to all First and Second Division clubs advising them that Best was on the transfer list and that the Reds would be interested in receiving offers for the 26 year old. Immediately there was interest from several clubs, including Oldham Athletic (who met the player and thought they had convinced him to sign according to the book "Manchester A Football History") and Manchester City. The Blues boss

Malcolm Allison wanted to sign Best but United, understandably, would not sell the player to their biggest rivals. Best himself had claimed in 1968 that he would love to play in City's forward line alongside the likes of Summerbee, Lee and Young.

Despite being transfer listed and interest shown, Best remained at Old Trafford although he wasn't to make another League appearance that season (1972-73). He did re-appear under manager Tommy Docherty for twelve League games in 1973-74. His last match being the 3-0 New Year's Day 1974 defeat at QPR.

At the age of 27 Best seemed far too young to be leaving United. Surely the Club and the player could have worked something out? Who knows what the Reds could have achieved in the mid-seventies had Best been able to focus on his football with the support of the Club?

After United, Best appeared for many clubs including the Jewish Guild in South Africa, Dunstable Town, Stockport County, Cork Celtic, Fulham, LA Aztecs, Fort Lauderdale Strikers, San Jose Earthquakes, Detroit Express, Hibernian, Bournemouth, and Brisbane Lions.

Once his playing days ended for good, Best performed media work and toured the after-dinner circuit with former Fulham team-mate Rodney Marsh and others. However, there remained a significant focus on his personal life, most notably his alcoholism. In 1990 he appeared, worse for wear, on the chat show Wogan and it appeared as if he had been deliberately encouraged to be outspoken. This was in real contrast to earlier appearances on the Parkinson show where Michael Parkinson, always a Best fan, would encourage him to recount the exploits of his life while also focusing on his brilliance as a footballer.

In March 2000 Best was diagnosed with severe liver damage, and two years later he received a liver transplant. Unfortunately, the former European Cup winner was unable to quit drinking for good and media stories in 2003 and 2004 focused on further issues, including a drink-driving offence in February 2004.

Best was admitted to the Cromwell Hospital in London suffering from a kidney infection in October 2005. The prognosis was grim and on 20 November the tabloid "The News Of The World" published an image of Best in his hospital bed with the message "Don't die like me." Five days later he died of a lung infection and multiple organ failure.

In the years that have followed Belfast airport has been renamed after him and various charity-activities, murals, mosaics and significant tributes have followed. He thoroughly deserves every accolade.

Football stars come and go, but George Best should be remembered for ever more for the excitement and entertainment he brought to United, Northern Ireland (where he made 37 appearances), and all the other clubs he appeared for. Best was a one-off, who delighted everyone who saw him play.

Leading League Scorer in:
1967-1968 - 28 goals, 41 appearances
1968-1969 – 19 goals, 41 appearances
1969-1970 – 15 goals, 37 appearances
1970-1971 – 18 goals, 40 appearances
1971-1972 – 18 goals, 40 appearances

40 – SAMMY MCILROY

Irishman Sammy McIlroy made his debut when an injury to Denis Law prevented him from appearing in the Manchester derby of November 1971 at Maine Road. It was a highly memorable first game for the 17 year old who opened the scoring for United before 63,326 noisy fans.

Even though Law returned for the next match, McIlroy managed to retain a place in the side for the next match – a 3-1 victory over Tottenham. An Old Trafford crowd of 54,058 saw the youngster score again.

By the end of the 1971-72 season McIlroy had made eight full appearances and eight substitute appearances in the League, and had netted four goals. In 1972-73 he only managed four (plus six as substitute) League appearances, but his progress was

impacted by a car crash in which he suffered a punctured lung and four broken ribs.

In 1973-74 he managed a total of 29 League appearances and topped the Club's goalscoring charts, but this was a desperate season and the Reds were relegated. McIlroy started the Division Two season that followed as substitute in the opening match, but went on to start every other League game that campaign as United won the Second Division title.

By 1976 McIlroy was one of United's most consistent and significant performers as he helped the Reds challenge for the title – they finished third in their first season back in Division One – and for the FA Cup where they were defeated by Southampton in the final. At one point it looked as if the game would go United's way as McIlroy's glancing header looked goal bound, but somehow the ball hit the bar instead.

The following year he was a key member of the side that defeated Liverpool in United's first FA Cup success since 1963. Then in 1979 he made his third FA Cup final appearance in four years when the Reds faced Arsenal. It became one of the competition's most memorable finals and McIlroy played his part well. One minute and 45 seconds from time, with Arsenal winning, he rushed into the area, squeezed past one defender, nutmegged a second before sending the ball past goalkeeper Pat Jennings for the equaliser. It was a highly dramatic and wonderful goal.

Sadly, Arsenal came straight back and netted the winner, but that should not detract from McIlroy's spirit and the determination that brought his goal.

McIlroy remained a key member of Dave Sexton's United side for the seasons that followed, however once Ron Atkinson arrived in 1981 it was clear the new manager would be bringing in players and making significant changes. Nevertheless he managed to start the 1981-82 season as United's number eleven, but Remi Moses arrived from Atkinson's old club West Bromwich Albion and McIlroy was moved to the sidelines. After twelve appearances that

season he was transferred to Stoke City for £350,000.

Stoke were a struggling side. After three years there McIlroy moved back to Manchester to appear for newly promoted City where he made 13 appearances, including the September 1985 Maine Road derby match which saw former Blue Peter Barnes play for the Reds.

Spells at Swedish club Orgryte IS, Bury, Preston North End and Northwich Victoria followed. He also enjoyed a wonderful career with Northern Ireland where he made 88 international appearances and played at the 1982 and 1986 World Cup finals.

While at Northwich he moved into management and later enjoyed a very successful spell as Macclesfield Town's boss. He guided the Cheshire club to successes in the Football Conference, the FA Trophy, and to promotion into the League and then the Second Division where they were on equal terms with his former club Manchester City.

He went on to manage the Northern Ireland team, and then Stockport. In 2005 he took over at Conference side Morecambe, initially on a caretaker basis, and managed them to promotion into the Football League. Further progress followed before, in May 2011, McIlroy left Morecambe by mutual consent after the 2010-11 season had seen the side struggle.

Leading League Scorer in:
1973-1974 - 6 goals, 29 appearances

GOLDEN GOALS

David Beckham

1996 v Wimbledon

Many goals over the years have been described as the greatest ever by a United player. Sometimes these become a talking point for a few days, sometimes for a few years but occasionally they are remembered for decades. Other goals often lose their significance as time moves on, unless they are netted in trophy-winning matches.

The idea of this 'GOLDEN GOALS' feature is to remember a significant or spectacular goal. We are not searching for United's greatest goal, but merely want to highlight some of the Reds' best efforts from a few years ago. Some of these may have slipped from memory, while others may have been talked of year after year. The Big Book Of United's hope is that modern day supporters learn more about some of these goals and help them be remembered and talked of for many more years.

The goal featured here was scored by David Beckham on the opening day of the 1996-97 season against Wimbledon at Selhurst Park. It became one of the most famous goals in United's modern history.

MATCH STATS

Date: 17 August 1996

Score: Wimbledon 0 United 3

Scorers: Eric Cantona (25th minute), Denis Irwin (38th minute) & David Beckham (90th minute)

Attendance: 25,786

Referee: D. Elleray

United Team: Schmeichel, Irwin, Neville P, May, Keane, Pallister, Cantona (McClair 79th minute), Butt (Johnsen 39th minute), Scholes, Beckham & Cruyff

PRE-MATCH

This was the first Premier League game of the season and came six days after the Reds had defeated Newcastle 4-0 in the Charity Shield. United were the reigning Premier League champions and this game was crucial to ensure the Reds title challenge started in the right way.

THE GAME

United cruised to a two goal lead and were totally in control against Joe Kinnear's Wimbledon team. As the game neared

its end David Beckham gained possession just inside his own half, right of centre. The young midfielder, who had been handed Mark Hughes' number 10 shirt in the close season, looked up and saw the Wimbledon keeper Neil Sullivan off his line.

The United star immediately sent a sixty yard shot flying over the 'keeper. The ball flew into the net close to the crossbar. It was a wonderful strike and one that helped cement Beckham's place as one of England's greatest stars.

Only ninety minutes into the new League season and Beckham's goal was already being talked about as the 'Goal of the Season'.

Later stories circulated about the boots that scored the goal. Apparently, it was revealed that the boots had been made for Rangers midfielder Charlie Miller and that they had 'Charlie' embroidered into them. Somehow they were sent to Beckham by mistake and the player had no choice but to wear them.

This game was also noteworthy as it saw the debut of £1.4m signing Jordi Cruyff, but it was Beckham who deservedly gained the headlines.

POST MATCH

The goal was not only viewed by many as the season's best strike, it was also voted in May 1998 as the third best goal of all time by a panel of experts pulled together by the magazine Four Four Two. It was also recorded as the goal of the decade.

Regardless of how the goal is remembered, the fact is that this goal helped to catapult Beckham into the public consciousness. United fans already knew what he was capable of but suddenly the wider football world, and ultimately the general population, began to talk about David Beckham.

Immediately there were calls for Beckham to appear in Glenn Hoddle's England squad and, sure enough, two weeks after scoring this goal the player made his international debut in a World Cup qualifying match with Moldova.

At the time former United hero David Sadler felt that the player's promotion was too soon, but he quickly changed his mind. In October, shortly after Beckham's second international, Sadler explained to the Manchester Evening News why he had been concerned for the player two months earlier: "When Beckham's wonder goal from the halfway line against Wimbledon settled into the back of the Selhurst Park net on the opening day of the season and immediately sparked a clamour for the young Manchester United star's elevation to full England status, I was a worried man.

"I thought it was all too early for him and the main reason for that was I was concerned how this sudden thrust into super stardom would affect Beckham's form for Manchester United. He wouldn't have been the first young England star to have suffered after an early call up."

Sadler admitted that Beckham's performances had caused him to change his mind: "I am having a rethink now on the Beckham situation. Far from the England status detracting from his club form, Beckham has continued to be outstanding for United despite all the newspaper attention. His form for England in the two matches he's played just proves that he takes everything in his stride."

UNITED'S FA CUP SUCCESSES

In 1990 United equalled the FA Cup record held by Aston Villa and Tottenham Hotspur of seven trophy successes. Villa had actually reached that milestone back in 1957, ironically in a final against United (United's third FA Cup final appearance), while Spurs had won their seventh FA Cup in 1982.

In 1991 Tottenham won their eighth FA Cup and this was equalled by the Reds in 1994. United took the total to nine in 1996 and continued to hold the record with each success over the next decade or so. In 2005 Arsenal took their total of FA Cup wins to ten but United were already at eleven wins by that point.

In 2011 the Reds remained the only side to have won the FA Cup on eleven occasions.

United's first FA Cup win came in 1909 during the days of Sandy Turnbull and Billy Meredith. That was the second major trophy won by the Reds, coming a year after the side had won the League title for the first time.

The longest period in between FA Cup successes for United stands at 39 years (1909-1948),

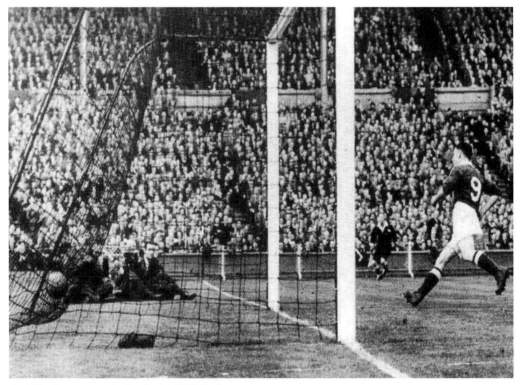

Jack Rowley scores his first in the 1948 final.

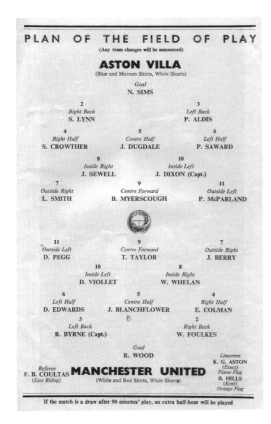

PLAN OF THE FIELD OF PLAY
(Any team changes will be announced)

ASTON VILLA
(Blue and Maroon Shirts, White Shorts)

Goal
N. SIMS

2		3
Right Back		*Left Back*
S. LYNN		P. ALDIS

4	5	6
Right Half	*Centre Half*	*Left Half*
S. CROWTHER	J. DUGDALE	P. SAWARD

8		10
Inside Right		*Inside Left*
J. SEWELL		J. DIXON (Capt.)

7	9	11
Outside Right	*Centre Forward*	*Outside Left*
L. SMITH	B. MYERSCOUGH	P. McPARLAND

11	9	7
Outside Left	*Centre Forward*	*Outside Right*
D. PEGG	T. TAYLOR	J. BERRY

10		8
Inside Left		*Inside Right*
D. VIOLLET		W. WHELAN

6	5	4
Left Half	*Centre Half*	*Right Half*
D. EDWARDS	J. BLANCHFLOWER	E. COLMAN

3		2
Left Back		*Right Back*
R. BYRNE (Capt.)		W. FOULKES

Goal
R. WOOD

Referee
F. B. COULTAS **MANCHESTER UNITED**
(East Riding) (White and Red Shirts, White Shorts)

Linesmen
K. G. ASTON
(Essex)
Flame Flag
B. HILLS
(Kent)
Orange Flag

If the match is a draw after 90 minutes' play, an extra half-hour will be played

THE FOOTBALL ASSOCIATION CHALLENGE CUP COMPETITION

THE FOOTBALL ASSOCIATION — CENTENARY YEAR

FINAL TIE
LEICESTER CITY
v
MANCHESTER UNITED

OFFICIAL PROGRAMME — ONE SHILLING

WEMBLEY

EMPIRE STADIUM

SATURDAY, MAY 25th   Kick-off 3 p.m.

which means that United's record of success since World War Two has easily eclipsed all other clubs – by the end of 2010 United had managed ten post war successes (Arsenal have achieved 8, Liverpool 7, Spurs 6 and Chelsea 6 during that time).

The following table shows each of United's FA Cup successes and, to give an indication of how United's record rated against the best in the land at the time, we include the team who held the record for the most number of FA Cup wins at the time of each Reds' success.

Season	Score	Runners-up	Attendance	Total FA Cup Wins	Team with most FA Cup successes
1908-09	1-0	Bristol City	71,401	1	Blackburn Rovers & the Wanderers 5
1947-48	4-2	Blackpool	99,842	2	Aston Villa & Blackburn Rovers 6
1962-63	3-1	Leicester City	99,604	3	Aston Villa 7
1976-77	2-1	Liverpool	99,252	4	Aston Villa 7
1982-83	2-2 (aet)	Brighton & HA	99,059		
	4-0 (replay)	Brighton & HA	91,534	5	Aston Villa & Tottenham Hotspur 7
1984-85	1-0 (aet)	Everton	99,445	6	Aston Villa & Tottenham Hotspur 7
1989-90	3-3 (aet)	Crystal Palace	80,000		
	1-0 (replay)	Crystal Palace	80,000	7	Aston Villa, Tottenham Hotspur & United 7
1993-94	4-0	Chelsea	79,634	8	Tottenham & United 8
1995-96	1-0	Liverpool	79,007	9	United 9
1998-99	2-0	Newcastle United	79,101	10	United 10
2003-04	3-0	Millwall	71,350	11	United 11

Listed below are the eleven most successful sides in the FA Cup at the time of publication. We also include the years of each club's first and most recent success, and have listed teams in order of their first success where two or more sides have the same number of wins.

United 11 – First 1909, Most Recent 2004

Arsenal 10 – First 1930, Most Recent 2005

Tottenham 8 – First 1901, Most Recent 1991

Aston Villa 7 – First 1887, Most Recent 1957

Liverpool 7 – First 1965, Most Recent 2006

Blackburn Rovers 6 – First 1883, Most Recent 1928

Newcastle United 6 – First 1910, Most Recent 1955

Chelsea 6 – First 1970, Most Recent 2010

West Bromwich Albion 5 – First 1888, Most Recent 1968

Manchester City 5 – First 1904, Most Recent 2011

Everton 5 – First 1906, Most Recent 1995

Matt Busby was the first United manager to win the FA Cup on more than one occasion with the Reds. In 1948 the FA Cup brought Busby the first trophy of his managerial career, and United's first major trophy since 1911: "There was so much talent, so many natural skills. At half-time skipper Johnny Carey and I urged the team to keep playing football, and the goals would come. They obliged and finally we won 4-2. I felt this could be the start of big things."

Busby's next FA Cup success came in 1963, after appearances in the 1957 and 1958 finals: "Bobby Charlton and Billy Foulkes had been with us for the finals in the fifties and they must have felt as delighted as I was when we put on such a wonderful display to beat Leicester City 3-1. I felt the same way as I had after the 1948 final, I knew instinctively that this was to be the start of a great run."

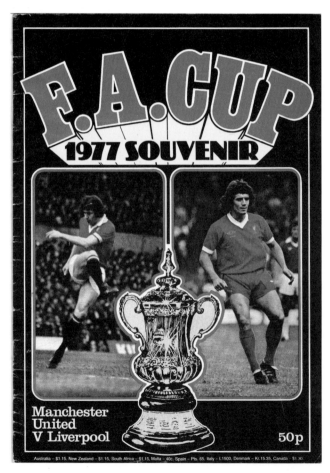

The Football Season Daily Reminder
January

1st January 1907

Jimmy Bannister made his United debut against Aston Villa. The game ended in a 1-0 victory with another debutant Sandy Turnbull scoring the only goal. Both players had joined the Reds following the infamous illegal payments scandal at Manchester City. 42 years later on New Year's Day United defeated Arsenal 2-0 in Division One (right).

2nd January 2002

Goals from van Nistelrooy (24th minute) and Scholes (50th and 62nd minutes) gave United a 3-1 victory over Newcastle before 67,646 at Old Trafford.

3rd January 1977

The Bank Holiday League campaign saw most games called off by snowy conditions forcing a backlog that was already greater than that experienced in 1963 – a season widely viewed as being the worst. Despite the weather, United's game with Ipswich was

played. Sadly, it ended in a 2-1 defeat on a very icy surface.

4th January 1964

The FA Cup holders beat Southampton 3-2 in an entertaining third round tie at the Dell.

5th January 1974

Lou Macari scored the only goal of the third round FA Cup tie at home to Plymouth before 31,810.

6th January 1968

West Ham were defeated 3-1 with goals from Aston, Best and Charlton.

7th January 2007

Solskjaer scored United's winner in the final minute of the FA Cup third round tie to Aston Villa. The game ended in a 2-1 victory.

8th January 1948

The FA Cup holders defeated Bournemouth & Boscombe Athetic 6-0 in the Third round.

9th January 1946

The FA Cup returned for its first season since the war but was played on a two-legged basis. The Reds defeated Accrington Stanley 5-1 in the second leg. The first leg had ended 2-2 in Accrington four days earlier.

10th January 1987

The first FA Cup tie played by United under Alex Ferguson ended in a 1-0 third round victory over Manchester City with a goal from Norman Whiteside.

11th January 1985

Colin Gibson, Mark Hughes

and Norman Whiteside scored to give the Reds a 3-1 victory at Oxford in Division One. In 1936 United defeated Reading 3-1 in the FA Cup third round – as this was the same scoreline rivals City enjoyed in their Cup match a cartoon was produced illustrating the fact.

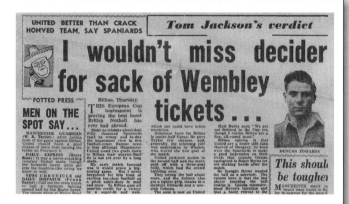

12th January 2008

Two from Tevez, one from Ferdinand and a hat-trick from Ronaldo gave United a 6-0 victory over Newcastle at Old Trafford. The game had been goalless at half time.

13th January 2007

Goals from Carrick, Park and Ronaldo gave United a 3-1 Premier League victory over Aston Villa before 76,073 at Old Trafford.

14th January 1905

Mackie and Arkesden scored as United drew 2-2 at home to Fulham in the FA Cup at Bank Street before 17,000 (right). The replay at Fulham ended goalless. The London club won the second replay 1-0 at Villa Park with 6,000 present.

15th January 1977

Lou Macari scored twice as the Reds beat Coventry City 2-0 at Old Trafford. The game hit the headlines because of an on-the-pitch scuffle between United stars Martin Buchan and

Gordon Hill. Hill told journalists: "Martin hit me when the Coventry attack got past us. They expect me to score goals and then drop back and pick up people. I am the World's worst defender. Still, there is no hard feeling between us – it all happened in the heat of the moment."

16th January 1957

Although United were

defeated 5-3 at Bilbao most journalists believed United would win the return European Cup quarter-final leg on 6th February (above). On the same date in 1904 United defeated near-neighbours Glossop 3-1 at Bank Street.

17th January 1923

A Jack Barber headed goal helped United to a 2-0 FA Cup victory over

Muhren and Coppell scored as Brian Clough's Nottingham Forest were defeated 2-0 before an Old Trafford crowd of 38,615.

23rd January 2010

Wayne Rooney scored all four goals as United beat Hull 4-0 at Old Trafford in front of 73,933. The goals came in 8th, 82nd, 86th and 90th minutes.

24th January 1970

Wilf McGuinness' United beat Joe Mercer's FA Cup holders City (left) 3-0 at Old Trafford before 63,417 in the FAC fourth round. Brian Kidd (2) and Willie Morgan (penalty) netted the goals.

25th January 1964

A Law hat-trick helped United to a FA Cup fourth round victory over Bristol Rovers. The game ended 4-1.

26th January 1952

Future England manager Alf Ramsey scored an own goal which helped give United a 2-0 Old Trafford victory over Ramsey's Spurs.

27th January 2010

The second leg of the all-Manchester League Cup semi-final ended in a 3-1 United victory at Old Trafford. Rooney's last minute goal gave the Reds a 4-3 aggregate victory in

---

Bradford City. The goal came following a corner taken by Joe Spence, however goalscorer Barber was unlucky when an injury later in the match put him out of action for a month. By the time he recovered he had to fight for his place again via the Reserves. At the end of March he dislocated his elbow and his United career was over. Altogether he made four United appearances and scored two goals.

18th January 1969

A Denis Law hat-trick and a George Best effort helped the Reds defeat Sunderland 4-1 in front of a home crowd of 45,670.

19th January 1977

Brian Greenhoff and Stuart Pearson ensured a 2-1 victory over Bristol City at Old Trafford in Division One.

20th January 1981

Owen Hargreaves was born at Calgary.

21st January 1989

West Ham were defeated 3-1 by United with goals from Gordon Strachan, Lee Martin and Brian McClair.

the first semi-final between the sides since 1969-70.

28th January 1939

Len Bradbury made his debut a successful one as he scored a header four minutes from time. This was the only goal of the Division One meeting with Chelsea at Stamford Bridge. Surprisingly, Bradbury only made one further appearance that season (a 7-1 defeat at Charlton) and war ultimately meant his League career was brought to a premature end.

29th January 2002

A hat-trick from Solskjaer gave the Reds a three goal lead at Bolton. Van Nistelrooy made it a 4-0 victory in the 84th minute.

30th January 1932

Tommy Reid netted a hat-trick as United beat Nottingham Forest 3-2 before 11,152 at Old Trafford in Division Two. Six years earlier the Reds achieved a 2-2 draw at Tottenham in the FA Cup fourth round (Hilditch leads United out above). Spence and Thomas scored United's goals. Joe Spence (left) again scored in the 2-0 replay victory on 3rd February 1926.

31st January 2010

Wayne Rooney scored the 100th League goal of his career with a 37th minute goal against Arsenal. The match ended in a 3-1 United win at the Emirates Stadium.

UNITED'S LEADING SCORERS

Our story of United's seasonal leading League goalscorers takes us on to the mid-1970s.

THE PROFILES
(PART FIVE)

41 – STUART PEARSON

Born at Cottingham, Hull on 21 June 1949, Stuart Pearson joined United in 1974 for a reported £200,000 fee from Hull City. He had originally joined the Tigers as an apprentice, and by the time he moved to Old Trafford he had made 129 League appearances for the club.

Playing in United's Second Division season of 1974-75, Pearson made his League debut, wearing the number nine shirt, in the 2-0 victory at Orient on the opening day of the campaign.

Known as a powerful goalscorer, Pearson found the net for the first time during the 4-0 defeat of Millwall in the second League match of the season. By the end of that season he had netted 17 League goals in 31 appearances and topped United's goalscoring charts as the Reds won the Second Division title under manager Tommy Docherty. More importantly he had established himself as one of the Club's more popular players.

Pearson topped United's League goalscoring charts again in his second season and was an

Stuart Pearson (centre) celebrating FA Cup success with Sammy McIlroy and Tommy Docherty.

ever-present in the FA Cup run that took the Reds to the 1976 final. Another final followed in 1977 and Pearson scored as Liverpool were defeated 2-1 at Wembley. His goal came five minutes after the break when he received a pass from Jimmy Greenhoff before shooting low under goalkeeper Ray Clemence's body. It gave United the lead, but Liverpool equalised two minutes later. Only five minutes after the opening goal, United scored the winner when Lou Macari's shot struck Jimmy Greenhoff and entered the net.

A third successive season at the top of United's League scoring charts followed for Pearson in 1976-77, and in 1977-78 he netted ten goals in thirty League games as he remained the preferred centre-forward. However, the arrival of Joe Jordan was a sign that manager Dave Sexton had started to view things differently, although injury also played its part, and the 1978-79 season opened in August with Jordan as United's preferred number nine. The following month Pearson joined West Ham for a fee of around £220,000.

At West Ham Pearson appeared in the 1980 FA Cup winning team and, after making

a goalscoring attempt himself, his shot set up Trevor Brooking for the only goal of the final. Any thoughts that his career had ground to a halt when he left Old Trafford were cast aside during this period as West Ham proved to be a popular and entertaining side. In 2011 Pearson explained his feelings to the West Ham website: "What a lot of people say is that when you leave Manchester United you go downhill, you can't match that. Well I proved that wasn't the case because I won three medals in the three years when I was at West Ham, and United didn't win anything in that same period. It was a great move."

He stayed with West Ham until the end of the 1981-82 season and then formed part of a controversial tour of South Africa as a member of Jimmy Hill's 'rebel' group of players. A spell in North America also followed before a knee injury, which had been problematic at various points in his League career, forced his retirement. He had endured three operations in 1979 alone and later admitted: "It was a bit of a mess and I was never quite the same afterwards."

Pearson embarked on another career, playing occasionally on the wing for Sale

RUFC, before returning to football as manager of Northwich Victoria in 1986. He also had a spell as a coach (and caretaker manager) at West Bromwich Albion, and as assistant manager to Frank Stapleton at Bradford City.

While at Old Trafford Pearson became an England international, first selected during Don Revie's reign. He made fifteen appearances for the national side.

Pearson's career may have been affected by injury at times, but for the fans that saw him play he will always be remembered as a centre-forward who played with vigour. While at Old Trafford he helped re-establish the side as one that was high in entertainment. His goals ensured the Reds rediscovered their trophy-winning ways after a dismal period prior to his arrival.

Leading League Scorer in:
1974-1975 - 17 goals, 31 appearances
1975-1976 – 13 goals, 39 appearances
1976-1977 – 15 goals, 39 appearances*

*Note: * Pearson & Hill had scored the same number of goals and had the same goalscoring ratio.*

42 – GORDON HILL

By the time Gordon Hill arrived at United in November 1975 he had already experienced football life at Staines Town, Slough, Southall, in the Third Division with Millwall, and on loan during the summer of 1975 at Chicago Sting in the NASL. An interesting record for a 21 year old.

Tommy Docherty brought him to Old Trafford for a fee of around £70,000, plus £10,000 due when Hill made his first international appearance, during the Reds first season back in the top flight. The winger made his debut on 15 November 1975 in the 2-0 victory over Aston Villa, with his first goal coming in his fifth League game at Sheffield United (4-1 United win).

By the end of his first season he had scored seven League goals in 26 appearances. He had also netted significant goals in the FA Cup run, most notably both of United's efforts in the 2-0 semi-final victory over Derby County at Hillsborough.

The following season, 1976-77, he made six international appearances for England and was a member of the United side that

defeated Liverpool in the FA Cup final. He also shared with Stuart Pearson the honour of being United's leading League scorer. This in itself was a tremendous achievement for a winger, but he bettered it in 1977-78 when he netted 17 goals in 36 League appearances to top the chart in his own right. However the Reds were now managed by Dave Sexton and his approach, demeanour and style of play was somewhat different to Tommy Docherty's. Hill's qualities were not viewed as essential, and in April 1978 he joined Derby County, then managed by his former boss Docherty, for a fee of £275,000.

After two seasons at Derby he joined Queen's Park Rangers – by this time managed by Docherty – but he only made 14 appearances there. Hill then tried his luck in the USA and Canada playing for a variety of clubs including Montreal Manic, Chicago Sting (again) and New York Arrows during the early 1980s.

A return to Europe came in 1985-86 when he joined Dutch side FC Twente, making 19 appearances, and then HJK Helsinki. He later had spells at Stafford Rangers, and Northwich Victoria, playing for Stuart Pearson before moving into management with Nova Scotia Clippers, Chester City and Hyde United.

In more recent times he became owner and head coach for a youth soccer club in Texas.

Leading League Scorer in:
1976-1977 – 15 goals, 39 appearances*
1977-1978 - 17 goals, 36 appearances

*Note: * Pearson & Hill had scored the same number of goals and had the same goalscoring ratio.*

43 - JIMMY GREENHOFF

By the time he arrived at Old Trafford in November 1976 for a fee of around £100,000, Jimmy Greenhoff had already found major success with both Leeds United and Stoke City. At Leeds he won the League Cup and the Inter-Cities Fairs Cup,

while his time at Stoke brought League Cup success in 1972.

He made his United League debut on 20 November 1976 in a 1-1 draw at Leicester City, alongside his brother Brian who had been a member of Docherty's side since 1973. His first United League goal came in the 4-0 victory over Everton on 27 December, and by the end of the season he had appeared in 27 League games and scored eight goals. However, his most significant goal that season came in the FA Cup final when a Macari shot deflected off his body for the goal that brought the Cup to United.

Known to United fans for his match-turning exploits, Greenhoff only managed 23 League appearances in 1977-78 due to injury. The following season he topped United's League scoring charts and helped the Reds progress to the FA Cup final. During that run his goals had proved vital – three games including the semi-final ended 1-0 with Greenhoff the scorer while he also scored another vital goal in a 1-1 draw.

Despite his positive contribution there had been further injury concerns causing him to miss several games towards the end of the 1978-79 season. In fact, during his United career two specialists had even suggested his playing days were over but his determination and enthusiasm for the Red cause ensured he returned to action.

He re-appeared in United's League team as substitute at home to Everton in March 1980, and then made the starting line-up on 5 April for the crucial meeting with Liverpool at Old Trafford. By this time Greenhoff was nearing his 34th birthday, but the player proved he still had something to offer as he scored the winner against United's title rivals.

Greenhoff missed the next three League games but did start the final three matches of the season as United looked to win the title. Two victories and a defeat followed, leaving the Reds two points short of champions Liverpool. For Greenhoff to have been selected for those final, crucial games, proves that his contribution and the quality of his play was still viewed highly.

The player started the 1980-81 season as Sexton's preferred number eight, but after a total of nine League appearances that year, he was transferred to Crewe in December. By that time Garry Birtles had arrived and Greenhoff was always likely to be a squad member rather than first team regular.

Spells at Toronto Blizzard, Port Vale – where he made 48 appearances – and Rochdale followed. At Spotland Greenhoff was Dale's player-manager during 1983-84. He also had time as a coach at Port Vale, before working in the insurance industry.

All in all, Greenhoff's time at Old Trafford was wonderful. His record at each of his clubs, but most significantly Leeds, Stoke and United was phenomenal and the fact that he continued to deliver for United into his mid-thirties despite injury concerns proves his qualities and commitment.

Leading League Scorer in:

1978-1979 - 11 goals, 33 appearances*

*Note: * Greenhoff's goalscoring ratio in 1978-79 was better than Steve Coppell who scored 11 League goals in 42 games that season.*

44 – JOE JORDAN

Scottish international Joe Jordan arrived at Old Trafford in January 1978 for a fee of £350,000 and immediately proved popular with United fans.

Prior to his arrival Jordan had been a key member of the Leeds United side that challenged regularly for the game's top honours. Often referred to as 'always the bridesmaids never the bride' Leeds always appeared more than capable of winning any game – or trophy – but ultimately they never quite managed to find the high level of success their players and team ethic suggested.

While at Elland Road Jordan appeared in the 1973 ECWC final, the 1975 European Cup final, and was part of the side that were First Division runners-up in 1971 and 1972. With a little bit of luck along the way those near misses could easily have brought trophy success. Nevertheless, Jordan did win a major trophy at Leeds - the 1973-74 League title.

His time at Leeds meant that prior to arriving at Old Trafford, United fans viewed him negatively as one of Don Revie's team of physical, spoiling players. As he was serving a suspension for activities while at Leeds many Reds wondered whether he was really a player that could fit into their side. However, manager Dave Sexton felt his United needed a different style and approach to that of his predecessor Tommy

Jordan's goal puts paid to Boro hopes

Manchester United .... 3 Middlesbrough 2

JOE JORDAN'S third goal in successive Old Trafford games enabled Manchester United, a competent rather than convincing side, to move into fifth place in the First Division after lowly Middlesbrough had twice fought back to equalise, writes **Denis Lowe.**

Two first-half headers by Lou Macari were cancelled out by David Mills and £70,000 newcomer Mick Burns, but Middlesbrough's chance of an unexpected point was squandered 14 minutes from time.

The tenacious Jordan had time and room to spare when Armstrong completely missed a cross from Grimes, United's substitute, and Stewart, ironically, was beaten by a mishit shot.

Burns benefits

"I thought Boro were bound to clear the ball, and I was a bit surprised when it reached me," said Jordan. "Still, we have managed 12 points by grafting for each one, and we will do much better when we really click."

United's huge following will share those hopes ,but Saturday's 45,402 crowd was almost 10,000 below the League average, and many supporters were unhappy when the defensive weaknesses exposed in the League Cup defeat by Watford reappeared early in the second half.

Roche then produced smart saves from McAndrew and Mahoney. McQueen chipped in with a timely tackle when Armstrong was clear, but the centre half, groggy after a collision with his goalkeeper, played Burns onside in the 66th minute, allowing the former Cardiff forward to score his sixth goal in seven appearances on this ground.

Earlier, Macari, a lively midfield force on his return after flu, had twice put United in front. The Scot added the finishing touch to McIlroy's corner in the third minute, but appeared to use a hand as well as his head when shrewd work by Albison and Greenhoff created a 31st minute opening.

Although Boro are already on many people's relegation short list Boam is still a tower of strength at the back, and the arrival of Burns will enhance the attack. There was nothing better in the match than the 26th minute scoring move, when Burns linked with Craggs to send Mills through.

Manchester United: Roche; Albiston Houston, McCreery, McQueen, Buchan Coppell, J. Greenhoff (sub Grimes 66) Jordan, Macari, McIlroy.

Middlesbrough: Stewart; Craggs Bailey, Mahoney, Boam, Ramage, Mills McAndrew, Ashcroft, Burns, Armstrong

Referee: K. McNally (Mold).

Docherty, and the boss made Jordan his first signing. The fee was around £350,000 and was claimed to be a record transfer between two English clubs, coming a few months after Hamburg had paid around £500,000 for Kevin Keegan.

Once Jordan made his debut United fans soon realised that the high level of commitment and determination he had shown at Leeds was likely to prove very successful for United.

By the end of his first season at Old Trafford, Jordan had made 14 League appearances and scored three goals, after making his debut in a drawn FA Cup tie at home to West Bromwich Albion on 28 January 1978. The following season he appeared in the side that reached the FA Cup final.

In 1979-80 Jordan topped the goalscoring charts with 13 goals from 32 League games as the Reds finished as runners-up to Liverpool. Interestingly, the Scottish international netted two goals in five separate League matches that season. As well as the goals, however, there was some controversy in 1980, particularly after a clash with Tottenham's Milja Aleksic resulted in the goalkeeper dislocating his jaw. Nevertheless, United fans loved Jordan's endeavour and the player was clearly a hero by this time. A point proved by his success in the annual supporters' player of the year vote when Jordan won the award in both 1980 and 1981.

The 1980-81 season was probably Jordan's best at Old Trafford, certainly as far as goalscoring statistics are concerned. He topped the scoring charts once again with a better ratio than the previous season. Despite his goalscoring and all-round contribution, the 1980-81 season was however Jordan's last at Old Trafford.

He joined AC Milan in July 1981 for a fee of around £175,000 but fans were far from happy at his departure. There was a genuine feeling that had he stayed the Reds may actually have won the title in 1981-82 under Ron Atkinson. The new manager guided United to third place, some nine points behind champions Liverpool, but there was a feeling that Jordan may just have contributed enough drive and bite to have turned some of the twelve drawn games into victories. As this was the first season of three points for a win, Jordan could have made all the difference.

Jordan spent two seasons at Milan. The first ended in relegation, but the second saw the player help bring the Serie B title to the San Siro with a total of 14 goals.

A move to Hellas Verona followed, and then Jordan returned to England to play for Southampton in 1984. In 1987 he moved to Bristol City where he later moved into management and guided the club to the semi-final of the League Cup and promotion in 1989-90.

As a manager he had spells at Hearts, Stoke, Bristol City again, and then caretaker-manager at Portsmouth. In November 2008 he joined Harry Redknapp's coaching team at Tottenham and helped them develop into regular contenders for European qualification.

Looking back on his entire career, it is clear Jordan was a very important player to each of his clubs, and he was also one of Scotland's all-time greats. Remembered for his bravery, commitment, never-say-die attitude, Jordan will always be a true hero to those that saw him in full flow.

Leading League Scorer in:
1979-1980 - 13 goals, 32 appearances
1980-1981 - 15 goals, 33 appearances

45 – FRANK STAPLETON

Ron Atkinson faced an immediate problem on his arrival at Old Trafford – the imminent departure of Joe Jordan to Milan. He moved quickly to sign Frank Stapleton from Arsenal in August 1981, although the proposed move soon hit problems as United's valuation of £650,000 was well below Arsenal's £2m.

These were the days of spiralling transfer fees and player values seemed to vary

enormously. As the 1970s had reached their end each selling club tended to ask for high fees in the hope that their rival club would stump up the cash, but by the summer of 1981 a more sensible approach was starting to be seen.

Ultimately, Stapleton's transfer was one of the first to be fixed by the League's new independent tribunal, which fixed the fee at £900,000 (£1.1m with levies and VAT). After the transfer Ron Atkinson described his new signing as the 'best centre-forward in Europe' – it's a good job he didn't say that before the fee was fixed!

Stapleton's heading prowess was legendary, and his ability to create as well as score goals had earned him a reputation as one of the best centre forwards in the League. He was United's leading scorer in his first three seasons at Old Trafford, thereafter turning provider rather than scorer.

He scored for United in the 1983 FA Cup Final, becoming the first player to score for two different clubs in a Wembley FA Cup Final - his first had come against United in the memorable 1979 final for Arsenal. It is worth noting that Arsenal's official statistics include that goal as one of 108 goals he scored in 300 appearances for the Gunners.

Stapleton had originally joined Arsenal as an apprentice in June 1972, after unsuccessful trials at both United and Wolverhampton Wanderers. He turned professional in September 1973, winning a regular first team place during the 1975-76 season.

He left United at the end of 1986-87, a season in which he was plagued by injury, to join Ajax. The move to the Netherlands was not successful and after just three games he was back in England, on loan at Derby County. After another loan spell, at Le Havre in October 1988, he joined Blackburn Rovers. He eventually retired from playing in 1994-95 after spells with Aldershot, Huddersfield, Bradford City (as player-manager), and Brighton.

Following his retirement, Stapleton coached New England Revolution in the MSL in 1996, and was briefly a specialist coach under Sam

Allardyce at Bolton Wanderers during the 2003-04 season.

All together he made 267 (plus 21 as substitute) appearances for United and scored 78 goals. He was, of course, also a key member of the Republic of Ireland side. He captained the Irish national team for the 1986 World Cup qualifiers and the 1988 Euro finals. By the time his international career came to an end he was Ireland's all-time leading goalscorer – a record that was overtaken by Niall Quinn a decade later.

Leading League Scorer in:
1981-1982 - 13 goals, 41 appearances
1982-1983 - 14 goals, 41 appearances
1983-1984 - 13 goals, 42 appearances

46 – MARK HUGHES

Mark Hughes was born near Wrexham in a town, Ruabon, with a great footballing pedigree. Many early Welsh internationals had come from the area while the local side Druids FC were one of the nineteenth century and early twentieth century's most significant Welsh sides. They were the first Welsh side to compete in the FA Cup and they won the Welsh Cup an astounding eight times, the last success coming in 1904.

Whether the town's footballing pedigree played its part in Hughes' ultimate development in the game is unlikely, but it is clear the player became an extremely successful and popular member of his national side over the years. He won 72 caps for Wales, as well as representing his country at schoolboy, youth and under 21 levels.

In March 1978, aged fourteen, Hughes joined United as an associate schoolboy. He signed his first professional contract in November 1980, although he had to wait almost three years for his senior debut, which came against Port Vale in a League Cup tie on October 26th 1983.

Hughes scored on his first full appearance, against Oxford United also in a League Cup tie, and by the end of 1983-84 he was established as Frank Stapleton's attacking partner. He was the club's leading scorer in both 1984-85 and 1985-86.

Bizarrely early in 1986, with the club challenging for the league title, United accepted a £2m bid from Barcelona for Hughes. Fortunately, the actual transfer was delayed until the end of the season but the sale of Hughes was not a good one. Even with the benefit of hindsight, it is hard to understand the Club's decision. Hughes, by his own admission, had been disciplined by the Reds but this was far from unique at Old Trafford during this period. It remains clear that there was no one in the reserves quite ready to replace him.

Hughes endured a torrid first season in Spain, managing five goals in 37 appearances, before his La Liga registration was cancelled to allow Steve Archibald to play. The departure of manager Terry Venables in September 1987 removed his last ally at the Nou Camp, and hastened the end of his career there. A television documentary made during this period focused on the differences between Hughes' time and that of Gary Lineker. Lineker seemed settled and at home in Barcelona, while the TV focus seemed to suggest Hughes was uncomfortable.

Hughes needed to move away from Barcelona and there seemed to be a possibility he could return to Old Trafford. It was suggested at the time in the media, however, that the former United star would have faced a huge income tax bill had he accepted a loan move back to United, now managed by Alex Ferguson. Instead he moved to Bayern Munich. He rediscovered his form in Germany, netting six goals in 18 Bundesliga appearances.

While in Germany, he gained a great deal of experience of the game that would later find its way into his managerial approach. Years later, while managing Manchester City, Hughes took his players on tours of Germany, often focusing on approaches he had gained as a player in the country.

In May 1988 Hughes returned to Old Trafford for a reported club record £1.8m fee.

During his second spell at United, Hughes was not as prolific a goal scorer as he had been first time round, but he was hugely influential. In fact he was probably more influential during his second spell. His goals were often in key games and usually spectacular.

Hughes scored twice in the 1990 FA Cup Final against Crystal Palace; both goals in United's 2-1 victory over Barcelona in the 1991 European Cup Winners' Cup Final; a last minute equaliser in the FA Cup semi-final against Oldham in 1993-94; and another in the Final against Chelsea.

The arrival of Andy Cole in January 1995 signalled the end of Hughes' time at Old Trafford. Twice PFA Player of the Year (in 1988-89 and 1990-91), the Welshman had won two Premier League titles, three FA Cups, the League Cup and European Cup Winners' Cup medals with United. In June 1995 Chelsea paid £1.5m for his services.

Hughes continued playing until July 2002 adding another FA Cup winner's medal (with Chelsea in 1997), two League Cup winner's medals (with Chelsea in 1998 and Blackburn in 2002), and a European Cup Winners' Cup medal in 1998 (with Chelsea). It is worth noting that those Chelsea successes came at a time when the London club were not the wealthy, money-no-object, side they later became, and so Hughes' achievements at Stamford Bridge should be viewed as truly significant. All successes should be viewed highly of course, but the point is that the Chelsea side was not packed with the world's greatest and most expensive players. It was a team in which Hughes had to work hard for to help bring success.

In 1999, while playing for Southampton, Hughes, was appointed the temporary Welsh team manager, alongside Neville Southall. He was later appointed on a permanent basis, and remained the Welsh boss until September 2004 when he took over as manager at Blackburn Rovers.

Hughes went on to manage Manchester City and Fulham, but he will always be remembered for his contribution to United's successes. He appeared in 453 (plus 14) United games and scored 163 goals, topping the Reds' goalscoring charts for five seasons, including the 1992-93 Premier League title winning season.

Leading League Scorer in:
1984-1985 - 16 goals, 38 appearances
1985-1986 – 17 goals, 40 appearances
1988-1989 – 14 goals, 38 appearances
1989-1990 – 13 goals, 37 appearances
1992-1993 – 15 goals, 41 appearances

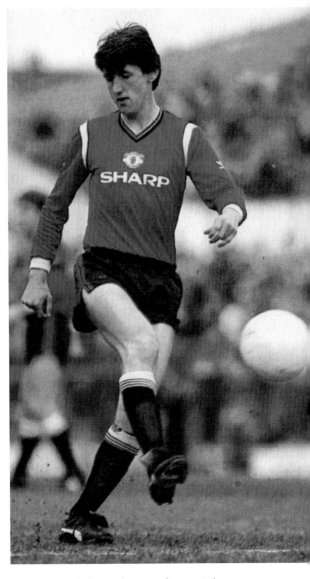

47 – PETER DAVENPORT

In March 1986 United's title challenge was faltering and the Club had agreed to sell the leading scorer, Mark Hughes, to Barcelona in the summer. Ron Atkinson identified Peter Davenport as the solution to both problems, and paid £570,000 to bring the striker to Old Trafford from Nottingham Forest.

He made his debut in the 1-0 defeat at Queens Park Rangers on 15 March 1986, replacing Hughes in United's attack. The defeat left United outside the top two for the first time that season. They eventually finished fourth with Davenport contributing just one goal, from the penalty spot, in eleven appearances and many questions were being asked by fans. Comparisons were being made with another former Forest star Garry Birtles.

Davenport joined Nottingham Forest in January 1982, having been spotted by Peter Taylor playing for Cammell Laird in the West Cheshire League. Quick and with excellent ball control, he played in the final five games of that season, but his progress was interrupted by injury. In fact, it wasn't until spring 1983 that the player established himself as a first team regular.

He was Forest's leading goal scorer in 1983-84 and 1984-85 and also at the time of his move to United.

Although Davenport continued his goal scoring form in his first full season at Old Trafford, netting 16 and leading the list, he never really established himself in the eyes of fans. He made 34 League appearances in 1987-88 as United mounted another title challenge, but 13 of those were as substitute and his return of just five goals reflected his increasing use as a wide man rather than central attacker. Ironically, the return of Mark Hughes that summer signalled the end of Davenport's career at United, and he was sold to Middlesbrough in November 1988 for £750,000.

His time at Ayresome Park was far from happy as the club were relegated in his first season and Davenport managed just four goals - although his first helped his new side to a 1-0 win over United on New Year's Day.

Davenport joined Sunderland in July 1990, suffered relegation again, but appeared for the Black Cats in the 1992 FA Cup Final against Liverpool. This was to be his only major cup final appearance. He later had spells with Airdrieonians, St. Johnstone, Stockport County, Southport and Macclesfield before finally hanging up his boots in 2000.

He replaced Sammy McIlroy as player-manager of Macclesfield in January 2000, having worked as a coach, and later assistant manager, at the club. He was dismissed in December 2000 and has subsequently held management positions with Bangor City, Colwyn Bay and Southport.

Davenport went on to work as a cover supervisor at a school in the Wirral, while studying for his teaching qualification.

Leading League Scorer in:
1986-1987 - 14 goals, 39 appearances

GOLDEN GOALS

Ryan Giggs

1992

v Tottenham

The idea of this 'GOLDEN GOALS' feature is to remember a significant or spectacular goal. The Big Book Of United's hope is that modern day supporters learn more about some of these goals.

Many goals over the years are described as the greatest ever by a United player. Sometimes these are remembered for ever, but it is also true that unless they happen to occur in a major trophy winning game goals can lose their significance as time moves on. This is especially true for goals during highly

successful seasons when there are plenty of key moments to consider. Focus often shifts to actual trophy success and so goals scored during the earlier stages of the season are often overlooked.

The goal featured here was scored by Ryan Giggs in a game with Spurs during the Premier League's first season. It came at a time when the Reds were hungry for success in the League – aren't they always!

MATCH STATS

Date: 19 September 1992

Score: Tottenham Hotspur 1 United 1

Scorers: Ryan Giggs (45th minute) & Gordon Durie (52nd minute)

Attendance: 33,296

Referee: R. Groves

United Team: Schmeichel, Irwin, Blackmore, Bruce, Ferguson, Pallister, Kanchelskis (Wallace 74th minute), Ince, McClair, Hughes & Giggs

PRE-MATCH

This first Premier League season had not started too well. Successive defeats at Sheffield United (2-1) and at home to Everton had brought some frustration to fans. However, the season soon turned around. A 1-1 draw at home to Ipswich on 22nd August was followed by five successive League victories. The most recent being a satisfying 2-0 away win at Everton to lift United up to third (United were 20th after the Ipswich draw).

Three days before the Spurs game United did however suffer a goalless draw at home to Torpedo Moscow before an official crowd of 19,998 at Old Trafford in the UEFA Cup. That day a young player by the name of Gary Neville made his debut.

THE GAME

A tight first half at fifteenth placed Tottenham, managed by Doug Livermore, seemed destined to end goalless. However, 18 year old Ryan Giggs soon proved what an immense talent he was with a brilliant solo goal in the 45th minute.

The young Welshman picked up the ball some 20 yards out and immediately knocked it past Dean Austin with ease. He then nutmegged Jason Cundy before picking the ball up on the other side of him.

Giggs then charged forward, rounded goalkeeper Ian Walker before firing home with his left foot at a tight angle as the Spurs' defence tried desperately to catch the youngster. The goal ensured a 1-0 lead at the interval.

Although Spurs equalised seven minutes into the second half, Giggs' goal ensured the Reds extended their unbeaten run to six League games as they looked to challenge for the title.

POST MATCH

United fans claimed Giggs' effort as the League's goal of the season and it was certainly a wonderful goal. It also proved to be highly significant. Had United lost that match then ultimately the defeat could have impacted the Reds' progression under Alex Ferguson.

The Reds unbeaten run lasted for ten consecutive League games and, although they were not quite the force they became later in the season, those results were important.

United went on to win the inaugural Premier League title – the Reds' first League success since 1967 – but more importantly this season helped develop the Club's modern era dominance and Giggs was there at the start.

BILLY MEREDITH

– THE FIRST UNITED LEGEND

Billy Meredith remains one of the most famous early stars of football. Stories of the great man's abilities have been passed down through the generations and, even today, his name often appears in the footballing and Manchester press.

In 2001 a group of Manchester football supporters contacted Billy's daughter Winifred to ask her permission to erect a new headstone at his grave. In April 1958 Billy had been buried in an unmarked grave. Although some authors have claimed that financial hardship was the reason for the grave being anonymous, the truth is somewhat different. According to his daughter Winifred, when she was in her mid-nineties, the decision to have an unmarked grave was her father's choice. He realised how popular football was and didn't want a fuss or for the grave to be some overblown shrine – but forty years after his death modern day supporters felt he deserved something more fitting.

Winifred, who had lovingly tended his grave throughout the intervening years, was delighted with the gesture. Thanks to the actions of various supporters, United, City, the PFA, and the Welsh FA each agreed to split the cost and a new headstone was erected.

The reason Billy's name has remained so important is simply because he was the first true Manchester hero. Not only that, but he was football's first true superstar. He was an immensely popular figure, appearing in all the sporting press of the day.

He was also, however, a highly controversial player. For years he campaigned for the rights of footballers and was always one of the first to air his views on the issues of the day. Although he was a very patriotic Welshman, as far as United fans were concerned it was Billy's role with the Reds that mattered most. This does him a bit of a disservice because his international career saw many highs and helped establish his name. It is also fair to say his time at Manchester City first brought Meredith to the attention of the English footballing public.

Meredith was Manchester's first true footballing star and, like the people who supported him, he acted like a typical Mancunian, even though he was not born in the region. His attitude to life and his commitment to the causes he believed in was total.

EARLY LIFE

Billy grew up during the 1870s and 1880s in Chirk, at that time part of an important coal mining area of Denbighshire, Wales. In fact at the age of twelve Billy started to work in the mines - mainly his activities revolved around moving the tubs of coal as they came through the tunnels. Sometimes he would guide ponies through the mines, other times he would push the tubs himself. Life was tough, but football was his chief release.

During his later career Billy looked back and talked of his family's interest: "All my brothers were players. Elias, the eldest, was fond of football, but he didn't play as much as Jim, a right full back, and Sam, a left full back, who went on to play for Stoke."

Sam actually left Chirk for football some years before Billy, but it was the younger man who would eventually become one of the most famous names in Britain. Billy, naturally, played for the local Chirk side, and even appeared for them in two Welsh FA Cup finals. He also appeared in games against English sides, usually the reserve sides of League clubs, and one of these games was against one of Manchester's prominent non-League sides Gorton Villa (an early rival to City's predecessors Ardwick). Chirk defeated Gorton Villa 10-1 in October 1892 with Billy in outstanding form.

The following season Billy played some games for Chirk, as well as League games for Northwich Victoria, and then officials from several more significant League clubs came with offers.

THE MOVE TO MANCHESTER

Billy's transfer to Manchester became one of early football's best stories, and gave some indication of the lengths clubs would go to sign players. The story as told by witnesses during the early years of the Twentieth Century is that two officials from Manchester City, believed to be two of the club's founding fathers Lawrence Furniss and John Chapman, arrived in Wales looking for the player that Furniss had spotted while refereeing a Northwich match. The two men were chased by locals and thrown into a duck pond. They then sought disguises and had to buy drinks for all of Billy's co-workers at the mine before they were allowed to speak to him.

They also had to face Billy's mother who, according to her son, said: "It is all very well for you gentlemen to leave your big cities and come to our villages to steal our boys away. You offer good money I know, and I suppose it pays you to do so, or you would not come. But a mother thinks of other things besides money. Our boys are happy

and healthy, satisfied with their work and their innocent amusements. You gentlemen come and put all kinds of ideas into their heads. Tell them they can get more money for play than they can for hard but honest work... if Billy takes my advice he will stick to his work and play football for his own amusement when his work is finished."

Whether Billy listened to his mother is not clear, however the young player did sign for Manchester City in October 1894. He also continued to commute to Chirk and work in the mine for at least a year, possibly four, after his transfer. Perhaps he needed to prove to his mother that he wasn't off to the big city simply to enjoy himself.

Within two weeks of signing he made his debut at Newcastle and then on 3 November he played his first home game at City's Hyde Road ground. The match was the very first League meeting between City and United's predecessors Newton Heath. The Heathens won the Second Division game 5-2 but Billy had scored both City's goals causing the Umpire newspaper to state: "The play of the young Welsh player, Meredith, was far superior to that of any other."

Billy had already started to impress and, once settled, Meredith was to help establish City as a major side.

THE FIRST SUPERSTAR

As Billy's career in England developed, so did City's. The two developed at a similar rate and it's fair to say their histories were intertwined. The ambition of the Blues was to achieve First Division football and a parity with the great clubs of the period such as Everton and Aston Villa. In 1896 City finished second in Division Two but promotion was not guaranteed for any side and the Blues failed in the end of season

Test Matches (similar to modern day play offs).

In 1899 however the Blues won the Second Division title with Billy scoring 29 goals in 33 games – he only missed one match. He was City's most important player by far. He had also been a Welsh international since 1895 and the national media were already aware of his immense talent. So much so that when he married his childhood sweetheart in 1901 one national sporting newspaper covered the story – this was unheard of at the time. He was the David Beckham of his day. The article started with: "William Meredith, City's crack outside-right and probably the cleverest man in his position throughout the United Kingdom, was married to Miss Negus in the early part of last week."

Billy's fame was to grow during the early years of the century and by the time of City's Cup run of 1904 he was football's most famous star. Rightly acclaimed as the greatest winger of the period by the Umpire newspaper in 1903, Billy's stature in the game grew after every match. By this time he was City's captain and after a cup tie with Sunderland in 1904 the Athletic News reported: "The City captain was the raider in chief and undoubtedly the most dazzling forward on the field. Assiduously supplied, the famous Welshman hardly ever failed to respond to the calls made upon him. His command of the ball as he threaded his way through the maze of his adversaries commanded admiration. Against a team of such class Meredith has not often given a more dazzling display. I have no wish to be guilty of exaggeration, but Meredith was the King of the Realm."

SUCCESS AND SCANDAL

Under Billy's direction the Blues won the FA Cup final for the first time and finished second in the League in 1904. It was a fantastic achievement. Billy became Manchester's leading personality and, again, his national fame continued to grow. Everyone loved him – it didn't matter whether you were Blue or Red. Every newspaper started to feature the player, while poems were sent in stressing his skills but also his importance to Manchester. There were even songs written about him. According to Billy's biographer John Harding, the following was a very popular song sung by the fans on the Hyde Road terraces during 1904:

> *Oh I wish I was you Billy Meredith*
> *I wish I was you, I envy you, indeed I do!*
> *It ain't that you're tricky with your feet,*
> *But it's those centres that you send in*
> *Which Turnbull then heads in,*
> *Oh I wish I was you,*
> *Indeed I do,*
> *Indeed I do....*

The Cup success saw Billy's role in Society develop further. Railway Companies and products such as OXO started to use him in their publicity, while local politicians encouraged him to support their campaigns. Everything Billy did was reported on. The Umpire newspaper summed it up: "Since the City have become famous it has been considered the proper thing to give every detail of their doings and I'm quite expecting to read that, while shaving, Meredith accidentally came across a little wart and the great international actually lost ten drops of his precious blood."

This higher profile also caused many footballing establishment figures to question what was going on behind the scenes at Hyde Road. The transfer of City from a lower than average Second Division side into FA Cup winners within ten seasons had caused some to question the general organisation of the club.

The southern-based FA were desperate to find an excuse for investigating the club and the Blues handed them that excuse on a plate. As with the Cup success in 1904, Billy was at the centre of the story.

Second placed City needed to beat Aston Villa and hope that Newcastle dropped a point at Middlesbrough on the last day of the 1904-5 season to bring the Blues their first League title. It was not going to be easy but, according to Billy, the City officials offered their players a £100 bonus if they won at Villa Park. The bonus was enormous at the time and Billy and his team were determined to succeed. However, the game became extremely confrontational with City's (and future United hero) Sandy Turnbull and Villa's Alec Leake the key protagonists. Due to its ultimate, positive impact on United, much of the story is covered within Turnbull's profile earlier in this book, but the key aspect, as far as Meredith's story is concerned is that the game brought an excuse for the FA to start investigations into Manchester's Blues.

At the start of August the FA announced their findings. The news caused an outcry and northern football was absolutely amazed when the announcement was made that Billy – and nobody else - was to be banned from football until April 1906. According to the FA, the City captain had attempted to bribe Alec Leake to throw the match.

Billy was devastated: "I am entirely innocent. Such an allegation as that of bribery is preposterous! I could never risk my reputation and future by such an action and I repeat that I never made such an offer. It is totally unjustified and grossly unfair. This sort of thing will demoralise Association Football. Manchester has not many friends among the Association officials. The FA was too influenced by Aston Villa. Manchester City is becoming too popular to suit some other clubs."

The controversy raged on for some time and the FA started investigating City's finances as well as player conduct. In May 1906 they announced that the Blues had been making illegal payments to their players for years. The maximum wage stood at £4 per week and the FA identified that Billy had been paid £6, and that others had been paid similar amounts. As a result the FA imposed the most severe penalty ever on to one of football's largest clubs. They decreed that 17 players were to be suspended until January 1907, and that the manager Tom Maley and former Chairman W. Forrest were to be banned sine die. They also suspended two directors. Inevitably there were also fines for the players – Billy was fined £100 – and for the club.

Ian Pringle, Billy's grandson, felt the heavy-handed approach by the FA changed Billy's thinking: "I don't think City were any worse than the other clubs at the time. I think Granddad knew that and that's why the injustice felt so strong. He was convinced that he and the Club had been singled out. It was clearly wrong."

AFTER THE SCANDAL

No club in the history of football had ever suffered to such an extent and all Mancunians were united in their disgust at the club's treatment. Worse was to follow for City as the FA made it clear that the banned players had to be transferred out of the club.

At that time City's misdemeanours were really no worse than any other major side and most football clubs knew this. The Football League, the media, and other northern clubs defended the Blues and accused the Southern-based FA of prejudice against the professional sides of the north (and the influence of the Football League).

Dismayed at the club's treatment, City's officials determined that those players banned from playing for City should sign for clubs the Blues identified with. City's officials wanted Billy and some of the others to sign for United. At that time the Reds had yet to find major success. Billy, as the most important member of the side, should have been worth a small fortune but his transfer to the Reds brought the Blues no

fee. Ironically, United paid Billy an amount of £600 which was, in effect, equivalent to his transfer fee.

Much has been written on Billy's transfer and how it came about, but the most accurate version is detailed in "Manchester A Football History" – it explains the scandal and the impact on both Manchester clubs.

All Mancunians were delighted that football's first true star was to remain in Manchester, although it's fair to say the rivalry between the Reds and Blues was not intense at this point in history. For Billy the move was a good one, especially as several other 1904 Cup winners joined the Reds at the same time.

FURTHER GLORY

Billy made his United debut against Aston Villa at Bank Street on New Year's Day 1907 – the day his ban was lifted. It is ironic that his grand return was against the side that had caused him so much pain almost two years earlier.

The attendance was approximately 40,000 – four times the size of the previous United home game and only the Reds' seventh attendance over 30,000 since they joined the League in 1892.

The Manchester Guardian reported: "When [Charlie] Roberts led out the United team with its famous recruits onto the field there was a scene of wonderful enthusiasm. A greater roar of cheering has probably never sounded over a football ground nor probably has a football ground ever been seen in a more remarkable animation. The vast motionless expanse of faces which stretched upward from the snow-heaped sides... became suddenly moved and transformed almost as a sea under a hurricane, and one saw nothing but an amazing tumult of waving arms and handkerchiefs."

United won the game 1-0 with both Billy and another of the former City players, Sandy Turnbull, making their mark. Turnbull headed the only goal from a Meredith centre. Billy later commented: "The crowd simply went mad, and during the next few days I got so many letters and wires congratulating me upon my return that I had to reply to them through the sporting press."

Prior to Billy's debut the Reds had earned 18 points from 21 games and were, it is fair to say, struggling. Their form suggested relegation, but once Billy, Sandy Turnbull, Herbert Burgess and Jimmy Bannister arrived from City United were transformed, earning 24 points from 19 games. The Reds ended the season 8th a mere nine points behind League champions Newcastle – not bad for a side that had looked certain to be struggling to avoid relegation at Christmas (had their pre-Meredith points ratio been maintained they would have ended the season fourth bottom of the division – a place, ironically, occupied by Billy's former club City).

United were able to pick up on the momentum City had enjoyed with those players in 1905, and the 1907-08 season became one of the most significant in Manchester's football history. The Reds won the Division One title with Billy playing more games than any other United player. Jimmy Bannister, Herbert Burgess and Sandy Turnbull were also consistent performers that season.

The Bolton Football Field recognised the significance of Billy and those players: "There can be no doubt that Meredith's advent in Manchester United's forward line has worked wonders in the general effectiveness thereof for, prior to his coming, the Clayton club were woefully weak in attack, being frequently at sixes and sevens with the result that the management were often at their wits' end as to which line of attack to adopt and in fact no especial line was adhered to for very long, so disappointing were the results. Now, however, all this has altered and despite the occasional weakness in United's inside trio, the line as a whole, of late, has given extreme satisfaction. A good deal of this

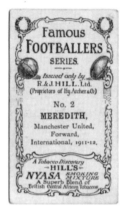

must be attributed to the prescience and power of the remarkably well-preserved Meredith who shows no decrease in ability. In his particular way, getting the maximum of results from the minimum of effort, Meredith undeniably is the greatest forward of all time and he looks like going on for a long time yet in first-class football."

Success in the League was thoroughly deserved and Billy was the star as United finished the campaign on 52 points – nine more than nearest rivals Aston Villa and a recovering Manchester City. Two days after the final League game Billy scored in the first ever Charity Shield match. That game ended in a 1-1 draw with QPR before a replay ended 4-0 to United at Stamford Bridge.

The following season Billy helped United to their first FA Cup trophy success. The Reds beat Bristol City 1-0 with a goal from Sandy Turnbull. Pre-match Billy received much of the focus as he had in 1904. This season though some suggested his fitness may be an issue. Before the FA Cup semi-final victory over Newcastle United he countered: "Personally I am satisfied that I am playing as well as I did last season when I was in better form than I have ever been in my life. The thing that pleases me is that I still have my speed."

It seemed that by this time in his career Billy was used to challenging the criticism of others. After the final, which most neutrals claimed was a poor one, Billy made it clear that he felt the game had been a good one:

"You can take it from me that the Final was not a poor game. It was a good game for dashing, keen, thrilling football, great goalkeeping and narrow escapes at either end."

Further success was to follow as the Reds won the League title for a second time in 1910-11. Again Aston Villa were runners up but this time only a point separated the two sides. Billy was still a key player – he appeared in 35 of the 38 games and only George Stacey had played in more games. Billy had also scored five goals.

Billy, by the start of the following season, was 38 but still an important Red. Unfortunately, United's trophy winning days were over – it would be another 37 years before the Reds were to find national success. The premature end to United's successful period was probably caused by the departure of manager Ernest Mangnall early in the 1912-13 season. A departure that ultimately led to Billy also leaving a few years later.

Despite Mangnall leaving, Billy remained with United until the outbreak of World War One. Throughout that time the Welshman remained an inspirational figure and his fame continued to develop. His fight for

MEREDITH GETS DOWN JUST TOO LATE.

player rights was well known – around the time of his move from City to United he played a leading part in the formation of the Players' Union, the forerunner of the PFA. In fact the Union was often described as 'Meredith's Union' as he was usually seen as the inspirational figure. He was certainly the most public player and it's fair to say that the injustices he had experienced after the illegal payments scandal at City had shaped his thinking.

Ian Pringle: "Billy had learnt the hard way how footballers could be treated. The scandal damaged him and it's no coincidence that he and some of the others unfairly treated at that time helped develop the Union. He was at United by that time, but it was that experience at City that drove him on."

During the First World War Billy returned as a player and a coach to City, despite still officially being a United man. There had been a number of petty disputes with the Reds' management and Billy was finding it hard to accept the treatment he and some of his fellow players were experiencing. At one point United had suspended him for insubordination. Then there was the match fixing scandal of Good Friday 1915.

United beat Liverpool 2-0 at Old Trafford – a scoreline that had received a significant number of bets. There were rumours of the match being fixed partly to help United in their fight against relegation, though this has since been discounted, and partly to make some money for some of the competing players. Ultimately an FA inquiry suspended four United players, including Sandy Turnbull, and four Liverpool players for life. Debates into the innocence of the players, most notably Enoch West, went on for years but Billy was viewed by most as an innocent bystander. Undoubtedly though the scandal helped shape Billy's future thinking but there were other issues. United even retained some of the £1,400 raised for him in a benefit match. Billy was appalled at the way they were paying him in instalments and he felt United were benefitting at his expense.

Billy's return to City was at the request of his former United manager Ernest Mangnall who still felt the Welshman had much to offer. After Billy's first game (a 1-1 draw with Liverpool on 11 March 1916) after returning, the Athletic News reported: "After an absence of close on eleven years, Meredith reappeared in the colours of Manchester City and though it was his first game of the season he could safely take credit to himself that he was unsurpassed by any other forward on the field. Naturally his pace has slackened and he didn't centre with the same facility of yore. He couldn't lift the somewhat heavy ball, but his feet have not yet lost their cunning and there was none that can back heel with such certainty as he."

He made 107 first team appearances for the Blues during the war but once it was over the Reds insisted he return to Old Trafford. Billy wanted to make his move to City a permanent one however: "Today I am kicking my heels in idleness because Manchester United have the power to fix a fee upon my head for my transfer to any club desirous of my services. True they have offered me the maximum wage and consequently the authorities turned down my appeal for a free transfer.

"But I am no sentimentalist. I am quite prepared to play for Manchester United and accept the wages offered. But before I accept those terms, I believe I have the right to make other demands.

"I maintain that it is the blackest injustice to place a price upon the head of a player for whom they paid no transfer fee."

To help settle the issue United offered to pay him £10 a week and £700 as settlement of the money they owed him for the benefit. Billy felt it was a pittance, but due to the

rules that surrounded player contracts at the time he could do nothing. During 1919-20 he appeared in 21 first team games for the Reds – all of these occurring after Christmas – and then the following season he made 14 first team appearances.

His last United appearance was in the 3-0 victory over Derby County on the final day of the 1920-21 season, while his final goal for the Reds came in a 2-1 defeat at home to Everton on 12 February that season.

The following July he returned to City on a formal basis. Billy made 25 League appearances in 1921-2, and one in 1922-3. The Blues moved to Maine Road at the start of the 1923 season and, incredibly, Billy went on to play in two League games at the new venue.

Playing at Maine Road in the stadium's first season meant that Billy became the only man to have played home matches at each of Manchester's four major League grounds (Hyde Road, Bank Street, Old Trafford, and Maine Road).

Appearing in the League once more was a significant achievement for Billy, but that wasn't all he achieved that season because, at the age of 49, he played a key role in City's FA Cup run, scoring at Brighton in the third round. One match – the fourth round tie against Cardiff – was watched by an incredible 76,166 which, at the time, was the largest football crowd in Manchester for any fixture including three FA Cup finals and numerous semi-finals.

Most people had come to see the legendary Welshman's quest for a Cup medal and for a few weeks it looked as if Billy might just make an appearance at the newly opened Wembley Stadium. It wasn't to be as City lost 2-0 to Newcastle in the FA Cup semi-final. It was to be Billy's last match.

Late 1940s, Billy Meredith with his grandson Ian Pringle.

For the next few years Billy's fame continued to grow. He was the star of a film, The Ball of Fortune, and became a popular presence at major events around Manchester and Wales.

His footballing life continued for some time when he became a founder member of Manchester Central FC, playing at the Belle Vue Athletics Stadium. Central hoped to fill the void left by City when they moved to Maine Road from east Manchester, but by the mid-thirties this enterprise had collapsed. Central's story was one which saw United and City combine to end the Central threat during extremely dark days for the Reds.

Billy had several years as a licensee – he'd been the licensee of the Church Hotel in Longsight while still a player during the early twenties – and he also enjoyed a series of benefit matches played in his honour in Wales and Manchester. Ian Pringle: "He also managed the Stretford Road Hotel for a time. I was there for a while as a very small child, and my dad [City captain Charlie Pringle] used to help him a bit.

"We moved to Scotland and, between the ages of 10 and 15, my parents used to put me on the train in Glasgow to go down to Manchester to see granddad at his home at 45 Burton Road, Withington. One time I was down with my Dad and my cousin Billy Driver, and my dad took us to Maine Road to watch a game. We walked from Granddad's house to the ground. City won that day and I remember dad and granddad talking about the ground holding the record for a crowd almost 85,000 – can you imagine? We saw them beat Luton 3-2 and Roy Clarke, another great Welsh international, scored (10th December 1955)."

The great man continued to follow football, in particular the Welsh international team. He was also present at many significant footballing events – in fact he attended every one of the nine FA Cup finals enjoyed by Manchester's sides from 1904 through to City's appearance in 1956 - until his death in April 1958 at the age of 83.

Ian Pringle remembers hearing the news: "I was 16 when he passed away at the age of 83. My mam and dad were at a Scotland-England international at Hampden on the day he died (19/4/58) and the news was in the Glasgow Evening Times. There were no telephones or anything, that's how the news reached us. We came down for the funeral of course. A lot of the stars of the day went to the funeral."

Billy was buried at Southern Cemetery. When he passed away, football and Manchester residents were still mourning the loss of the victims of the Munich disaster, and as a result Billy's death received considerably less coverage than it would normally have warranted.

Proving that interest in the player never died, in 1977 Manchester City Council named a street close to Maine Road after Meredith, and in 1985 'Football Wizard', a biography of his life, was published. In 1997 BBC2 Wales broadcast a television documentary about him.

Billy Meredith's position in Manchester football is a major one. He was Manchester's first successful captain and helped to create both City and United's trophy winning heritage, and deserves to be recognised forever more as one of Manchester's leading citizens. Without Meredith neither club would have established their name.

Today, over 100 years after United's first League title success Billy's name stands clear as football's first true superstar and a man idolised by all Mancunians. He remains a truly iconic figure.

Player Career Stats – Billy Meredith

Typical Height & Weight: 5'8"   10st. 7lbs (recorded while a City player)

5'9"   11st. 4lbs (recorded while a United player)

Born: Chirk, 30 July 1874

Died: Withington, Manchester, 19th April 1958

Appearances:

Season	League		FA Cup		Other (Test Matches & Charity Shield)		Totals	
	App	Goals	App	Goals	App	Goals	Apps	Goals
Northwich								
1893-94	12	5	0	0			12	5
Manchester City								
1894-95	18	12	0	0			18	12
1895-96	29	12	0	0	4	1	33	13
1896-97	27	10	1	0			28	10
1897-98	30	12	2	0			32	12
1898-99	33	29	1	1			34	30
1899-1900	33	14	2	0			35	14
1900-01	34	7	1	0			35	7
1901-02	33	8	3	0			36	8
1902-03	34	23	1	0			35	23
1903-04	34	11	6	2			40	13
1904-05	33	8	2	1			35	9
Manchester United								
1906-07	16	5	2	0			18	5
1907-08	37	10	4	0	2	1	43	11
1908-09	34	0	4	0			38	0
1909-10	31	5	1	0			32	5
1910-11	35	5	3	0			38	5
1911-12	35	3	6	0	1		42	3
1912-13	22	2	5	0			27	2
1913-14	34	2	1	0			35	2
1914-15	26	0	1	0			27	0
1919-20	19	2	2	0			21	2
1920-21	14	1	0	0			14	1
Manchester City								
1921-22	25	0	0	0			25	0
1922-23	1	0	0	0			1	0
1923-24	2	0	4	1			6	1
	681	186	52	5	7	2	740	193

FEB 6TH 1958 THE FLOWERS OF MANCHESTER

W211

6th February will always be remembered above all other dates in United's history.

The Football Season Daily Reminder

February

1st February 1984

Darren Fletcher was born in Edinburgh.

2nd February 2002

A goal from Phil Neville opened the scoring in the sixth minute against 15th placed Sunderland, but Kevin Phillips equalised six minutes later. David Beckham made it 2-1 in the 25th minute and by half time it was 4-1 to the Reds. Van Nistelrooy scored after 28 minutes to make it 3-1 and then again from the penalty spot a minute before the break.

3rd February 1937

In Division One United drew 1-1 with Preston North End. The goalscorer was Billy Wrigglesworth playing only his second League game for the Reds. The match was watched by 13,225 at Old Trafford.

4th February 2007

A tense first half ended with United taking the lead via a Ronaldo penalty in the 45th minute. Three second half goals (Vidic 48, Scholes 54 and Giggs 77) ensured a 4-0 victory for League leaders United over 9th placed Tottenham.

5th February 1985

Cristiano Ronaldo was born in Funchal, Portugal. On the same day Carlos Tevez was celebrating his first birthday in Argentina.

6th February 1956

United defeated Athletic Bilbao 3-0 (below, United won 6-5 on aggregate) in the quarter-final of the European Cup. The game, watched by 70,000 at Maine Road, was a thoroughly exciting

affair and prompted journalist Frank Swift to write a newspaper article highlighting the wonderful performance of German referee Albert Dusch: "The best display of controlled, decisive refereeing I have seen this season. It earned him the respect and admiration of crowd and players alike."

7th February 1948

Goals from Warner (25th minute) and Mitten (85th) gave United a 2-0 fifth round FA Cup win over Charlton at Leeds Road, Huddersfield. A home United crowd of 33,312 witnessed the tie played in Yorkshire as United's landlords City were also drawn at home. Charlton's 'keeper Sam Bartram was chaired off the field at the end after an outstanding display that kept the score down. On the same date in 1970 George Best netted six goals in a memorable game with Northampton Town.

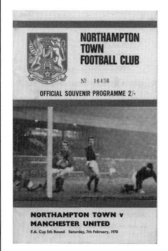

8th February 1936

Four goals from Tom Manley helped the Reds defeat Port Vale 7-2 as United pushed for promotion. The game was watched by 22,265 at Old Trafford.

9th February 2003

The Manchester derby ended in a 1-1 draw at Old Trafford. Van Nistelrooy scored the opener in front of 67,646. At the time this was the second highest attendance for an Old Trafford derby match (record was set at 68,796 in 1936).

10th February 2002

Two goals from Solskjaer (33rd and 74th minute)

brought a 2-0 victory at Charlton in the Premier League. On the same date in 1951 Matt Busby's United defeated FA Cup holders Arsenal, captained by Joe Mercer, 1-0 in the FA Cup fifth round (opposite).

11th February 1933

The Reds drew 3-3 at Preston in Division Two.

12th February 1949

United defeated Yeovil 8-0 in the fifth round of the FA Cup at Maine Road. The attendance was 81,565 (to this day the Reds' third highest home crowd) and was over 32,000 more than the previous meeting between the sides in 1938 at Old Trafford.

13th February 1988

Chelsea were defeated 2-1 by the Reds in Division One with goals from Bruce and O'Brien.

14th February 1976

Goals from Macari (7th minute) and Daly (33rd) helped United take a two goal lead over Leicester in the FA Cup fifth round tie. Leicester made it 2-1 in the 60th minute and had a goal disallowed in the closing minutes, but United held on.

15th February 1985

Strachan (6 minutes) and McGrath (87th minute) gave United a 2-0 victory over Blackburn in the FA Cup fifth round. Strachan had the chance to increase United's lead but sent his penalty over the bar.

16th February 2010

AC Milan were defeated 3-2 by United at the San Siro in the Champions League knock-out stage first leg.

17th February 1905

Full-back Billy Dale was born in Manchester. Dale joined United as an amateur in April 1925 and remained with the Reds until 1931, making 68 appearances. At the time of his arrival the Manchester Evening Chronicle reported: "The trialist from Sandbach Ramblers kicked and tackled like a League player."

18th February 1953

Full-back Johnny Carey played the League game at Sunderland as United's 'keeper. The match ended in a 2-2 draw before 24,263. During a remarkable United career Carey played in every position except outside-left.

19th February 1958

The highly emotional fifth round FA Cup tie with Sheffield Wednesday ended in a 3-0 United win before a crowd of 59,848. This was the Reds first game after the Munich disaster. The goals were scored by debutant Shay Brennan (2) and Alex Dawson.

20th February 1909

United defeated Blackburn Rovers 6-1 in the FA Cup third round. The game was remarkable as it saw two hat-tricks by players with the surname Turnbull – Sandy scored in the 15th, 56th and 90th minutes while Jimmy netted in the 50th, 51st and 85th minutes.

21st February 1959

Goals from Charlton and Viollet brought a 2-1 Division One victory at home to Wolves. In the fifties United and Wolves were viewed as the game's biggest rivals.

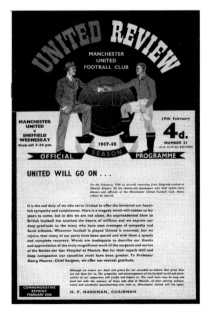

22nd February 1913

United and Oldham played out a goalless draw in the FA Cup third round at Boundary Park. The replay ended in a 2-1 defeat to David Ashworth's Oldham (above).

23rd February 1963

£56,000 signing from Celtic Pat Crerand made his debut in the 1-1 draw with Blackpool before 43,121.

24th February 2007

Despite McBride opening the scoring for Fulham in the 17th minute, United defeated the London side 2-1 in the Premier League. Giggs equalised in the 29th minute and Ronaldo scored the winner two minutes from time.

25th February 1984

Kevin Moran scored twice to give United a 2-1 victory at home to Sunderland.

26th February 1973

Ole Gunnar Solskjaer was born at Kristiansund.

27th February 1971

Shoot magazine profiled George Best giving details of his lavish lifestyle and his £30,000 house (right).

28th February 1948

United defeated Preston 4-1 in the FA Cup quarter-final at Maine Road (left). The match was watched by 74,213 with goals from Pearson (33rd & 78th minutes), Rowley (80th) and Mitten (23rd).

29th February 1964

The Reds drew 3-3 with Sunderland in the FA Cup sixth round at Old Trafford. The replay ended 2-2 at Roker Park and a crowd of 54,952 at Leeds Road, Huddersfield, witnessed a 5-1 United victory in the second replay.

What Football Means to George Best

TOO SMALL and too frail for big-time football — that was the general verdict on the fourteen-year-old George Best, of Belfast. Good enough, but not big enough.

So what career should the football-mad lad follow? Well, his dad, Richard Best, worked in the Belfast shipyards, helping to build the sea-going monsters that sailed out of Belfast Lough.

But it was hard work. Often there was grave unemployment. And little money. George himself dreaded being sent to work there, just an unidentified cog in a huge wheel. His dad agreed. So the idea was born that George should leave school at fifteen and become an apprentice printer.

A good, safe, well-paid job. There was always room for a good craftsman.

In the end, though, the Manchester United scouting system discovered the puny Irish lad, took him to Old Trafford and built him up physically. He became not only good enough, but BIG enough.

There's a picture of George, back in Belfast, sitting at the type-setting machine that could have been his "office" for a whole

working life. Only George had made the grade in soccer by then — and sat there in an expensive suit, silk handkerchief peeping from a pocket and hand-made shoes.

Says George: "In fact, football is the only life I know. It's brought me everything I have today. I've packed more living into nine years than most people could do in ninety."

Soccer brought him first the name. George Best is known around the world. Gradually that name developed the power to pull fans into areas other than football grounds. To his boutiques, starting with one on the main shopping road at Sale, near Manchester, then to Edwardia right in the middle of the city.

It brought him advertising deals which currently involve oranges, chewing gum, boys' ties, sportswear, football books, women's fashion, men's fashion, plastic footballs and eggs. Plus a varied selection of fast cars, a £30,000 house (pictured above) with a room specifically built to hold his own collection of clothes.

Says George: "But that's just the material side. I don't rate it as important as having

travelled the world in comfort, watching great sporting stars in action.

"But if I'd been stuck in Belfast, I'd probably still regard a ferry trip to Liverpool as a memorable journey."

George agrees that football has also brought him responsibility — in that his activities are followed by millions.

"I try to keep out of trouble, because I realise I can influence some youngster in the wrong way. I had a good record for years, then I slipped. But I'm working on improving my temperament . . ."

PERSONALITY BUG

He brought the show-biz personality-bug to soccer. He's more than matched his gimmickry with his sheer on-the-park skills. He's been both English Footballer of the Year and European Footballer of the Year.

Just think. George Best, instead of setting up goals for United, could have been sitting at a printing machine setting up STORIES of goals scored in local leagues round the dockyard city of Belfast.

UNITED'S LEADING SCORERS

Our story tracing the players who have topped the seasonal League goalscoring charts for the Reds through to the start of the 2011-12 season moves on to the reign of Alex Ferguson.

THE PROFILES (PART SIX)

48 – BRIAN McCLAIR

Born in Belshill, the same Lanarkshire town that Matt Busby came from, Brian McClair had enjoyed a successful career with Celtic before joining United in 1987. With the Scottish giants he won the Scottish Cup and the Premier Division. He was also both the Scottish Football Writers' Association footballer of the year and the Scottish Players' Player award.

Prior to Celtic he had made forty appearances over two seasons for Motherwell and had even had a spell at Aston Villa at the start of the 1980s, though he never actually appeared in their first team.

McClair arrived at United for a fee of £850,000 in July 1987, although Celtic had valued the striker at £2m. A similar transfer six years earlier would probably have cost United a figure closer to Celtic's valuation, but football fees had tended to stagnate a little in the mid-eighties after over valuations at the start of the decade.

The new signing made his League debut for United on 15 August 1987 at Southampton. This was to be Alex Ferguson's first complete season as manager after his arrival the previous November. McClair's first goal came in his third League game when the Reds defeated Watford 2-0 before 38,582 at Old Trafford, and this was followed a week later with his second for United.

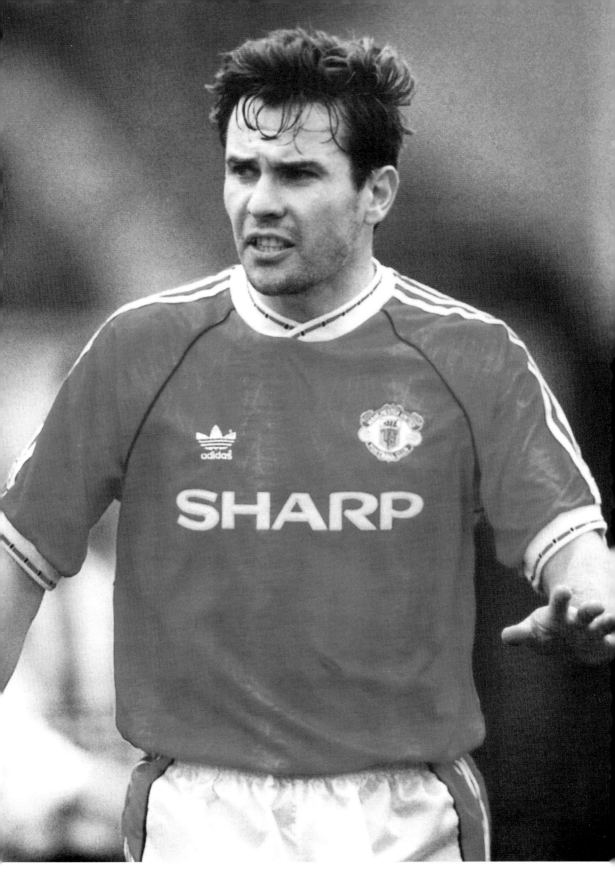

On 31 August 1987 McClair helped United defeated Chelsea 3-1, bringing the Reds 11 points from their opening five games, and taking them to the top of the League for the first time in over a year. The Sun's Peter Fitton explained: "Brian McClair put Manchester United on top of Division One for the first time in 19 traumatic months yesterday – with a goal he didn't even see. 'It was pure instinct,' confessed the Scottish international striker after his mid-air bicycle kick cracker."

McClair described the goal: "You could call it a strike in a million – the sort that could have ended up anywhere. I knew it was past the Chelsea 'keeper, but I didn't see it going in. I was tumbling on my back at the time. I wondered when I hit it why I didn't go for it with my head. It was a bit high, and the referee might have judged it dangerous play."

The new signing continued to score significant and impressive goals throughout the season, including a hat-trick in the 4-1 victory over Derby County on 2 April, and he ended 1987-88 as United's top scorer with 24 goals – the most since George Best netted 28 in the 1967-68 season. He was also the Reds only League ever-present.

The following season saw the return of Mark Hughes, which shared the goalscoring burden, but this was a transitional period for United. Ferguson's side was in the process of being shaped and several youngsters, most notably Lee Sharpe, Lee Martin and Mark Robins, were starting to appear alongside several new signings. McClair played more of a midfield role, ending the 1988-89 campaign as one of three ever-presents. He was second highest scorer with ten goals, but the following season was more concerning for United overall. A worrying League campaign, during which there were chants of "Fergie Out", brought only five goals for McClair in 37 League appearances. Fortunately, the season was salvaged with success in the FA Cup over Crystal Palace. McClair appeared in both the final and its replay, and had contributed significant goals in the 3-2 fifth round victory over Newcastle, the only goal of the quarter-final at Sheffield United, and in the 2-1 semi-final replay over Oldham at Maine Road.

Further success followed for the Reds when they won the ECWC in 1991 and, as history now proves, Alex Ferguson's side were to go on and dominate football for most of the twenty years that followed. McClair had appeared in the ECWC final against Barcelona and also topped United's League goalscoring charts that year.

As time progressed the contribution of some of the Reds early nineties stars has often been overlooked, but it is fair to say that without the likes of McClair United's trophy-winning heritage may never have reached the level it has.

In November 1991 McClair scored the only goal of the European Super Cup game with Red Star Belgrade and he also netted the only goal of the League Cup final the following April, bringing United their fourth trophy in three seasons. It was also his 100th senior goal for the Reds and came in a season when he topped United's goalscoring charts for the third and final time.

Appearances became less frequent in the years that followed, but McClair remained a valuable member of the first team squad. He netted the fourth goal in the 1994 FA Cup final and contributed a great deal as the Reds continued to find success. His role may have changed from out and out striker to a more subdued midfielder, but his commitment and drive remained.

In 1997 a crowd of more than 44,000 attended his testimonial game with Celtic and at the end of the following season he was given a free transfer. He returned to Motherwell for a few months.

In 1998 he became Brian Kidd's assistant at Blackburn Rovers, and then in 2001 he became manager of United's reserves. Great success followed, particularly in 2004-05 when they won four significant trophies.

At the start of 2006-07 McClair became

director of United's Academy, and continued to prove that first team manager Alex Ferguson had been right to sign the player for a bargain £850,000 during his first close season at Old Trafford.

McClair's all-round contribution to the Red cause has been high both as a player, and behind the scenes. It is unlikely he will ever be regarded by the media and younger fans as Ferguson's greatest signing, but the truth is that without him much of what United became would not have been possible. McClair encapsulates in one player everything that brought the Reds modern day glory.

Leading League Scorer in:
1987-1988 - 24 goals, 40 appearances
1990-1991 - 13 goals, 36 appearances
1991-1992 - 18 goals, 42 appearances

49 – ERIC CANTONA

Frenchman Eric Cantona may only have spent five years at Old Trafford, but in that time he made such an impact that his name is now ingrained in the culture of Manchester United to such an extent that fans are still singing his name at matches around 15 years after he retired.

Glorious goals, assists and an imperiously raised collar were all trademarks of the Cantona era, as was controversy.

From his early days at Auxerre, it was clear he was a player with tremendous ability but also a propensity for getting into trouble. Cantona had served suspensions for a variety of misdeeds with media reports claiming he had kicked a ball at the crowd; thrown his shirt away after being substituted; and thrown his boots in the face of a team-mate. The final straw in France, though, came when Cantona was accused of throwing the ball at the referee in protest at a decision. The player was initially punished with a one month ban. However, this was increased to three months after he allegedly called each of the members of the disciplinary committee idiots. Cantona responded in disgust by announcing his retirement from football at the age of 25.

This retirement proved to be short-lived and the player came over to England to try to kick-start his career in early 1992 with a trial for Sheffield Wednesday, who were at that point amongst the challengers for the title. When Trevor Francis requested that Cantona should extend his trial period by an extra week, he refused and ended up signing for Leeds United in February 1992 instead.

Cantona was an instant success at Elland Road and was instrumental in taking the title to Yorkshire. He scored nine goals in 28 appearances and provided a number of assists in a profitable partnership with Lee Chapman.

Despite his contribution to Leeds' title success – the last season prior to the formation of the Premier League - and the fact that he started the 1992-93 season with hat-tricks against Liverpool and Tottenham Hotspur, Cantona's relationship with Howard Wilkinson had rapidly become strained.

At the same time, United had begun their latest bid to end their title hoodoo in an unconvincing fashion. After Alex Ferguson had brought trophy success both domestically and in Europe the main focus of the Reds was to win the League title for the first time since 1967. However, the 1992-93 season had begun poorly. The team were struggling for goals and had only won six times in the opening 16 League games. To make matters worse, new signing Dion Dublin had broken his leg and was ruled out for six months. This left United short of striking options. Brian McClair and Mark Hughes were there of course, but by the middle of November the Reds had only netted 14 goals.

Around this time, Leeds made an enquiry about the availability of United full-back Denis Irwin. Their interest was rebuffed, however one thing led to another and Cantona exited Elland Road, made his way across the Pennines and joined the Reds for a fee of £1.2 million. A transfer that even in 1992 seemed like a bargain, particularly as Ferguson needed to find someone to replace Dion Dublin.

Eric Cantona has been framed. He's not the kind of guy who would say 'Pretentious moi?' at all. Nor is he a master of the martial arts. He just happens to be the best footballer to play on these shores since George Best. At least that's what Alex Ferguson said when he talked to

It's often overlooked now, but the injury to Dublin was the catalyst to the arrival of one of the Reds' biggest stars. Had Dublin been fully fit and been able to perform at the level he did later in his career at Coventry, it's highly likely Cantona would not have joined United.

Although Cantona did not make his debut for United until early December, his arrival coincided with an upturn in form for the team. After beating Arsenal 1-0 at Highbury in the League game prior to his debut, the Reds went on a run that saw them only lose two League games in the rest of the season that followed.

Cantona made his League debut as a substitute in the Old Trafford derby match on 6 December, and went on to contribute nine League goals that season. However, his importance could not be measured by simply the number of times he put the ball in the net. As experienced at Leeds, Cantona provided a number of scoring opportunities for his team mates, and his tremendous self-confidence was vital for a team that had not won the league since the Sixties – a

statistic that brought much ridicule from Liverpool supporters, especially when they pointed out the number of successes they had experienced in the interim and the fact that two other significant rivals, Leeds and Manchester City, had enjoyed League title success more recently (though only one season more recently in City's case).

The gloating and boasting of the other clubs, plus the intense media focus on those League title-less years meant that United's 1992-93 title win was celebrated like no other. It was not only historic for the club though, but also for Cantona as he became the first player to win back to back English League titles with two different clubs. It is worth noting that because he won the title in his last season in France, he had actually won three consecutive winner's medals with three different clubs overall.

Cantona was the man who had helped transform the season and bring that elusive first title. From that point on the Reds were unstoppable and Cantona was idolised. The 1993-4 season was, if anything, even better than the previous campaign. United not only retained their title, but also won the FA Cup and reached the League Cup Final. The FA Cup was particularly memorable for Cantona as he scored two penalties to consign Chelsea to a 4-0 defeat. He also won £100 after Dennis Wise bet him that he'd miss the first penalty.

1993-94 did, however, have its low points and, as well as a disappointing European campaign, Cantona was sent off three times during the season, including twice in consecutive matches in March.

Worse was to come the following season when the player was sent off at Selhurst Park. As he made his way off the pitch, Cantona reacted angrily to abuse he was receiving from a fan and he launched a 'kung-fu' kick at the Crystal Palace supporter. The action stunned those watching in the ground and at home, and it was replayed ad infinitum on the day, with media commentators dissecting every moment. The resulting furore saw Cantona arrested and convicted for assault. On appeal his two week prison sentence was reduced to 120 hours of community service.

As for football itself, he was initially banned by United for four months, but this was doubled by the FA. Inevitably, Cantona missed the remainder of the 94-95 season, as well as the beginning of 1995-96.

Cantona's unavailability proved crucial as United went trophy-less for the only season of his stay in Manchester. His importance was also underlined by the fact that Alex Ferguson flew to Paris to persuade Cantona to reconsider when he requested a termination of his contract.

With perfect timing, Cantona made his return from suspension in a game against Liverpool in October 1995. His impact was immediate and Cantona not only set up a goal for Nicky Butt within two minutes of the start, but he also scored a penalty in the 2-2 draw. However, his true importance was not to be felt until the second half of the season, where in tandem with a number of Schmeichel clean sheets, Cantona scored the winner in five significant 1-0 victories,

most notably against a Newcastle team that was several points ahead in the league when the two sides met in March.

Cantona also went on to score an outstanding winner in a fairly tepid FA Cup Final against Liverpool, as well as earning personal success as the PFA and Football Writers' Player of the Year.

This success was not replicated on the international front, as Cantona was ignored by France for the Euro' 96 competition, despite being a prominent part of the English advertising campaign – "66 was a great year for English football. Eric was born."

After finishing the season on such a high, it was a surprise that Cantona decided the following year to retire from professional football. He went out on a high though, captaining the side to their fourth title in his five years at Old Trafford. His final season also coincided with United's best run in the Champions League since the end of the Sixties as the team reached the semi-finals before a disappointing exit to Borussia Dortmund.

Much has been made of the fact that Cantona did not dominate matches in Europe or lead United to the kind of success that he had domestically. However, there are some mitigating factors that need to be remembered. At this point, United were very much finding their feet in Europe's top competition, and their buccaneering 4-4-2 style of play from the Premier League left them susceptible to conceding when playing in Europe.

More damagingly, this was the era of the 'three plus two' foreigners rule, which meant that for Champions League fixtures, even Scottish and Welsh players were regarded as foreigners. Therefore, United had to field a team that was weaker than the team they were using domestically. The most famous - or possibly infamous - example of this was when both Cantona and Schmeichel were dropped for a game at the Nou Camp and United were hammered 4-0.

Since leaving top flight football, Cantona

has had a varied career, including a spell captaining the French Beach Football side. He has also embarked upon an acting career, even inspiring Ken Loach to write a film based upon Cantona being a spiritual guide for a Manchester postman - the well-received "Looking for Eric." He has also set up the media company Canto Bros and produced a TV documentary on the Manchester derby for French television.

Recently, Cantona has become involved in football once again, when it was announced at the start of 2011 that he was to be the Director of Soccer at the New York Cosmos as they bid to re-establish themselves as a team in North America. In August 2011 his new side faced United in a testimonial for Paul Scholes.

Leading League Scorer in:
1993-1994 - 18 goals, 34 appearances
1995-1996 – 14 goals, 30 appearances

GOLDEN GOALS

Eric Cantona

The idea of this 'GOLDEN GOALS' feature is to remember a significant or spectacular goal. The Big Book Of United's hope is that modern day supporters learn more about some of these goals.

The goal featured here was scored by Eric Cantona in a game with Sunderland shortly before Christmas 1996.

MATCH STATS

Date: 21 December 1996

Score: United 5 Sunderland 0

Scorers: Ole Gunnar Solskjaer (35th & 47th minutes), Eric Cantona (43rd minute penalty & 79th minute) & Nicky Butt (58th minute)

Attendance: 55,081

Referee: P Durkin

United Team: Schmeichel, Neville G, Neville P, May, Irwin, Pallister (McClair 46th minute), Cantona, Butt, Solskjaer (Poborsky 54th minute), Scholes & Giggs (Thornley 63rd minute)

PRE-MATCH

This was Sunderland's first visit to Old Trafford in the Premier League following their promotion under manager Peter Reid. Inevitably 1995-96 title winners United were favourites for success in this fixture, but results had been a little mixed in the weeks leading up to the game. Successive score draws in the two preceding Premier League games (West Ham 2-2 & Sheffield Wednesday 1-1) brought a few concerns United's way, however these were minor in comparison with an infamous 6-3 defeat in grey at Southampton on 26 October, a 2-0 loss at Leicester in the League Cup and 1-0 defeats to Fenerbahce (at home) and Juventus in the Champions League.

Most media pundits wrote off United's chance of retaining the title, but Alex Ferguson continued to believe that the League could be won. It was important this game saw United at their best to ensure Ferguson was right and his doubters proved wrong.

THE GAME

The Reds were dominant and opened the scoring in the 35th minute when Solskjaer headed home from about five yards out after a save by Sunderland's Lionel Perez in the Stretford End goal.

Eight minutes later Nicky Butt was brought down by Perez in the penalty area, and Eric Cantona placed the resulting spot kick low and to the left to give United a two goal advantage.

Two minutes into the second half a Sunderland free kick came to nothing for the visitors as Peter Schmeichel made a rather simple catch. However, the Danish 'keeper immediately saw Solskjaer free close to the half way mark but still within United's half of the pitch. The 'keeper threw the ball straight to Solskjaer who immediately surged forward, avoiding the threat of Sunderland's Kubicki, before sending the ball past an advancing Perez. At 3-0 the game was already over, but United wanted to prove their title credentials. They relentlessly pushed forward and then, only 13 minutes into the half, a Ryan Giggs corner was headed home by Nicky Butt.

The Reds could have sat back and taken it easy, however this was not United's way, certainly not while Eric Cantona was playing and, sure enough, the Frenchman continued to give his all.

Eleven minutes from time, Cantona was slightly inside the Sunderland half when he received a pass. With his back towards the Sunderland goal he quickly worked the ball round, turned to launch his attack, and dodged two of Peter Reid's men who were paying him close attention. He then moved with ease between the players.

One of them, Paul Bracewell, followed and tried to put the United star under pressure, but Cantona continued to move forward with ease. He passed the ball to Brian McClair, who moved the ball a yard or so, while Cantona continued to head for goal. McClair then returned an expert pass to the advancing Frenchman as he neared the penalty area.

The United captain despatched an inch-perfect chip beyond the Sunderland goalkeeper and in off the top of the far post. A marvellous goal. Cantona celebrated in an equally memorable style – he simply turned, collar up, looked towards the main stand as if he was taking the scene in, then he raised his arms and turned. He then put his arms around McClair.

POST MATCH

The goal itself may not have been the deciding factor in the game, but it did help re-enforce the view that United were a dominant force and that they could win a successive League title.

This 5-0 victory was followed by a ten game unbeaten run, including eight victories, in the Premier League. Those results lifted United to the top of the table by the end of January, where they remained for the rest of the season. The Reds also reached the semi-final of the Champions League for the first time since the sixties.

For the scorer of the fifth goal against Sunderland however, this season saw the end of his United career. Eric Cantona announced his retirement on 18 May 1997, and this goal against Sunderland was one of many highlights the Frenchman gave the Reds during a wonderful career.

The Football Season Daily Reminder
March

1st March 1977

Ashley Grimes signed for United in a reported £20,000 transfer from Bohemians.

2nd March 1957

A 64th minute penalty, scored by Johnny Berry, gave United a 2-1 lead over Bournemouth in the FA Cup sixth round. Bournemouth had taken a 35th minute lead but Berry equalised in the 57th minute.

3rd March 2007

In a game that saw Scholes sent off and the media claim United only had one shot, the Manchester Reds won the Premier League meeting with Liverpool at Anfield with a 90th minute goal from O'Shea. On the same date in 1945, the wartime meeting with Oldham (pictured) ended in a 3-2 victory at Maine Road.

4th March 1995

Andy Cole scored five against Ipswich to create a new goalscoring record. No player had netted so many goals in a Premier League game before – it would be over four years before the record was equalled (by Alan Shearer for Newcastle against Sheffield Wednesday). United scored nine that day – another record for the Premier League.

5th March 1977

United beat Championship challengers Manchester City 3-1 with goals from Coppell, Hill and Pearson at Old Trafford, causing the media to suggest the Reds stood an outside chance of the League title.

6th March 1909

The FA Cup tie at Burnley was abandoned after 72 minutes due to a snow blizzard. The Reds had been losing after a Burnley goal in the 15th minute. On the same date in 1926 United defeated Fulham 2-1 in the FA Cup quarter-final.

7th March 1908

Despite a goal from Jimmy Turnbull and significant

effort from Sandy Turnbull, the Reds were defeated 2-1 at Fulham in the FA Cup fourth round (above).

8th March 1977

In a re-match of the previous season's FA Cup final, United defeated Southampton 2-1 thanks to goals from Jimmy Greenhoff (5th and 69th minutes). Referee Clive Thomas had dismissed Southampton's Jim Steele for 'persistent misconduct'. Southampton announced they had returned 5000 tickets to the Reds for this 5th round replay because their fans did not want to have to confront United's.

9th March 1976

A 96th minute extra-time goal by Sammy McIlroy was the difference when Wolves and United met in the FA Cup quarter-final replay at Molineux. The game ended 3-2 before 44,375.

10th March 1909

The replayed FA Cup tie with Burnley ended in a 3-2 victory. Burnley had taken the lead in the 16th minute but ten minutes later Halse equalised. Jimmy Turnbull scored the other United goals (29th & 62nd minutes). Victory meant the Reds had

qualified for their first FA Cup semi-final (below).

11th March 1963

The fourth round FA Cup tie against Aston Villa ended 1-0 to United. The previous round had made history as the United-Huddersfield time had been postponed a record seven times in total due to an appalling winter.

12th March 1988

Newspaper baron Robert Maxwell revealed that he was launching a bid to take over United. It was rumoured he was prepared to pay £5 for shares valued

16 DAILY SKETCH, MONDAY, MARCH 29, 1909.

News in Pictures. Pictures in News.

SHEFFIELD SEMI-FINAL : MANCHESTER UNITED'S VICTORY OVER NEWCASTLE.

Robert Maxwell

Max in moves for United

By GEORGE SCOTT

MILLIONAIRE publisher Robert Maxwell is building up a stake in Manchester United, it was reported last night.

Maxwell recently bought five per cent of the club's shares—and one of the companies he uses in such deals has been active again.

Major shareholders at Old Trafford have been receiving tempting offers to sell, it was revealed.

Failed

A broker has offered £5 a share—£1 above the odds—on behalf of an un-named bidder.

Maxwell, chairman of Derby County, tried to take control of United over four years ago, but his £10 million offer was rejected.

And only last November he failed to buy Elton John's shareholding at Watford for £2 million.

He backed down after the Football League management committee ruled against him.

at £4. Four years earlier he had launched a £10m takeover plan.

13th March 1948

Derby were defeated 3-1 at the Hillsborough, Sheffield in the FA Cup semi-final. A hat-trick from Stan Pearson (30th, 34th and 55th minutes) brought a deserved victory. The Guardian's famous reporter, Don Davies, felt that despite Derby's battling qualities the result was appropriate: "justice removing the bandages from at least one eye, refused to allow so fair and gallant a team as Manchester United to be baulked of its prize."

14th March 1979

A crowd of 54,510 witnessed a 2-0 United victory over Tottenham in the FA Cup quarter-final replay at Old Trafford.

15th March 1965

Two goals apiece from Connelly and Herd helped United to a 4-1 home win over Fulham in Division One as the Reds pushed for their first League title since 1957.

16th March 1963

Chelsea were defeated 2-1 in the FA Cup fifth round. Albert Quixall, who scored the second goal, later admitted: "The win against Chelsea really put us on the Wembley

trail, and probably for the first time we realised that Manchester United were only a stone's throw and two more matches from what is every footballer's dream… to play in the Cup Final at Wembley."

17th March 2007

Three goals in the opening half hour set United up for a 4-1 victory at home to Bolton in the Premier League.

18th March 1967

Leicester were defeated 5-2 with goals from Aston, Charlton, Herd, Law and Sadler. After two successive draws the victory was an important one and ensured the Reds continued to challenge for the title.

19th March 1977

The FA Cup quarter-final against Aston Villa was meant to be an easy win for the Reds. Villa were midway through a protracted League Cup final – both the original game and the replay, played 3 days before the United FA Cup tie, had ended in draws and a second replay had yet to be played. Despite Villa's distractions they actually raced in to a first minute lead. United ultimately fought back and goals from Houston (25th minute) and Macari (76th minute) made it 2-1.

Ray Ranson & Lou Macari,
United 3 City 1, 5 March 1977

20th March 1971

A brace from George Best brought a 2-1 victory at Stoke City.

21st March 1908

Goalkeeper Herbert Broomfield made his debut at Woolwich Arsenal. Despite only managing 9 first team appearances Broomfield was once described as "A man who does not waste words, unassuming and a loyal clubman." He went on to be the Players' Union secretary and was a key figure during its formation.

22nd March 1986

The Manchester derby ended 2-2 at Old Trafford. In 1891 Newton Heath defeated Stockport 3-1 on the same date in the Manchester Cup semi-final.

23rd March 1957

Within 15 minutes the Reds had raced into a two goal lead in the FA Cup semi-final against Birmingham City at Hillsborough. Goals from Johnny Berry (13th minute) and Bobby Charlton (14th minute) against the previous season's FA Cup finalists

were enough to see United progress to Wembley.

24th March 1962

A crowd of 31,322 witnessed a 1-1 draw with Sheffield Wednesday. Bobby Charlton (right) scored the United goal.

25th March 1972

Crystal Palace were overwhelmed as United secured a 4-0 victory at Old Trafford.

26th March 1958

The FA Cup semi-final replay ended in a 5-3

United chasing a record

By RONALD CROWTHER

MANCHESTER UNITED are now within easy reach of the all-time season attendance record for any club in the Football League. Even before last night's derby their average had reached 56,619.

This is running ahead of the record of 56,473 set up by Newcastle United in season 1947-48.

With a sell-out assured for the visit of Liverpool to Old Trafford and the championship struggle almost certain to keep enthusiasm on the boil, there can be little doubt that a new record will be set up.

In the history of the Football League there have been only five instances of clubs topping 50,000 average for a season. United, who with 53,984 last season went nearest to Newcastle's record, have done so twice.

In season 1958-59—the one after Munich—they had an average of 53,033. The other clubs to exceed 50,000 were Tottenham in 1960-61, the season of their League and FA Cup double, with 53,315, and Everton, in their championship season of 1962-63, with 51,460.

Newcastle's record still stands out as a football phenomenon, because it was established in Division Two. Admittedly it was a promotion season, but that early post-war side, with great personalities such as Jackie Milburn, Joe Harvey, Frank Brennan, Jackie Fairbrother, George Stobart, and Tommy Pearson, did not finish up as champions. In the final table they were three points behind Birmingham City.

Growth

Manchester's pulling power this season when as League champions, they are also fighting for the European Cup, is not surprising. But last season, when they topped 50,000, they were in no European competitions.

When I asked manager Matt Busby if he could explain this growth of interest he told me : 'I believe it to be a combination of things. The World Cup gave English football a big boost. And, as I see it, it is becoming more and more a family entertainment.'

Secretary Les Olive added: 'We have noticed that many more women are coming to games, particularly teenagers. I believe our facilities have added to the attractiveness of football at Old Trafford, where we have seats for 18,500 people.'

In their bid for the record United lead a trend that is bringing greater prosperity to the game generally. For the overall picture is one of Football League gates running at a figure of more than a million and a quarter up on last season.

By the end of the season they may be two million up on 1966-67, and in that season they rose by 1,695,616 on the previous one. That was the biggest seasonal gain for 19 years.

United victory at Highbury over Fulham. The initial game had resulted in a 2-2 draw at Villa Park.

27th March 1909

United's first FA Cup semi-final ended in a 1-0 victory (Halse, 65th minute) over Newcastle at Bramall Lane.

28th March 1968

The Daily Mail reported that United were on schedule to break the Football League's average attendance record. At the time Newcastle held the record with an average attendance of 56,473 set in 1947-48. The article commented that there had only ever been five instances of teams exceeding 50,000 – two of these were achieved by the Reds. Ultimately, United did beat the record with an average of 57,552.

29th March 1980

Goals from Jordan and Thomas brought a 2-0 victory at Crystal Palace.

30th March 1963

Despite conceding a shock fifth minute goal, United beat Coventry City 3-1 in the FA Cup quarter-final at Highfield Road.

31st March 1945

A hat trick from Jack Smith helped United to a 4-0 win over Burnley in wartime football. Billy Bryant opened the scoring with a spectacular goal in a first half in which the Reds could attack at will.

UNITED'S LEAGUE CUP SUCCESSES

In 1992 United won the League Cup for the first time. It was the third major trophy of Alex Ferguson's reign as manager and was therefore a highly significant success at the time. Playing against United that day was Nottingham Forest who shared the record number of wins with Liverpool at the time.

From 1992 to 2010 United appeared in five further finals, winning the trophy on three occasions.

The following table shows each of United's League Cup

successes and, to give an indication of how United's record rated, we include the side with the most number of League Cup wins at the time of each Reds' success.

Season	Score	Runners-up	Attendance	Total Lge Cup Wins	Team with most League Cup successes
1991-92	1-0	Nottingham Forest	76,810	1	Liverpool & Nottm Forest 4
2005-06	4-0	Wigan Athletic	66,866	2	Liverpool 7
2008-09	0-0	Tottenham H	88,217	3	Liverpool 7
		(aet; Utd won 4-1 on penalties)			
2009-10	2-1	Aston Villa	88,596	4	Liverpool 7

By the end of 2011 the five most successful sides in the League Cup (with the number of times each has been League Cup final runners-up in brackets) were:

Liverpool 7 (3)
Aston Villa 5 (3)
Chelsea 4 (3)
United 4 (4)
Nottingham Forest 4 (2)
Tottenham Hotspur 4 (3)

UNITED'S LEADING SCORERS

Our story of all the players who have topped the seasonal League goalscoring charts for the Reds through to the start of the 2011-12 season moves on to United's first Ukrainian star.

THE PROFILES
(PART SEVEN)

50 – ANDREI KANCHELSKIS

A pacey and powerful right winger, Kanchelskis was born in Kirovograd, Ukraine (then a part of the Soviet Union) in 1969. He began his career with local side Zvezda as a 17 year old, and joined Dynamo Kiev. Due to Dynamo's status as a police team, his two years there fullfilled his compulsory national service requirement.

During his Dynamo days he made his first trip to England for a friendly tournament. He played at Wembley against Liverpool and Porto, scoring the winning goal against the Portuguese.

In 1990 he joined Shakhtar Donetsk, the team he had supported as a boy. Success with the USSR in the final of the Under-21 European Championships soon followed. A little more than a year later, he found himself flying out of the Ukraine to an unknown destination in England, knowing only that he was to be going for a trial at a northern club. It was all very mysterious and reinforced the stereotypical view of what life in east Europe was like.

The club he was travelling to was, of course, Manchester United. After a successful trial an initial fee of £650,000 (increasing to £1.42m with appearance clauses) was paid to secure his services. Kanchelskis arrived in time to make an inauspicious debut in the penultimate league game of the 1990-91 season - a 3-0 defeat to Crystal Palace at Selhurst Park.

The following season saw Kanchelskis make 42 appearances for the club in all competitions. He scored his first goal for the Reds in a 2-0 home win against Sheffield United in November 1991. Receiving the ball in the centre circle, Kanchelskis made a typically athletic run into the box, turned the Blades central defence, came inside and rifled a cracking shot into the top corner over a hapless Simon Tracey.

The Ukrainian would score a further seven goals during the 1991-92 campaign and although United ultimately fell short in their quest to win the league title, Kanchelskis picked up his first piece of silverware in English football when the Reds lifted the League Cup for the first time after a 1-0 victory over Nottingham Forest at Wembley.

For the opening three games of the inaugural Premier League season of 1992-93, Kanchelskis started, but with United winning just a point from the nine available, he was relegated to the bench. Appearances came in fits and starts mainly as a substitute, marginalised in favour of Lee Sharpe who had returned from illness (Meningitis). Alleged disagreements with Alex Ferguson saw Kanchelskis make no home starts after the defeat by Wimbledon on 28 October 1992, and it was reported that he was sent to train with the reserves.

Between New Year and the end of the season he made six starts and chipped in two more goals. His overall contribution that campaign was enough to ensure a Premier League Champions medal when he replaced Brian McClair against Blackburn on 3 May 1993, just minutes before United lifted the trophy for the first time in 26 years. Having endured a difficult and mixed season, which had been compounded with personal tragedy off the field, Kanchelskis seriously considered leaving the club. Alex Ferguson, however, convinced him to stay for another season with assurances that spending this period of his career at United would improve his game.

Kanchelskis was a far more influential member of the squad in 1993-94 when, despite being handed the number 14 squad number, he was a first XI player. He made a total of 47 appearances, scored ten goals and provided twelve assists. A victim of the UEFA 'foreigner rules', he made no appearance for United in their first Champions League campaign, and he was sent off for handling a shot on the line in the League Cup final defeat by Aston Villa. He missed the semi-final of the FA Cup against Oldham due to injury, but was able to play in the replay where he scored the opener - a stunning solo goal where he came inside from the right wing, past a line of defenders before placing a shot from the edge of the box into the top right corner.

That season he also picked up a second Premier League medal and started the FA Cup final - facing up to compatriot and former under-21 teammate Dimitri Kharine in the Chelsea goal. Kanchelskis won United's second penalty when he was fouled by Frank Sinclair in the second half on the way to a 4-0 win to complete United's first double.

1994-95 started off as the previous season had ended and Andrei even found himself part of Ferguson's European squad, featuring in five Champions League matches and scoring against Gothenburg. His first goal of the season was a magnificent angled volley in a 1-1 draw at Nottingham Forest, and more followed in wins against Liverpool and Everton as well as a crucial brace at Blackburn.

A place as a United legend was cemented with a hat-trick against City in the 'Demolition Derby' of 10 November 1994. Setting up Eric Cantona for the first goal, the favour was returned by the Frenchman for Kanchelskis' first goal of the night as he came back to haunt Simon Tracey – the goalkeeper he'd scored his first United goal against three years earlier. A further five goals against Crystal Palace, Leicester, Norwich, Manchester City (again) and Arsenal took Kanchelskis' tally for the

233

season up to 14 in the League (plus one in the Champions League), however the goal against the Gunners was to be almost his last kick for the club as he was ruled out of the rest of the season with a hernia. Meanwhile, missing the Ukrainian as well as the suspended Cantona and an injured Giggs, United slumped. They lost the title on the last day by a single point to Blackburn Rovers and the FA Cup final by a solitary goal to Everton.

It was the Merseyside cup-winners who Kanchelskis joined the following Autumn, when Joe Royle signed him for a club record £5m. A breakdown in relations with Ferguson was cited as the reason he had handed in a transfer request, and a protracted transfer ensued. The player went on to emulate the feats of his final season at United during his first at Everton, scoring 16 League goals despite being injured early in the campaign when he faced United at Goodison Park. Two goals in an away win at Anfield in the Merseyside derby ensured he enjoyed a similar rapport with Toffees fans as he had with United supporters.

The Ukrainian's spell at Goodison Park did not last long however, and after an underwhelming start to 1996/97, he was sold to Fiorentina for £8m. Just two years later, having been in and out of the team at the Italian outfit, Kanchelskis returned to Britain with Rangers where he picked up an array of medals during a four year spell, including two Scottish League titles.

In early 2001 he had an eleven game period on loan to the club he had once tormented, Manchester City, who were managed by his former Everton boss Joe Royle. He was not able to halt City's slide to the drop, but he did score in a 4-2 defeat by Liverpool in the FA Cup.

After his contract with Rangers came to an end, Kanchelskis once again returned to English football, this time with Southampton. However, he made only two substitute appearances before his contract was cancelled. He moved to Saudi Arabian

club Al-Hilal on a four month deal in 2003. Following that, he finished his playing career in Russia with Saturn and Krylia Sovetov.

In 2007 Kanchelskis became a director of FC Nosta Novotroitsk before becoming manager of Torpedo-Zil two years later. In 2011 he became manager of FC Ufa of the Russian Second Division.

Leading League Scorer in:
1994-1995 - 14 goals, 30 appearances

51 – OLE GUNNAR SOLSKJAER

When Ole Gunnar Solskjaer joined United in the 1996 close season very little was expected of him. He had come from Molde in the Norwegian Tippeligaen for a reported fee of £1.5m and, although he'd impressed in an international friendly against Northern Ireland the previous March, he was largely unknown outside of his homeland.

In recent years he has come to be seen as a low cost alternative to Alan Shearer, who had joined Newcastle for £15m – an astounding amount at the time - during that same summer, but at the time of Solskjaer's arrival in Manchester, Alex Ferguson was still trying to engineer a transfer for the England striker from Blackburn Rovers. Had Rovers financier and chairman Jack Walker been willing to deal with United, Solskjaer may have been confined to playing a bit-part role at United, and been presented with far fewer chances to stake a claim for a place in the team.

Solskjaer made his debut against Blackburn Rovers in the Premier League game at Old Trafford in August 1996. United were 2-1 down after an hour and Solskjaer came off the substitutes' bench replacing David May. Nine minutes later he scored the equaliser. Latching on to a hopeful forward header from fellow substitute Jordi Cruyff on the edge of the box, Solskjaer fired off a powerful volley that Tim Flowers could only palm away back to the Norwegian for him to place his second attempt into the bottom right. A slightly unfair reputation as United's 'super sub' was instantly forged and this was

soon followed by the press dubbing him the 'Baby-faced Assassin'.

Solskjaer's first season coincided with Andy Cole's extended spell out of the side through broken legs and pneumonia, and so the Norwegian played often alongside Eric Cantona as United led the table for much of the season on their way to another Premier League title. Cole had returned in time to combine with Solskjaer in a vital game against challengers Arsenal where the Englishman set him up for the crucial second goal - United winning 2-1. Against all odds and expectations, he ended the season as the Club's top scorer with 18 league goals (19 in all competitions).

Eric Cantona retired in the summer, but all hope that this would provide Solskjaer any further opportunities to start quickly vanished, as Teddy Sheringham was signed from Spurs as the Frenchman's replacement. Throughout Solskjaer's time at Old Trafford he had a great reputation as one of the club's finest and most lethal finishers, however he also had incredible competition for his place in the team as United signed a succession of new strikers, from Yorke to van Nistelrooy, Forlan, Saha and Rooney. It was much to his credit that he stayed to fight for his place and played with such enthusiasm and commitment throughout his Old Trafford career.

Having been knocked out of both the FA Cup and Champions League (though they did reach the quarter-final) by March 1998, United's only chance of silverware that season was in the Premier League, where they trailed Arsenal by seven points going into the home match against Newcastle on 18 April. United went a goal down minutes into the game and although they equalised through Beckham before the interval, they simply could not find the winner they needed. With every United player camped in Newcastle's box as the clock ticked down, Robert Lee received the ball and quickly broke into United's half with only Peter Schmeichel ahead of him. Desperate to keep the title challenge alive, Solskjaer raced back to challenge Lee on the edge of United's box. Making contact in a seemingly clumsy manner he was sent off by referee Uriah Rennie. The match ended 1-1 and United ended the season trophyless.

Solskjaer resisted overtures from Tottenham in the summer of 1998 and he appeared at Wembley in the season's opener, the 1998 Charity Shield which ended in a 3-0 defeat to Arsenal. This was an unpromising start to the season, and offered no clue as to what would follow. Although given just 17 starts, Solskjaer scored an impressive 18 goals in all competitions. First came a brace against Charlton (9 September), then followed goals against Brondby, Bury, Forest and Leeds. Two vital goals were scored at his north London suitors, Spurs in a 2-2 draw on 12 December. Then, a sign of what was to follow, as Solskjaer came off the bench in the 81st minute with United a goal behind to Liverpool in the fourth round of the FA Cup. Dwight Yorke bagged an 88th minute equaliser before the Norwegian all but stole the ball from Scholes' feet in the Liverpool box, and fired low into the left of the goal to break the Liverpool fans' hearts in injury time.

Two weeks later at the City Ground, Solskjaer again came on as a late substitute. The Reds were 4-1 up and Ole was instructed by coach Jim Ryan to go and keep possession by playing it simple – there was no need to search for more goals with a victory comfortably in the bag. Whether Solskjaer listened or whether he simply got carried away isn't clear, but in a twelve minute spell he put four past a luckless Dave Beasant. The player scored another two goals against Everton and Sheffield Wednesday in the League and, although he missed several weeks due to injury, he was on the bench when United wrapped up the title with a 2-1 win against Spurs on 16 May 1999. He was granted a place in the starting FA Cup final eleven against Newcastle, and helped the Reds to a 2-0 victory, ensuring Solskjaer collected a second double in just three seasons.

Four days after the FA Cup final came the defining moment of Solskjaer's career. At the Nou Camp against Bayern Munich in the final of the Champions League, United were trailing 1-0 to the Germans after a Mario Basler free kick had left Schmeichel rooted to the spot. With a mere nine minutes remaining, the Norwegian replaced Andy Cole as United clung on to the hope of hitting a stubborn and well-disciplined Bayern on the break. Thirty seconds into injury time, Sheringham turned in a scuffed shot from Giggs after a David Beckham corner and the Reds had hope of success. According to legend UEFA officials had already placed Munich's ribbons on the trophy.

A few seconds later, following another corner from Beckham, Solskjaer wove himself into the fabric of the club's history with the winner. Bayern were crushed, United were triumphant, and the glorious treble was sealed.

Solskjaer had further successful seasons at United where he helped the club to consecutive titles and forged partnerships with a succession of strikers, including 2001-02 when he combined with Ruud van Nistelrooy in a partnership that yielded 60 goals between them. He played alongside Nistelrooy and Scholes in attack during 2002-03 as well as appearing often as a winger as his 57 appearances - the most of any United player that season - helped the Reds to another championship trophy.

The Norwegian continued his wide role successfully in the wake of David Beckham's sale to Real Madrid the following summer as United won the FA Cup for the eleventh time in 2003-04, although a knee injury picked up in September kept him out of action for six months.

Knee problems haunted him for this period of his career, and he underwent surgery which caused him to miss all of the 2004/05 season and much of the following campaign - he played only around an hour of league football in 2005/06.

At 32 years old, it looked as though

Solskjaer's career was winding to an end, however he made a remarkable return in 2006-07, scoring eleven goals in 32 appearances as United regained the league title after a gap of four years.

Solskjaer announced his retirement in August 2007 after having undergone further surgery on his problematic knee which he failed to fully recover from.

In May 2008 he took over as the United reserve team coach, winning the Manchester Senior Cup and the Reserve League North before accepting the job as manager of his former club Molde in November 2010. He continued with United until January 2011 before managing Molde for the first time in the Norwegian league on 18 March 2011.

Leading League Scorer in:
1996-1997 - 18 goals, 33 appearances

52 - ANDY COLE

Andy Cole actually started his career at Arsenal in 1988, but after making a solitary League appearance for them, he was sold on to Bristol City in the third tier of English football. His Arsenal appearance had come as a substitute against Sheffield United in Division one on 29 December 1990. However, it is worth recalling that he had actually also made 13 League appearances and scored three goals during a loan spell at Fulham in 1991.

Despite his Fulham spell, it was at Ashton Gate that Cole began to show his true potential, rifling home a number of goals in his short time with Bristol City at a rate of almost a goal every two games.

However, it was when he moved on to Newcastle United in 1993 that Cole really caught the eye. Kevin Keegan signed him in February 1993 and he hit the ground running at St James's Park, scoring a goal a game as Newcastle gained promotion to the Premier League.

This form continued apace in the top flight as Cole struck up a hugely productive partnership with Peter Beardsley. The player hit 41 goals in all competitions in his first season in the Premier League, breaking the club's seasonal goal scoring record. He also won the PFA Young Player of the Year Award for 1994.

Cole started the following season well, scoring 12 goals before Christmas. It therefore came as a great surprise to supporters in both Newcastle and Manchester, when the news broke in January 1995 that the player was moving to United. He signed as part of a deal worth around £7million that also saw young winger Keith Gillespie move in the opposite direction.

The expectations on Cole were huge. His record for Newcastle was outstanding, but he was basically the focus for all of their attacks and therefore likely to make a greater impression than his colleagues. At Old Trafford, Cole's responsibilities were increased beyond just goal scoring, and there was also an emphasis on the importance of team play. It also could be said, though Newcastle fans may disagree, that Cole had to share the spotlight more at United than at Newcastle. Put simply, he was no longer his club's biggest star as the United team included players such as Keane and Cantona.

Despite the step-up, and a perception in some areas that Cole found his first half season to be a challenge, he still managed to score a very respectable 12 goals in 18 league games. This included five goals in a single match when Ipswich were defeated 9-0 as United sought to retain the League title for a third season. It should be remembered that this was all the more impressive as Eric Cantona was suspended for the latter part of the season. Ultimately though, the season was to end frustratingly for Cole as the final match ended in a 1-1 draw with West Ham handing the title to Blackburn.

In terms of statistics, Cole appeared less successful in front of goal in his first full season at Old Trafford, hitting only 14 goals in all competitions. However, he did score some significant goals including the winner against Chelsea in the FA Cup Semi Final

and a goal in the final game of the season against Middlesbrough that helped United regain the league title.

An horrific injury almost put paid to the 1996-97 season for Cole as he suffered breaks to both legs when he was on the receiving end of a terrible tackle from Neil Ruddock in a reserve game in the October. However, despite the injury and the emergence of Ole Gunnar Solskjaer as a threat to his position, Cole managed to return to full fitness and participate in 20 Premier League games.

He made up for lost time the following season though, returning to goal scoring form and enjoying the responsibility of being the senior striker following the retirement of Eric Cantona. Although the season was to end without a trophy for the club, Cole did achieve some personal success and his 25 goals in all competitions (including 2 hat-tricks in 3 games) saw Cole voted runner-up in the PFA Player of the Year awards.

1999 was a standout year for both Cole and Manchester United. Despite the increased competition for places at Old Trafford, with Dwight Yorke joining the club, Cole enjoyed considerable success. As well as scoring over 20 goals, he formed part of one of the finest forward pairings in Europe with Yorke. The partnership garnered over 50 goals and they caught the eye repeatedly with their link up play. This was most perfectly exemplified in a thrilling 3-3 draw with Barcelona at the Nou Camp.

Cole also continued to score goals at significant moments. He hit the winning goal away to Juventus to secure United's passage into the Champions League final, and also scored in the vital win on the last day of the season against Tottenham that sealed the title. The Club, of course, went on to win the Treble.

He continued to find the net and be the senior striker for United until the arrival of Ruud van Nistelrooy in 2001. The Dutchman's form and a tactical change that saw United prefer a 4-5-1 for big league games and European matches, saw the number of starting opportunities reduced for Cole. Rather than settle for being a bit part player, he opted to move away from Old Trafford and signed for Blackburn Rovers in December 2001. He enjoyed almost instant success by scoring the winning goal in the League Cup final.

Spells at Fulham and Manchester City followed, before he moved to Portsmouth in August 2006. Brief periods at Birmingham (on loan), Sunderland, Burnley (on loan), and Nottingham Forest came before retirement in November 2008.

Given the success he had at club level, it is something of a surprise that Cole did not receive more international recognition. He was only picked for England on 15 occasions in 7 years, and the first four of those caps were under four different managers. It was not until Sven Goran Eriksson took the helm in 2001, that Cole received an opportunity to have any kind of run in the team.

Perhaps managers were of the same mind-set as Glenn Hoddle who, when asked to justify his omission of Cole, claimed that the striker required six or seven chances to be able to score. However, Cole's goal record at Newcastle and United, plus his trophy haul for the Reds, proved his qualities as a striker. As does the fact that, at the time of going to press, he remains the second highest scorer in Premiership history with 187 goals. Ultimately England's loss was definitely United's gain.

Leading League Scorer in:
1997-1998 - 15 goals, 33 appearances

ATTENDANCE FACT FILE

We all know that United are English football's best attended club. Since the dawn of the Premier League the Reds have been head and shoulders above the rest, but when did United's popularity first reach a level way ahead of their rivals, and how does the Reds worst attended seasons compare?

United's top five average attendances of all time have been recorded in the five seasons since 2006. They are also the League's best ever averages. The six next best United seasonal averages all came in the period between 2000 and 2006.

Old Trafford's capacity did restrict attendances throughout the period from the early 1990s when ground redevelopments and legislation saw the capacity drop from approximately 56,300 in the mid-eighties to around 45,000 in 1995. However, before the nineties Old Trafford, like the majority of other grounds, was not sold out game after game.

Here we pinpoint the growth in the Reds support via average attendances.

First average over 10,000:   1902-03* – 11,875
(11th best in League; Best – Aston Villa 19,650)

First average over 20,000:   1906-07* – 20,725
(4th best in League; Best – Newcastle 33,650)

First average over 30,000:   1920-21 – 35,020
(6th best in League; Best – Newcastle 41,100)

First average over 40,000:   1946-47# – 43,945
(4th best in League; Best - Newcastle 49,379)

First average over 50,000:   1947-48# – 54,890
(3rd best in League; Best - Newcastle 56,283)

First average over 60,000:   2000-01 – 67,544 (Old Trafford, best in League)

First average over 70,000:   2006-07 – 75,826 (Old Trafford, best in League)

Note: * = at Bank Street, # = at Maine Road, all others at Old Trafford

Highest all-time average: 75,826 (2006-07, best in League).

Lowest all-time average: 4,650 (1901-02, 23rd best in League; Best – Aston Villa 19,175)

Alongside the incredible growth in support there have been some disappointing lows, most notably in the 1930s. The following shows the lowest ten averages since the Club reformed as United in 1902:

11,685 (1930-31, 34th best in League; Best - Arsenal 37,106)

11,875 (1902-03, 11th best in League; Best – Aston Villa 19,650)

12,325 (1914-15, 15th best in League; Best – Manchester City 21,000)

13,011 (1931-32, 30th best in League; Best – Arsenal 40,547)

13,950 (1905-06, 8th best in League; Best – Aston Villa 21,850)

15,400 (1904-05, 6th best in League; Best – Newcastle 21,250)

Looking across the Bank Street ground at the turn of the last century.

16,950 (1909-10, 9th best in League; Best – Tottenham Hotspur 27,000)

17,200 (1911-12, 11th best in League; Best – Chelsea 26,400)

17,375 (1908-09, 7th best in League; Best – Newcastle 28,400)

18,338 (1933-34, 16th best in League; Best – Arsenal 40,750)

Lowest post-war average: 33,358 (1961-62, fifth best in League;
Best – Tottenham Hotspur 45,576)

Highest pre-war average: 35,020 (1920-21, sixth best in League; Best – Newcastle 41,100)

Record lowest individual attendance: 3,507 V Southampton, 02/08/31 (at Old Trafford).
Note: this excludes all estimated attendances pre-1925.

Lowest post-war home attendance: 8,456 V Stoke City, 05/02/47 (at Maine Road)

Lowest post-war attendance at Old Trafford: 11,968 V Fulham, 29/04/50

Highest United attendance at Old Trafford: 76,098 V Blackburn Rovers, 31/03/2007

Record highest individual attendance: 83,260 V Arsenal, 17/01/48 (at Maine Road). This is
also the Football League's record crowd.

It is worth recalling that since 1994 a United home game - often all the Reds home games –
has been the seasonal highest in the League every year. Between 1925 (when attendance
figures were properly calculated) and the 1994 close season, United home games topped
the League's seasonal charts in: 1947-48, 1972-73, 1973-74, 1974-75 (in Division Two), 1975-
76, 1976-77, 1977-78, 1978-79, 1979-80, 1981-82, 1982-83, 1983-84, 1984-85, 1985-86, 1986-87,
1988-89, 1989-90, 1990-91, & 1991-92.

In 1930-31 United attracted a home crowd of 3,679 for a top flight game with Leicester
City at Old Trafford. This was the lowest Division One attendance that season and remains

Old Trafford in 1969

United's lowest top flight crowd at Old Trafford. The following season a lower crowd watched a home Division Two game with Southampton, however this was not the Second Division's worst attendance.

The highest ever attendance the Reds have played a competitive game in front of stands at 135,000 in April 1957 at Real Madrid. United have played in front of four 100,000 plus crowds in European football, excluding finals. The most recent came in 1994 when United faced Barcelona at the Nou Camp before 114,273.

Ignoring neutral venues, the highest domestic attendance for a competitive away match played by United is 78,000 for the Maine Road derby match with City on 20 September 1947. At the time of going to press, this is the thirteenth highest away attendance the Reds have played in front of (excluding neutral venues). Some incorrectly claim a lower figure of approximately 71,500 for this game, however the figure of 78,000 is the total number of spectators submitted to the Football League by City's secretary Wilf Wild in 1947. This higher figure included season ticket holders and other ticket-bearers who had been excluded from the lower figure.

The next best away attendances for domestic competitive United games stand at:

77,920 at Goodison Park, Everton V United, FA Cup 5th round, 14 February 1953

74,723 at Maine Road, City V United, FA Cup 4th round, 29 January 1955

72,077 at Goodison Park, Everton V United, Division One, 4 September 1957

70,882 at White Hart Lane, Spurs V United, 22 September 1951

70,483 at Maine Road, City V United, 28 December 1957

SPOT THE DIFFERENCE

For this edition of *The Big Book Of United* we have trawled through our archive, photograph libraries nationwide, players' collections and those of United supporters in a bid to find varied images. We're never satisfied and strive to identify varied photos wherever possible. Once in a while we discover similar – but different - images of the Reds.

Today, for your enjoyment we thought we'd share two similar photographs from 1905-06.

The images come from different collections and neither is fully dated, however it is clear that these were taken at the most a few seconds apart. Seeing this has caused us to analyse the photos looking for differences. We believe there are at least seven differences. See how many you can spot. The photos were taken from slightly different angles so that adds to the possible differences.

Our differences appear on the next page.

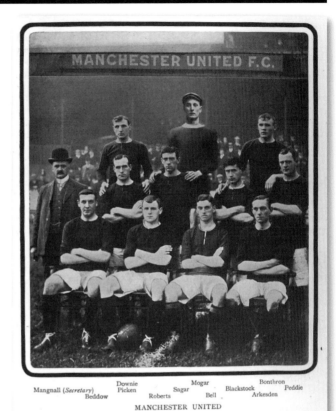

Mangnall (*Secretary*)
Beddow
Downie
Picken
Roberts
Sagar
Mogar
Bell
Blackstock
Arkesden
Bonthron
Peddie

MANCHESTER UNITED

Back Row: ALEC DOWNIE.   H. MOGER (Goalkeeper).   R. BONTHRON

E. J. Care, Manchester.
Middle Row: J. MANGNALL (Secretary).   J. PICKEN.   C. SAGAR.   T. BLACKSTOCK.   J. PEDDIE.   FRED BACON (Trainer).
Bottom Row: J. BEDDOW   C. ROBERTS.   ALEC BELL.   T. ARKESDEN.

SPOT THE DIFFERENCE
– THE ANSWERS

The differences we identified are:

Downie's right hand and arm have moved.

Moger's head seems higher in one photo (his name is also incorrectly spelt on one image)

Mangnall, Sagar and Bell all appear to be gazing directly at the camera in each photo and must therefore have changed their head angle slightly

Trainer Fred Bacon has been removed from one photo.

The Manchester United sign and stand roof has been altered to make them clearer on one photo.

There may be others, but clearly a special mention must be made of Bonthron (back row far right) who appears to have the most relaxed team picture pose of the team. His casual style seems so different to that of the players on the front row.

UNITED'S LEADING SCORERS

Our story of all the players who have topped the seasonal League goalscoring charts for the Reds through to the start of the 2011-12 season moves on to the 21st Century.

53 – DWIGHT YORKE

Born in Tobago in 1971, Dwight Yorke was first noticed, at least as far as English football was concerned, by Graham Taylor. At that time the former England boss was managing Aston Villa and had taken his side on a tour of the West Indies.

Yorke had a trial and was given a playing contract. He made his Villa debut against Crystal Palace in March 1990 and went on to establish himself as first an attacking winger and then a centre-forward for Villa. He found success in 1996 when he scored the third goal as Villa defeated Leeds 3-0 in the League Cup final.

In August 1998 Yorke's departure from Villa proved highly controversial. Some fans claimed he had made no effort in a game at Everton after asking for a transfer request. Villa had been trying to negotiate with United a player exchange with the Midlands' club hoping to sign Andy Cole, but Yorke's reported decision to move forced Villa's hand.

In the end United paid around £12.6m to Villa but fans felt it was little compensation even if the fee made him the sixth most expensive player at the time.

At United, Yorke immediately settled into the side following his debut in the goalless draw at

West Ham on 22 August 1998. That season he made 48 (plus three as substitute) appearances in all first team competition as the Reds went on to win the historic treble. He also topped the Reds' goalscoring charts – a feat he achieved again the following season when he netted 20 goals in 29 (plus three as substitute) League games as United won the title again.

2000-01 was a little difficult for the player and appearances were fewer though his goalscoring ratio remained impressive as he netted nine goals in 15 (plus seven as substitute) in the Premier League. Media stories on his private life seemed to have an effect on his playing career and, after only six (plus ten as substitute) appearances in all competitions during 2001-02 Yorke moved on.

Two years at Blackburn followed, where he played alongside Andy Cole for a while, before he moved back to the Midlands with Birmingham City. Of course, his successful period at Aston Villa was an issue for some fans, although he only actually stayed with Birmingham for one season.

In 2005-06 he joined Australian side Sydney FC and went on to help them find success in the first A-League Grand Final where they defeated Central Coast Mariners before a crowd of over 41,000. Yorke was voted the final's best player award and in many respects he was perceived through the football world as the face of the Australian League.

In 2006, after a spell training with United and a last farewell game in Australia, Yorke joined Roy Keane's Sunderland for a fee reported as £200,000 at the time. Despite rumours of a possible return to Australia the player remained with Sunderland until 2009, when he was released at the end of the season. He went on to become Trinidad and Tobago's national team assistant manager.

As an international footballer Yorke had an impressive career with his home country, and captained Trinidad and Tobago at the 2006 World Cup finals.

Despite his achievements at Villa, Sydney and for his national team, he will always be remembered by United fans for the enjoyment he demonstrated whenever he scored a goal wearing the famous red shirt.

Leading League Scorer in:
1998-1999 - 18 goals, 32 appearances
1999-2000 – 20 goals, 32 appearances

54 – TEDDY SHERINGHAM

By the time he arrived at Old Trafford in the 1997 close season, Teddy Sheringham was an established England international and a well-known Premier League footballer after first appearing in the English game's top flight with Millwall in 1988. Sheringham had been with Millwall from school and formed a great partnership with Tony Cascarino as the London side stunned the football world.

Although Millwall's period in the top flight was not to last, Sheringham's contribution to the club ensured they challenged for a return in the season that followed. During this period he became the League's highest scorer, and he broke several club goalscoring records before being sold to Nottingham Forest in July 1991.

While playing for Brian Clough, Sheringham helped Forest reach the 1992 League Cup final – where they lost to United – and he was also a member of the side that defeated Southampton 3-2 in the last Full Members' Cup Final (known by its sponsored name of the Zenith Data Systems Cup).

He started the following season, the first since football was restructured and the Premier League was formed, with Forest but moved to Tottenham for £2.1m shortly into the campaign.

It was while at White Hart Lane that Sheringham's career really blossomed and he ended the first Premier League campaign as the competition's highest goalscorer with 22 goals (including one with Forest). He topped Tottenham's goalscoring chart in 1993-94 with 14 goals from a mere 19 games after injury had restricted his opportunities.

Once fit, the player helped Tottenham finish

seventh and reach the FA Cup semi-final in 1994-95, however Spurs were unlikely to make the final push for the League at this point.

In June 1997, at the age of 31, Sheringham joined United in a reported £3.5m deal as a replacement for Eric Cantona. It was widely reported at the time that the former Spurs star had claimed the motivation for his move was to win trophies, something the media claimed was unlikely at Spurs. This, understandably, angered some Tottenham fans and whether the player was quoted accurately or not became irrelevant as they made their feelings known when he made his League debut for United at White Hart Lane. In the 60th minute of his debut he failed to score from a penalty, which delighted the home fans, but ultimately he had the last laugh as the Reds won 2-0.

As far as United fans were concerned Sheringham was, of course, unlikely to fill Cantona's boots. The Frenchman had been the difference that first finally brought the League title to Old Trafford after such a long absence and then helped the Reds appear invincible. This perhaps contributed to a first season that many saw as difficult for the player. Nevertheless he still managed to net nine goals in 28 (plus three as substitute) appearances.

Shortly into the 1998-99 season some felt Sheringham's time at United was up, especially when Dwight Yorke signed from Villa. His appearances became limited and he also had to have a knee operation in February 1999. The following March his former club Tottenham won the League Cup, prompting some London fans to talk about Sheringham's alleged desire to win honours as the reason for leaving. Once again though, Sheringham was to have the last laugh as a dramatic turn of events led to the player ending the season with the greatest honours the European game had to offer.

Sheringham ended the 1998-99 League season with seven (plus ten appearances as substitute) as United won the League. His total appearances and contribution were enough to earn a Premier League medal, but greater success was to follow.

The Reds had reached both the FA Cup final and the European Cup final, setting them up for a possible treble. The first of these finals saw Sheringham on the substitutes' bench when, after only eight minutes Roy Keane had to be replaced through injury. Sheringham came on and within two minutes he had given United the lead when he rifled a low drive under the Newcastle 'keeper.

United went on to win the FA Cup 2-0 with Sheringham heralded as the man of the match, but even this achievement was to be overshadowed four days later as the Reds faced Bayern Munich in Barcelona.

The story of the 1999 Champions League final is well known, however it is worth highlighting that United were still losing 1-0 after a sixth minute goal by Munich's Mario Basler when Sheringham came on as substitute in the 67th minute. There seemed to be no way back as Munich came close to scoring in the fifteen minutes or so that followed.

The game was reaching the end of normal time when the fourth official raised the board indicating that there were to be three minutes of added time. The Reds were preparing to take a corner at this point and, as with so many occasions during Alex Ferguson's reign, a feeling that salvation might be close at hand started to engulf United fans in the Nou Camp. Goalkeeper Peter Schmeichel moved into the Munich penalty area as David Beckham sent the corner flying towards him. The ball went slightly over Schmeichel's head before Yorke sent the ball back into the crowded area. Somehow the ball arrived at Ryan Giggs' feet whose shot then landed in front of Sheringham who sent a right foot shot into the bottom corner of the goal to make it 1-1.

Neutrals started to assume that the final would go into extra time, but within thirty seconds of the re-start United forced another corner. This time Beckham's corner was headed down by Sheringham before Solskjaer managed to send the ball into the roof of the goal to make it 2-1 to the Reds. Bayern Munich were stunned.

Shortly afterwards the whistle went and United had won their second European Cup. Sheringham had gained three medals in less than two weeks, easily eclipsing his Full Members' Cup medal with Forest, and his place in United's history was secure.

The 1999-2000 season saw him appear more for the Reds in the League and in Europe than during the treble winning season, and he earned a second Premier League medal. By this time many football pundits had started to suggest that his career had reached, or was at least nearing, its end, but the player soon confounded his critics with an amazing 2000-01 season.

Although he only managed 23 starts, plus six appearances as substitute, in the Premier League, he topped United's scoring charts with fifteen goals. He was voted the player of the year by both the PFA and the Football Writers' Association.

Despite the strength of his play the 35 year old's opportunities at United were expected to be limited during 2001-02 and, with his contract at its end, the player decided to move back to Spurs on a free transfer instead of accepting a one year United contract.

Back at Spurs Sheringham helped the club to a League Cup final appearance and a ninth placed Premier League finish, but moved on at the end of 2002-03 when he joined newly promoted Portsmouth. During his season at Fratton Park he became the oldest player to score a hat-trick in the Premier League.

Spells at West Ham, where he helped the Hammers to success in the Championship play-offs, and Colchester followed before he retired in 2008.

Sheringham enjoyed a long and ultimately very successful career. He may only have been with United for a small period of his entire playing life, but the accolades he gained while with the Reds were thoroughly deserved.

Leading League Scorer in:
2000-2001 – 15 goals, 29 appearances

55 - RUUD VAN NISTELROOY

Numerous strikers have come to Old Trafford and struggled to cope with the expectations placed upon them, or at the very least taken their time to settle in. Ruud van Nistelrooy, however, was different. He hit the ground running and went on to score an abundance of goals for United, being the first player in decades who gave the impression that there was the possibility he could score in every game he played.

However, van Nistelrooy's career with United was almost ended before it began, when he ruptured his knee ligaments in training with his club PSV Eindhoven in 2000 before his transfer could be completed. Alex Ferguson stayed in touch with van Nistelrooy throughout his rehabilitation and, after a successful recovery, Ruud made his way to Manchester in a deal worth around £19 million.

van Nistelrooy made his competitive debut in the Charity Shield against Liverpool in August 2001. Although United lost 2-1, the Dutchman did score the Reds' consolation. He also went on to score a lot more goals that season, including 23 goals in only 32 league games. When he found the back of the net with a penalty in a 2-1 victory over Blackburn on 19 January 2002, he scored for the eighth consecutive Premier League match. This set a new Premier League record, but one that van Nistelrooy himself would break at the end of the following season by scoring in ten consecutive league games.

Premier League defences were not alone in being terrorised by United's Dutchman. He was also prolific in Europe, scoring 10 goals in 14 matches and finishing as the top scorer in the Champions League in 2001-02.

As well as impressing the Old Trafford

faithful, he also impressed his peers, taking home the PFA Player of the Year award in his debut season. Previously he had also won the Dutch equivalent in 1999 and 2000.

Despite the personal success, van Nistelrooy and Manchester United finished his first season without a major trophy. However, this was to be remedied in his second season when van Nistelrooy managed to outstrip the achievements of his debut season. Overall, he managed an eye-popping 44 goals in just 52 matches, including 14 in 11 in Europe. van Nistelrooy's relentlessness helped United to overhaul an Arsenal side that had been eight points clear at the start of March, and thus he secured his only Premier League winner's medal.

van Nistelrooy had the chance to potentially scupper Arsenal's ambitions the following season in a match billed as 'The Battle

of Old Trafford'. In the dying moments of the match, the Reds were awarded a penalty and, despite missing his previous two penalties for the club, van Nistelrooy stepped up to take it. The ball was smashed against the crossbar and Arsenal escaped with a point leaving them with the advantage. Overall, the Dutchman was in sharp form in front of goal throughout the season. The FA Cup, however, provided him with his second major honour in English football as his two goals helped United to a comfortable 4-0 victory over Millwall in the final.

Injuries reduced van Nistelrooy to only 17 league appearances in 2004-5, but the following year, he started the season in blistering form, scoring an impressive ten goals in the opening 12 games. However, as the season wore on, Louis Saha's excellent form after returning from injury meant that the Dutchman was not always the first name on the team sheet. In the run-up to the League Cup final against Wigan, rumours started to filter through to the media that relations between van Nistelrooy and Sir Alex Ferguson had become strained. Although this was denied, van Nistelrooy was an unused substitute in the final and he also started the following six games on the bench. Matters reached a nadir when van Nistelrooy left Old Trafford before the last game of the season against Charlton after he learned that he was going to be on the bench.

van Nistelrooy's time at Old Trafford came to an end in the Summer of 2006 when it was announced that he would be moving to Real Madrid for 24 million euros.

Although his career at Old Trafford did not end in a manner that either the club or he would have liked, van Nistelrooy was able to leave Manchester with his head held high. In five seasons, he scored an astonishing number of goals for the United and broke a number of records, becoming the club's record goal scorer in Europe with 38 goals from 47 appearances.

After leaving United, van Nistelrooy continued to be highly successful and scored a number of goals for Madrid. He won La Liga twice and the Pichichi (top goal scorer) award before injuries took their toll. He moved on to Hamburg in January 2010 and then Malaga in June 2011.

The number of goals, and the rate that he scored them for each of his clubs coupled with his impressive strike rate of 1:2 at international level, make Ruud van Nistelrooy probably the best out-and-out goal scorer to grace Old Trafford since Denis Law.

Leading League Scorer in:
2001-2002 - 23 goals, 32 appearances
2002-2003 - 25 goals, 34 appearances
2003-2004 - 20 goals, 32 appearances
2005-2006 - 21 goals, 35 appearances

56 – WAYNE ROONEY

In October 2002, at just 16 years of age, Everton striker Rooney first grabbed the attention of the nation with a stunning last minute winning goal against Arsenal - a feat which made him the youngest goalscorer in Premier League history at the time. It also ended Arsenal's 30 match unbeaten run. The BBC Young Sports Personality of the Year followed in December, and in February 2003 he became the youngest player to be capped by England when he appeared in a friendly against Austria. Rooney broke another record when he became the youngest England goalscorer when he found the net against Macedonia during qualification for Euro 2004.

Another impressive season at Everton in 2003-04 was followed with a series of superb displays for England in Euro 2004. Interest in the player grew but Evertonians were convinced Rooney would not leave Goodison. In 2002 he had lifted his shirt to reveal a slogan: "Once a Blue, Always a Blue." Despite Rooney's sentiments, several clubs made their interest clear with Newcastle seeming likely to sign the player at one point. Then, on 31 August 2004, a deal was agreed with Everton that saw Rooney move to United for a reported fee of £27m, a world record for a teenager.

The former Evertonian was injured at the time of the move and did not make his United debut until 28 September 2004 in a Champions League match against Fenerbahçe. Ryan Giggs opened the scoring, but Rooney scored a hat-trick to ensure a great start to his United career. He memorably scored United's second as they beat the "Invincibles" of Arsenal a month later as well as the only goal in a 1-0 away win against Liverpool in January.

Rooney's first season as a Red was a personal success as he scored a total of 17 goals in all first team competitions, and formed a good understanding with his new team mates. However, United finished third in the league, 18 points behind a runaway, newly wealthy Chelsea - who won the title

with a record 95 points having spent close to £200m in a desperate bid to catch up with United and Arsenal - and six behind Arsenal, who also beat United on penalties in the FA Cup final.

Rooney's promising partnership with van Nistelrooy was disrupted in 2005-06 as the Dutchman was often dropped towards the end of the season. By the end of the campaign, Rooney had developed a promising relationship on the field with Ronaldo, and bagged 19 goals in all competitions including two in the 4-0 League Cup final win over Wigan. He produced a man of the match performance in that final.

In the league, United had improved but needed to beat Chelsea at Stamford Bridge in late April to have any chance of regaining the title. United lost 3-0 and with just minutes remaining, Rooney sustained

a broken metatarsal after a Paulo Ferreira tackle. This put his involvement in that year's World Cup in doubt and the news became one of the major talking points of the early summer. Rooney collected a second successive PFA Young Player of the Year award while his foot was still in plaster.

Following treatment, including a spell in an oxygen tent, Rooney travelled with the England squad and recovered sufficiently in time to feature in the second match of the World Cup tournament. England made it to the quarter finals where they met Cristiano Ronaldo's Portugal. Following a tackle on Ricardo Carvalho, Rooney was red carded by referee Horacio Elizondo while Ronaldo appeared to be encouraging the referee to send his United team mate off. Further controversy arose when Ronaldo was caught on camera appearing to wink at his manager in the dugout following Rooney's dismissal. Much was made in the media of the incident with many newspapers alleging that there had been an irreparable breakdown in the relationship between the two, and predicting the imminent sale of Ronaldo to Real Madrid.

Despite the furore, the first day of the 2006-07 season saw both Rooney and Ronaldo start against Fulham. Within 20 minutes, United were 4-0 up and the pair had combined for the fourth - Rooney with a perfect cross for Ronaldo to head home. As Rooney scored United's fifth goal, it was apparent that the World Cup incident was not an issue.

Ruud van Nistelrooy's transfer to Madrid had meant that Rooney forged a strike partnership predominantly with Luis Saha, who enjoyed his best season at United, and a rejuvenated Ole Gunnar Solskjaer. Unfortunately, the England international was suspended early in the season after he had received a red card in a tournament in Amsterdam. An appeal had been lodged, citing the example of two Liverpool players who had escaped a domestic ban after they were dismissed in the same tournament three years earlier, but it was unsuccessful.

Rooney's hat-trick at Bolton in October 2006, four days after his 21st birthday, brought to end an eight League game goal drought, and it wasn't until the turn of the year that he started to score regularly again. This coincided with United's best run of form in the League for years as the Reds also pushed on in the FA Cup and Champions League.

April 2007 was memorable as Rooney scored a brace against Watford in the FA Cup semi-final victory at Villa Park, four days after scoring in the 7-1 Champions League quarter-final demolition of Roma.

In the Champions League semi-final first leg he scored another two goals as United came from behind to beat AC Milan, and four days after that he slotted home United's third as they came from 2-0 down to beat Everton 4-2 in a crucial Premier League fixture.

Though United were knocked out of the Champions League in the return leg in Milan on 2 May, they returned to Manchester and took on City at Eastlands three days later. A 1-0 win followed by Chelsea's draw the next day at Arsenal, handed United their 16th top flight title. Chelsea had their revenge at Wembley in the FA Cup final when neither Rooney or his team mates could find the net. Didier Drogba's injury time winner was enough for the London blues. At the time of writing, the FA Cup remains the only major domestic trophy Rooney has not won.

By the end of the 2006-07 season it was clear that United were no longer missing van Nistelrooy. The Reds had scored 83 goals in the league alone, their best tally for five years.

Argentinian striker Carlos Tevez was added to United's ranks in the summer of 2007 as Solskjaer retired and Saha struggled with injuries once more. After a month out due to an injury sustained in the opening fixture against Reading, Rooney struck up an explosive partnership with the Argentine, silencing pundits who had doubted that they could combine well due to their perceived similarities. They combined to produce one of the goals of the season against Middlesbrough - Tevez flicking the ball over a defender to Rooney who controlled the ball inside the box and back heeled it into the on-rushing Argentine's path to finish past Mark Schwarzer.

Rooney's season looked like it was in danger of ending prematurely when he suffered an injury in the crunch game at Chelsea in late April, causing him to miss the Champions League semi-final second leg against Barcelona. He returned in time for the final League match of the season at Wigan and started the Champions League final in Moscow. The 2007-08 season was one of the most successful in the club's history and the short-lived triumvirate of Rooney, Tevez and Ronaldo produced 79 goals as United sealed the Premier League and Champions League double.

The following season saw yet more competition up front as Dimitar Berbatov was added to the squad and, with Ronaldo still in scintillating form in front of goal, Rooney was occasionally deployed wide on the left in order to accommodate as many of United's attacking players as possible. The first silverware of the season was collected by United when Rooney scored the only goal in the FIFA Club World Cup final against LDU Quito in Japan.

It was not until the new year, however, that Rooney started to score regularly and he chipped in with vital goals against the likes of Chelsea, Wigan, Newcastle and Blackburn. Following a defeat to Liverpool and with United losing 2-0 at Fulham, Rooney was dismissed for apparently kicking away the ball with only two minutes to go. This caused him to miss the vital League game against Aston Villa on 5 April 2009. Fortunately, 17-year-old Federico Macheda made sure he was not missed when he scored an injury time goal to ensure a 3-2 victory.

Rooney returned to action two days later to help steer United through to the Champions League semi-finals with a goal against Porto in the first leg. Eighteen days later he was instrumental as United came back from 2-0 down against Spurs to win 5-2, scoring two goals and setting up two. Those goals were to be his last of the season as he was unable to find the net in the next seven games, including the Champions League final against Barcelona. Despite this he did collect another Premier League championship medal as the Reds proved the dominant force domestically.

Following the sale of Cristiano Ronaldo to Real Madrid and Carlos Tevez's move to Manchester City, Rooney found himself under more pressure to produce goals and to play as a more traditional forward. Bolstered by the addition of Antonio Valencia to United's number, Rooney found himself less of a creator of goals and more of a goalscorer.

He opened his account against Chelsea in the Community Shield in August 2009 and scored frequently and consistently, from

then on. Previously his United career had been marked by prolonged dry patches in front of goal, but in 2009-10 he seemed to be consistently productive in front of goal.

Rooney scored the winner against Birmingham in the Premier League opener that season; scored a brace against Wigan; netted in wins against Arsenal and Spurs; and opened the scoring in the 4-3 thriller against City. He bagged a hat trick against Portsmouth and scored four against Hull, wonderfully assisted by a resurgent Nani. Four days later he hit an injury time winner past City in the second leg of the League Cup semi-final and another four days later scored as United put on a footballing masterclass at Arsenal, winning 3-1 on 31 January 2010.

The former Evertonian also scored two goals at the San Siro as the Reds beat AC Milan in the last 16 of the Champions League. He repeated the feat in the return leg, United winning 4-0 at Old Trafford, just three days after Rooney headed the winner at Wembley in the League Cup final against Aston Villa. Another brace came against Fulham in March, and Rooney made up for missing a penalty against Liverpool that month by slotting home the rebound as United kept pace with Chelsea at the top of the Premier League table.

When United travelled to face Bayern Munich in the Champions League quarter finals, Rooney opened the scoring after just two minutes but, as the match drew to a close, he sustained an ankle injury tackling Mario Gomez. Almost simultaneously, United conceded a sloppy goal.

Rooney left the Allianz Arena on crutches and it was feared that his season was over. The player was unavailable when United faced Chelsea in a potential title decider at Old Trafford on 3 April. The London side won 2-1 courtesy of a Didier Drogba goal that almost everyone was convinced was offside. Perhaps understandably, Rooney was rushed back into action four days later for the second leg against Bayern. Visibly uncomfortable and lacking his usual pace, the Bayern players targeted Rooney. To add insult to injury, United crashed out on away goals.

Four days later he missed the game against Blackburn and United's available strikers were unable to break the deadlock. The game ended 0-0, ultimately proving costly to United's drive to win a fourth consecutive title. Rooney played on 17 April as United beat City in injury time for the third time that season, but he missed the next match as the Reds defeated Spurs 3-1. He was deemed fit enough to start the last two games of the season – both victories - as United finished the League campaign in second place, just a point behind Chelsea.

Despite the continuing problem with his ankle injury and the fact that he had not scored since March, Rooney was once again highlighted in the media as England's great hope for winning the 2010 World Cup. The campaign was disastrous in all aspects. Rooney failed to score, but he wasn't the only one. After a series of poor team performances, England were eliminated in the second round by Germany. The player made some comments, picked up live on television as he left the field, criticising England fans. Inevitably, there was a media backlash.

It was hoped that Rooney could put these issues behind him as 2010-11 kicked off, but his form suffered. A penalty against West Ham was a bright moment, but there was significant criticism at times. According to the media, the player appeared to disagree with his manager about the condition of his ankle, and Rooney was dropped to the bench or rested entirely on several occasions. The alleged dispute appeared to escalate when in October, before United's game against Bursaspor, Ferguson revealed that Rooney had asked to leave the club. The player then released a statement claiming that his position was not due to any disagreement with the management, but because of a perceived lack of ambition at the club. It was an astounding comment and fuelled much debate about the state

of the game when a leading player at the most successful club of the modern era could suggest his side lacked ambition. Protests outside Rooney's house and graffiti threatening his life appeared in the city centre when it was suggested the player was about to sign for rivals City.

In the middle of the protests, it was felt that Rooney had played his last game for United. Then he signed a new contract with United, before being sent to Nike's facility in America to regain form and fitness. He returned to action in late November, coming on as a substitute against Wigan. The reception from supporters was mixed, and it was clear he had a lot of work to do to regain the trust and support of many Reds.

Rooney's road to redemption began when he scored a penalty as United beat Rangers in the next Champions League match on 24 November 2010. His goal against West Bromwich Albion on New Year's Day was his first from open play in over nine months.

His form gradually improved, and he took a step back into the hearts of United fans when he scored the goal of the season with a stunning overhead kick to give the Reds a 2-1 win over City in the League. Further goals followed against Wigan and Chelsea before another against Arsenal set up the Reds for the first all-Manchester FA Cup semi-final since 1926. The first ended in a City victory at Bramall Lane, this time the game would be staged at Wembley. However, as he secured his hat trick in another thrilling comeback against West Ham on 2 April 2011, he celebrated by swearing in what was perceived as an abusive manner directly into a television camera.

Despite a written apology, Rooney was handed a two match ban, which the club appealed against without success, causing the player to miss the semi-final. His absence was felt as United were defeated 1-0 by City, the eventual FA Cup winners.

Rooney was free to appear in the Champions League quarter final against

Chelsea, and he scored the only goal of the first leg as United won at Stamford Bridge for the first time in nine years. He also scored in the away leg of the Champions League semi-final at Gelsenkirchen as United defeated Schalke 6-1 on aggregate, setting up another final against Barcelona. This time the two European giants would meet at Wembley.

Domestically, after having beat nearest rivals Chelsea 2-1 in May, United needed just one point from their last two games. After 70 minutes of a tense and nervy United performance at Blackburn, Mexican striker Javier Hernandez was brought down in the box by Rovers' keeper Paul Robinson. It fell to Rooney to calmly put away the penalty that sealed a record 19 league titles for United. Two weeks later, despite scoring a great goal in the Champions League final to take the score into half time level at 1-1, United were overcome by an astonishingly brilliant Barcelona.

Although he has often fallen foul of the authorities and occasionally upset supporters, Rooney remains one of the most significant players in United's modern history.

Leading League Scorer in:
2004-2005 - 11 goals, 29 appearances
2009-2010 - 26 goals, 32 appearances

GOLDEN GOALS

Ryan Giggs **1994 v QPR**

The idea of this 'GOLDEN GOALS' feature is to remember a significant or spectacular goal.
The Big Book Of United's hope is that modern day supporters learn more about some of
these goals. The goal featured here is our second Ryan Giggs effort. It was scored in a
game at Queens Park Rangers in February 1994.

MATCH STATS

Date: 5 February 1994

Score: QPR 2 United 3

Scorers: Andrei Kanchelskis (18th minute), Clive Wilson (44th minute penalty), Eric Cantona (45th minute), Ryan Giggs (59th minute) & Les Ferdinand (65th minute)

Attendance: 21,267

Referee: G. Poll

United Team: Schmeichel, Parker, Irwin, Bruce, Kanchelskis, Pallister, Cantona, Ince, Keane, Hughes, Giggs.

PRE-MATCH

The Reds were challenging on three fronts by the time this match was played and had already progressed to the fifth round of the FA Cup (where they would face Wimbledon) and the semi-final of the League Cup (against Sheffield Wednesday). United were also looking to retain the League title and were undefeated in the previous twenty League matches. In fact they had only lost one League game all season (at Chelsea on 11 September). However, Loftus Road was not the easiest of grounds to perform at and QPR had ended the previous season fifth.

THE GAME

Although United had deservedly taken the lead through Kanchelskis in the 18th minute, QPR had fought back with a penalty scored by Mancunian Clive Wilson shortly before the break. Cantona made it 2-1 shortly afterwards, but with almost an hour gone the match remained fairly tight. United were the dominant force, but Gerry Francis' QPR side remained a threat.

As the game neared the hour mark Giggs scored the goal that some regard as his finest ever – yet as this book shows there are several other contenders. The twenty year old Welshman seized a loose ball from former Red Ray Wilkins inside the QPR half and then proceeded to work his way forward. As he did so he dodged a lunge from Darren Peacock, and with great balance and poise he strutted past three other Rangers men. The run was impressive and was finished off with an exquisite shot into the bottom right hand corner of the net from slightly inside the penalty area. Goalkeeper Jan Stejskal stood no chance.

As Giggs headed towards the stand to celebrate the QPR penalty box seemed full of exasperated defenders left struggling to compete with the United star's play. After receiving the congratulations of his teammates Giggs performed with Paul Ince the memorable goal celebration they had perfected - they held out their hands in front of themselves and moved backwards as they started to crouch (watch a DVD or video of the celebration to fully appreciate it!).

Despite taking a 3-1 lead the match was far from over and Les Ferdinand made it 3-2 with 25 minutes remaining. Ultimately though United gained the three points they needed to stress their superiority.

POST MATCH

Immediately after the match Journalists and others in the media claimed Giggs was the new George Best – for years they had tried to compare modern day stars with the legendary Irishman – and the goal became one of the most talked about of the year. It was certainly viewed as the goal of the season and as Giggs' career developed some continued to claim this as his greatest ever goal.

For United, the goal proved to be an important one as they pushed for the title. Victories in the following League and cup games gave the impression that a historic treble was possible, but then defeat in the League Cup final to Aston Villa killed off that hope. In the end United did become only the sixth side in history to achieve the historic League and FA Cup double (Preston, Aston Villa, Tottenham, Arsenal and Liverpool had preceded them). An amazing feat in its own right.

The Reds had won the League on 92 points, eight more than nearest rivals Blackburn and 15 more than third placed Newcastle.

The Football Season Daily Reminder

April

1st April 1972

Best, Charlton and Storey-Moore helped United beat Crystal Palace by the odd goal in five.

2nd April 1898

Newton Heath won 3-1 at Grimsby Town despite the home side being on top for most of the game and having three penalties awarded to them. Two of the spot kicks were saved by goalkeeper Frank Barrett who had an outstanding match.

3rd April 1983

Goalkeeper Ben Foster was born at Leamington Spa.

4th April 1979

A 78th minute Jimmy Greenhoff header brought the only goal of the Liverpool-United FA Cup semi-final replay at Goodison Park.

5th April 1980

United defeated Liverpool 2-1 at Old Trafford. This was a crucial game in the title race, however Liverpool did go on to win the title by two points with United second.

6th April 1907

The first Division One Manchester derby staged at Bank Street ended in a 1-1 draw before a crowd of around 40,000. Fans were so keen to see the match that some took to the roof for a better view.

7th April 1956

Fans celebrate (above) as United's 2-1 victory over Blackpool brought the 1955-56 League title to Old Trafford. Attendance 62,277.

8th April 1990

United and Oldham drew 3-3 in the FA Cup semi-final at Maine Road in front of 44,026.

Salford Quays TOYOTA

9th April 1963

Charlton and Stiles helped United win 2-1 at Joe Mercer's Aston Villa.

10th April 1925

Two goals from Pape gave the Reds a much needed 2-0 victory over Stockport County. United had lost 1-0 at Derby the previous week and needed to ensure their promotion challenge was brought back to life. The County game was the first of seven unbeaten games that assured the Reds promotion in second place from Division Two.

11th April 1990

Alex Ferguson's United defeated Joe Royle's Oldham 2-1 after extra-time in the FA Cup semi-final replay at Maine Road. The game was watched by a surprisingly small crowd of 35,005 – the first game had attracted around 9,000 more.

12th April 1980

An Andy Ritchie hat trick helped United to a 4-1 victory over Tottenham in Division One.

13th April 1985

The FA Cup semi-final ended in a 2-2 draw after extra time at Goodison Park between United and Liverpool.

14th April 2007

The Reds won the FA Cup semi-final at Villa Park. The game ended in a 4-1 victory over Watford with goals from Rooney (2), Ronaldo and Richardson. The following day Old Trafford staged the Chelsea-Blackburn semi.

15th April 1978

Norwich City were

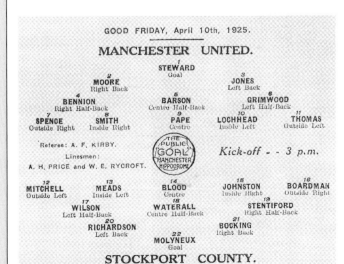

GOOD FRIDAY, April 10th, 1925.

MANCHESTER UNITED.

1
STEWARD
Goal

2   3
MOORE   JONES
Right Back   Left Back

4   5   6
BENNION   BARSON   GRIMWOOD
Right Half-Back Centre Half-Back   Left Half-Back

7   8   9   10   11
SPENCE   SMITH   PAPE   LOCHHEAD   THOMAS
Outside Right Inside Right   Centre   Inside Left   Outside Left

Referee: A. F. KIRBY.

Linesmen:
A. H. PRICE and W. E. RYCROFT.

THE PUBLIC GOAL MANCHESTER HIPPODROME

Kick-off - - 3 p.m.

12   13   14   15   16
MITCHELL   MEADS   BLOOD   JOHNSTON   BOARDMAN
Outside Left   Inside Left   Centre   Inside Right   Outside Right

17   18   19
WILSON   WATERALL   STENTIFORD
Left Half-Back   Centre Half-Back   Right Half-Back

20   21
RICHARDSON   BOCKING
Left Back   Right Back

22
MOLYNEUX
Goal

STOCKPORT COUNTY.

defeated 3-1 at Carrow Road with goals from Coppell, Jordan and McIlroy.

16th April 2011

United and City met in the first all-Manchester FA Cup semi-final for 85 years. It was the first time the two sides had faced each other at Wembley Stadium. Four months later they were to meet there again in the Community Shield.

17th April 1985

The Liverpool-United FA Cup semi-final replay ended 2-1 to United. Liverpool had taken the lead with a 39th minute headed own goal from Paul McGrath, before Robson (47) and Hughes (58) ensured victory.

18th April 1981

West Bromwich Albion were defeated 2-1 at Old Trafford in front of 44,442.

19th April 1947

Goals from Pearson (2), Rowley and an own goal from Higgins ensured a 4-0 victory over Blackburn. It was an important victory as United challenged for the League title. Ultimately, they ended the first post war League campaign second to Liverpool.

20th April 2002

Third placed United defeated fifth placed Chelsea 3-0 at Stamford Bridge.

21st April 2007

Despite a third minute goal from Kieran Richardson – the second League goal of his United career – the eventual League champions could only manage a 1-1 draw at home to Middlesbrough.

22nd April 1961

Two goals each from Charlton and Setters brought a 4-2 victory over Preston North End.

23rd April 2008

United and Barcelona played a goalless match in the first leg of the Champions League semi-final. Six days later a 14th minute Scholes goal gave the Reds a 1-0 victory before an Old Trafford crowd of 75,061. The first leg was watched by 95,949. On the same date in 1977 Steve Coppell and Jimmy Greenhoff scored in the 2-1 defeat of Leeds in the FA Cup semi-final (below).

24th April 1937

United were relegated after a frustrating 1-0 defeat at West Bromwich Albion. The most interesting aspect of the game was the Daily Express's match report which started: "This was a hard game – hard to sit through. I'd have gone home long before the end if it hadn't been my duty to stay. Lots of spectators

1912-13

THE LAST TURN.

THE OLDHAM ATHLETE: "And now Ladies and Gentlemen, before the curtain drops, I will conclude my performance by extracting a couple of league points from this ball of cotton."

started in 1938 when he signed as an amateur until the mid-fifties. He later became a member of the coaching staff while his son won the League title with United in 1967. Well known Manchester journalist Henry Rose commented at the time of Aston senior's testimonial: "Johnny Aston was a wonderful player, a great clubman, one who always put team before self – a glowing example to the young up and coming player."

26th April 1913

United ended the season fourth after a goalless game at Boundary Park gave their opponents a ninth placed finish on the last day of the Division One season.

27th April 1963

A solitary goal from Denis Law (22nd minute) was enough to send United through to their fifth FA Cup final. The Reds beat

melted away. Both teams were supposed to be fighting for safety-first points. But I've seen more fights in a schoolboy's game on a village green."

25th April 1956

An 'All Star XI' played United in a testimonial for John Aston senior. Aston had made 282 League and Cup appearances for the Reds during a career that

MANCHESTER UNTD 1
(Law)
SOUTHAMPTON 0
(at Villa Park)

Here's United goalie DAVE GASKELL dealing with a high ball during the semi-final tie against Southampton at Villa Park. A solitary goal by DENIS LAW was enough to see United through to Wembley

Moger on ground after making a Cup Final save, 24 April 1909.

Southampton at Villa Park in the semi-final.

28th April 1945

A hat trick from Billy Wrigglesworth ensured a 3-1 victory over Doncaster Rovers in the second leg of the Northern War League Cup quarter-final. The match was watched by 31,728.

29th April 2009

United defeated Arsenal 1-0 in the first leg of the Champions League semi-

final before 74,733 at Old Trafford. John O'Shea (below) was the scorer. The Reds went on to win the tie 4-1 on aggregate.

30th April 1983

Former West Bromwich Albion star Laurie Cunningham made his full United debut in the 1-1 draw at Norwich. He had already made two substitute appearances

(scoring in the 2-0 win over Watford on 23rd April). Cunningham was trying to resurrect his Football League career and joined his former boss Ron Atkinson on loan from Real Madrid. Ultimately, he only managed 3 (plus two substitute) appearances for the Reds. Sadly, on 15th July 1989 he died in a car crash at Madrid.

26 April 1952 - United 6 Arsenal 1 clinches the title.

BASKETBALL

In October 2009 the Financial Times reported that the British Basketball Association, set up in 2007, was targeting American owners of British football clubs, in particular the Glazer family, with the aim of creating a new basketball league of eight sides to commence in November 2010. That date was later revised to November 2012. Despite the reports it seemed unlikely that a Manchester United side would appear in the new league however.

The Reds have, of course, already had their own basketball side. In 1985 United took over the Manchester Giants and the club was renamed Manchester United. Some Giants fans then set up Stockport Giants, but it is fair to say that the new name did bring added benefits to the original club and the sport.

Under the United name the side briefly flourished, winning the National League title in 1986. Plans were made to build an 8,000 capacity venue on car parking at Old Trafford and the

future looked bright for a while. However the optimism did not last and United pulled the plug on the venture in 1988. The franchise was sold, and the club was remodelled as Manchester Eagles.

In 1990 the side merged with the Stockport Giants and, as Manchester Giants once more, the club eventually moved to the MEN Arena. While there they attracted 14,251 fans to a game with London Leopards – a British record. Many high points followed, however the end of the nineties saw the club struggle. The team was disbanded during the 2001-02 season while playing at the Velodrome, next to United's former Bank Street ground.

The Manchester Cup. This was the competition that established Newton Heath's name and reputation during the 1880s.

HEATHEN QUOTES

Before Manchester United became world renowned the Club was very much a small team based in east Manchester. The Club developed and joined an enlarged League in 1892. A decade later they reformed as Manchester United. The following snippets give an indication of the way the Club was reported in the press during the 19th Century.

"The annual athletic festival in connection with the Lancashire & Yorkshire Railway Cricket & Football Club, Newton Heath, was commenced on Saturday on the Club Cinder Path, North Road, before an assembling of about 3,000 spectators."

The Manchester Courier, 22nd August 1887 talking of the Club's annual athletic festival. The piece went on to mention football: "A football contest, under Association rules, six a side, was won by W. Tait's team (Newton Heath L&YR)."

***

"Newton Heath, after beating Accrington the week before, went down before Bell's Temperance on Saturday. Oh, what a fall it was there! People are asking what Newton Heath are doing in the Lancashire Junior Competition. Surely Powell's smart lot are not hard up for a cup."

The Gorton Reporter, 17th September 1887 after the Heathens had been defeated in the Lancashire Junior Cup 2-1 on 10th September 1887. At that time it was felt the Heathens should have been above competing for that cup.

***

NEWTON HEATH L.Y.R.
Cricket and Football Club

FIXTURES for Season 1888-89

President:
F. ATTOCK, Esq.

Vice=Presidents:
The Hon. A. J. BALFOUR, M.P.
The Hon. C. E. SCHWANN, M.P.
Sir JAMES FERGUSSON, Bart., M.P.
C. R. Creswell, Esq.   W. H. Rothwell, Esq.
J. Grimshaw, Esq.   H. G. Sadler, Esq.
J. Taylor, Esq., J.P.   I. Hilton, Esq.
C. P. Scott, Esq., J.P.   W. Torkington, Esq.
G. Turton, Esq.   Alderman W. Brown.
W. S Laycock, Esq.   Councillor Payne, &c.

Treasurer: Mr. J. HANDLEY.

Financial Secretary:
Mr. GEORGE FARROW, 637, Oldham Road, Newton Heath.

Corresponding Secretary:
Mr. T. SADLER, 7, Marsden Street, Newton Heath.

Committee:
Mr. J. Panter.   Mr. T. Rigby.
Mr. T. Jackson.   Mr. J. Whitehead.
          Mr. J. B. Dodd.

Captain (1st Team): Mr. JOHN POWELL.
Captain "Swifts": Mr. JOHN EARP.
Club House: SHEARS HOTEL.

No. 13.— THE NEWTON HEATH TEAM.

"There was a lot of shouting over at Newton Heath last Saturday when five thousand spectators assembled on the North Road venue to see the tussle between these old time rivals Newton Heath and Ten Acres."

The Gorton Reporter, 17th November 1887 reporting on the size of the crowd watching the derby between two sides from Newton Heath. Ten Acres were one of the Club's main rivals during its formative years. In 2010 FC United revealed that they were planning a stadium at Ten Acres Lane, Newton Heath, however the plan ultimately did not receive the appropriate backing.

***

"The second half was also all in favour of the Newton Heath men, as they were constantly pressing and goals were scored by J Davies, J Doughty (3), R Doughty and another. Newton Heath winning a very one sided game. The cup was presented to Powell by Mrs Colbeck."

The Umpire, 29th April 1888 reporting Newton Heath's easy 7-1 victory over Denton in the Manchester Cup final at Whalley Range.

"Newton Heath played a very stubborn game at Burnley and for a considerable time appeared to possess a fine chance of winning, especially when they scored the first goal, but afterwards the other fellows 'weighed in' and put on four, winning by four to one. Burnley have thus captured three points out of Newton Heath who, like Notts Forest, are finding it more difficult to beat League teams than those of last year's Alliance."

The Gorton Reporter, 24th September 1892 after the Heathens had succumbed to a 4-1 defeat at Burnley in only their third League game.

"Newton Heath fairly came out of their shell and notched their initial win in the League Tourney with no uncertain notch. Considering their League position in the League table – having played seven games without a single win – they found it necessary to alter their team somewhat. The 'Wolves' came short-handed being minus Rose, Topham, Wykes, Baker and Johnson. The result of the numerous changes in both teams is seen with the score of ten goals to one in favour of the Mancunians.

"The Heathens surprised themselves by scoring goal number one in thirty seconds and at half time led by 6-1, and to the great and unmistakeable delight of their partizans, they popped goal after goal through the disorganised defence, until the score reached double figures and, for once in a way, Manchester is happy out Newton Heath way. On this form matters are looking up at Cottonopolis, and we may next expect to hear of Manchester team 'a winning of The Cup'."

The Gorton Reporter, 22nd October 1892 after Newton Heath won their first League game. The score was an incredible 10-1 over Wolverhampton Wanderers.

***

"Bravo Newton Heath. They are springing themselves. After performing so well against the 'Wolves' they go to the Olive Grove where it took Sheffield Wednesday all their time to get the best of them."

The Gorton Reporter, 29th October 1892 after Newton Heath lost 1-0 at Sheffield Wednesday on 22nd October 1892. Despite the defeat this was viewed as a creditable result.

***

"Bob Donaldson used to wait in the goalmouth for free kicks to fall over his head. Then he went in and anything in the way had to go down."

Heathens' star Fred Erentz talking in 1922 about his playing colleague Bob Donaldson (right). Donaldson was known for a physical method of scoring during the Club's earliest League seasons (the rule about charging a goalkeeper didn't come in until 1894 and many strikers used a 'barging' technique).

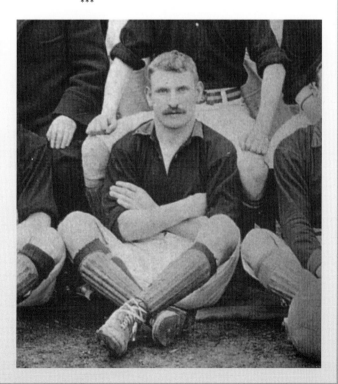

UNITED'S LEADING SCORERS

Our story of all the players who have topped the seasonal League goalscoring charts for the Reds finally reaches the end of 2010-11 season.

THE PROFILES
(PART NINE)

57 – CRISTIANO RONALDO

The legend goes that having been so impressed with Cristiano Ronaldo's performance against United as they took on Sporting Lisbon in a friendly, the players begged Alex Ferguson to sign him. The truth appears to be slightly different. United were already interested in the 18 year old and so were other English clubs. In fact, Liverpool had been very keen. So much so that the Merseysiders' then-assistant manager Phil Thompson was aghast when United announced the £12.24m acquisition of the tricky Portuguese winger as he was sure that Liverpool had an option on a £4m deal for him.

Ronaldo made an impressive debut as a substitute against Bolton Wanderers on 16 August 2003 as United won 4-0. He scored his first goal against Portsmouth in a 3-0 home win the following November. He was also a key figure when United faced City in the fifth round of the FA Cup. That day he set up van Nistelrooy for United's second and scored the third three minutes later with the match ending 4-2.

After beating Fulham and Arsenal in the competition, United took on an unfancied Milwall in the final at Cardiff's Millennium Stadium. Ronaldo had a shot cleared off the line before Gary Neville supplied a deft chip for the Portuguese to head home the opener. The Reds went on to win 3-0, claiming an eleventh FA Cup, and the player had been a key contributor during the season, although he had only made 24 starts and 15 substitute appearances during the campaign.

Ronaldo became more established within the starting XI during the 2004-05 season, starting 40 games and scoring nine, most notably the brace in a 4-2 away victory over Arsenal in February 2005. He scored one and set up the other in the 2-0 FA cup fifth round win at Everton eighteen days later, scored against Fulham in the quarter final, and turned in a man of the match performance against Newcastle in the semi-final. The defeat in the final against Arsenal on penalties meant that United ended the season trophyless for the only season while Ronaldo was at the Club.

After a quiet start to 2005-06, a sublime display against Bolton at the turn of the year kick started Ronaldo's season. He scored two against Fulham in a 4-2 League win on 4 February and bagged another couple against as United beat Portsmouth a week later. By the end of the season he had notched a dozen goals including one as United beat Wigan to win the League Cup for the first time.

Ronaldo was part of Portugal's 2006 World Cup squad as they progressed to the quarter finals where they met an England side featuring Wayne Rooney. Following a tackle on Ricardo Carvalho, Rooney was red carded by the referee while Ronaldo appeared to be encouraging the referee to send his United team mate off. Further controversy arose when Ronaldo appeared to wink at his manager in the dugout following Rooney's dismissal.

Despite the expectation of animosity, the two forwards struck up a thrilling partnership back in Manchester. They demolished Fulham in the first game of the 2006-07 season, and Ronaldo produced the best form of his United career so far. He almost doubled his goal tally of the previous season as United swept to the top of the table, into the Champions League

semi-final and booked a place in the first FA Cup final to be staged at the rebuilt Wembley. The potential that had been seen in him in previous seasons was realised, and the glimpses of individual skill turned into moments of genius. The previous criticism that he could be something of a show-pony with little end product was all but forgotten as he demonstrated an ability to change a game in United's favour almost single handedly - the 88th minute winner against Fulham in February being a particularly memorable example.

It was Ronaldo who coolly slotted home the penalty at Eastlands that ultimately sealed the title for United with a 1-0 victory over City. In addition to his Premier League medal, he received the PFA Young Player and Players' Player of the Year awards, and was voted player of the year by United fans.

2007-08 started ominously. After a goalless home draw against Reading, United travelled to Portsmouth where they dropped another two points and Ronaldo was sent off after clashing with Richard Hughes. A three match ban meant he missed the Manchester derby, which United lost 1-0.

Ronaldo returned to score winning goals away against his former club Sporting in the Champions League during September, and Birmingham in the Premier League. It was a knack he was able to reproduce consistently throughout the season, his goals won games against Kiev, Blackburn, Fulham, Everton and Sporting (again) in the weeks that followed. However, after putting the Reds 1-0 up, Ronaldo missed a penalty at West Ham in late December and the Irons came back to win 2-1, leaving United trailing Arsenal by two points at the turn of the year.

In January, he scored his first United hat trick in a 6-0 win against Newcastle, taking his tally to 22 goals in all competitions. Yet another Ronaldo goal was enough to defeat Olympique Lyonnais as the Reds progressed to the quarter finals of the Champions League. Sadly, he was unable to score against Portsmouth in the FA Cup quarter

final as they lost to Pompey and missed out on a chance of a second treble, but he did manage to do so in each of his next seven matches. Crucial goals were scored against Derby, Bolton and Middlesbrough before Ronaldo scored his 38th goal of the season from the penalty spot in a 2-1 victory that ended the Gunners' title challenge with United needing two wins for the title.

Against Barcelona in the Champions League semi-final first leg on 23 April United were awarded a penalty for handball seconds into the tie. Ronaldo stepped up but sent the ball high and wide, leaving United wondering whether they would live to regret not having taken that opportunity as the game ended goalless. In the return leg however, Ronaldo set up Paul Scholes to score the game's solitary goal sending United to an all English final against Chelsea.

In the Premier League, Ronaldo's three goals in the last two games secured the title with United finishing 2 points clear of Chelsea. By this stage he had scored 41 in all competitions. He bagged his 42nd in the Champions League final as Wes Brown delivered a pinpoint cross for the Portuguese to head past Petr Cech to put United 1-0 up. After Frank Lampard equalised for Chelsea, the game went to extra time and, with neither team able to take advantage, it came down to a penalty shootout to decide the winners.

Ronaldo had developed a style of taking penalties that involved a stuttering run up, presumably so he could trick the keeper into committing early. However, on this occasion, it failed spectacularly. Cech remained rooted firmly to his spot and with no run up, Ronaldo took a weak kick that the Chelsea keeper saved with ease. United were on the brink of defeat when John Terry slipped as he took what could have been Chelsea's final kick. Ronaldo was reprieved as Edwin van der Sar saved from Nicolas Anelka to win the final for United.

The build-up to the Champions League final in Moscow was marked by the rumours of Ronaldo's imminent switch to Real Madrid, and despite his goal in United's third European Cup triumph, it was the transfer saga that was the talk of the summer. Ultimately, he was convinced by his manager and team mates to stay for another season.

The start of the 2008-09 season was disrupted by an ankle injury which had necessitated an operation, but on his return, Ronaldo was soon back on form. Important goals were scored against Bolton, West Ham, Everton and Blackburn as United battled a resurgent Liverpool in the Premier League. The Portuguese won the Ballon d'Or and was voted FIFA world player of the year becoming the first United player to hold that title.

He helped the Reds to victory in the Club World Cup and collected his second League Cup as the Reds saw off Tottenham at Wembley. In Europe, United looked like becoming the first team to successfully defend the Champions League title as Ronaldo produced imperious performances against Inter, Porto and Arsenal as they progressed to the final against Barcelona. The domestic title was settled in United's favour after a draw with Arsenal, the Reds winning a record equalling 18th League championship.

The 2-0 defeat to Barcelona in Rome on 27 May 2009 was to be Ronaldo's final game for United. Little over a month later it was announced that he was to join Real Madrid for the record sum of £80m. An absolutely astounding amount and one the Reds could hardly turn down.

In 2010-11 Ronaldo became the first player to score forty goals in La Liga, and became the highest goalscorer in Real Madrid's

history when he ended the season with 53 club goals, four more than the previous best tally of 49 scored by the legendary Ferenc Puskas.

Leading League Scorer in:
2006-2007 - 17 goals, 34 appearances
2007-2008 - 31 goals, 34 appearances
2008-2009 - 18 goals, 33 appearances

58 – DIMITAR BERBATOV

Dimitar Berbatov first came to the attention of United fans when he appeared for Bayer Leverkusen against the Reds in the Champions League semi-final in April 2002, and scored the following September as the sides met again.

The Bulgarian striker began his career at his hometown club, Pirin, before moving to CSKA Sofia in 1998. In 2006, after an impressive five year spell at Leverkusen, Berbatov signed for Tottenham Hotspur for a fee of around £11m after interest from Liverpool and Celtic. This made him the most expensive Bulgarian player ever.

An impressive debut season in the Premier League saw him score a dozen goals and secure a place in the PFA team of the year. The 2007-08 season saw Berbatov help Spurs to an 11th place finish after a poor first half of the season. He grabbed four goals in a thrilling 6-4 victory over Reading and earned a League Cup winner's medal after scoring a penalty in the 2-1 victory over Chelsea in the final. Throughout this time at Spurs there were regular stories linking him to a potential move to United in the media.

When the 2008-09 season began, Berbatov was still at Spurs, but was not picked for any of their games as it was widely known that Alex Ferguson had expressed an interest in the player. Some media reports quoted Ferguson as saying that he expected to sign the player, prompting Spurs to complain to the Premier League claiming that the Reds had broken League rules.

On the last day of the transfer window, most expected Berbatov to sign for United, but Spurs still did not seem keen on the move.

The London club had negotiated with Manchester City to sign Vedran Corluka, and shortly after Corluka's transfer was made public, news filtered through that the Blues had been bought by businessmen from Abu Dhabi. An astounding series of events followed as a man claiming to be a spokesman for City's new owners claimed the Club had a number of transfer targets and that at least one major signing would be made before the day was out. It wasn't long before Berbatov appeared to be the man the Blues wanted.

Tottenham announced they had accepted an offer from City as rumours focused on the player's whereabouts. Ultimately, Berbatov arrived in Manchester and was met by Alex Ferguson, while City manager Mark Hughes was on a golf course explaining to journalists that the Blues had a number of targets and that no one had even spoken with Berbatov yet.

As the minutes ticked by, the pressure mounted for United to complete their deal. Shortly before midnight, United agreed a transfer with Spurs, ultimately paying a club record fee of £30.75m. Moments later City announced they had signed Robinho – a man who had seemed destined to sign for Chelsea.

Berbatov made his United debut at Anfield where he set up Carlos Tevez's 3rd minute goal, although the game ended in a 2-1 defeat. Berbatov's addition to the squad saw him used extensively alongside Wayne Rooney in the attack, starting 29 of the remaining 35 league matches while Tevez was utilised mainly as a substitute. Berbatov scored his first and second United goals against Aalborg in a 3-0 Champions League away win at the end of September, and his first in the League against West Bromwich Albion at Old Trafford in a 4-0 romp on 18 October. The Bulgarian's most productive spell in his first season came in the Christmas and New Year period when he assisted Tevez's winner at Stoke City, and scored the only goals against Middlesbrough and Bolton in the Premier League, as well

as the winner in the 4th round FA Cup tie against his former club Spurs. Berbatov scored the winner in the away match at Newcastle on 4 March, and United's fifth in a thrilling 5-2 victory over Spurs in April as the Reds came from two goals behind to strengthen their grip on the title. It had looked as if the League was slipping away from them and into the hands of arch-rivals Liverpool. Ultimately, United topped the table with 90 points, with Liverpool four points behind in second place. Berbatov's match-winning goals had been worth nine points alone and were crucial to United equalling Liverpool's record title haul of 18.

Despite the importance of his goals, Berbatov needed to work hard to win over some United fans who criticised his work rate. They were also not amused when he had a weak penalty saved against Everton in the FA Cup semi-final as United were beaten 4-2 in a shoot-out.

The 2008-09 season ended with Berbatov making an appearance as a substitute in the Champions League final – the second time this had happened in his career - although he was again on the losing side as United were defeated 2-0 by Barcelona.

2009-10 was less successful for both the player and the club. Berbatov scored 12 goals - all of which came in the League - as United missed out on the League title to Chelsea by a single point. He did provide the assist for Michael Owen's equaliser in the League Cup final against Aston Villa, but that was the only silverware the club won that season.

Significantly, Berbatov was unable to provide goals during the latter stage of the campaign when leading scorer Wayne Rooney was unavailable due to injury. A home loss to Chelsea was followed by an away-goals elimination from the Champions League at the hands of Bayern Munich, and a goalless draw at Blackburn ultimately defined United's disappointing season. Around the same time, having become the Bulgarian national team's all-time top scorer, Berbatov retired from international football.

Berbatov's first appearance of 2010-11 came against Chelsea in the Community Shield. Replacing Wayne Rooney at half time, he turned in a splendid performance, topped off with a sumptuous chipped goal from outside the box as United won 3-1. He opened the scoring in the first League match against Newcastle and scored United's third goals against both West Ham and Everton.

His best performance, as far as many fans are concerned, in a United shirt came against Liverpool in a 3-2 home win on 19 September 2010. It had looked to be an easy victory for United as Berbatov scored his second with a stunning overhead kick in front of the Stretford End, but defensive errors handed Liverpool two goals before the Bulgarian sealed his hat trick with a fine header from John O'Shea's perfect cross. It would be over two months until he found the net again, however. On 27 November Berbatov became only the fourth player in Premier League history to score five goals in a single match as United demolished Blackburn Rovers 7-1 at Old Trafford.

In January, Berbatov registered his third hat trick of the season as the Reds thrashed Birmingham 5-0 and three days later he bagged a brace at Blackpool as United turned around a two goal deficit to win 3-2. Finding himself increasingly being deployed from the bench in favour of new signing Javier Hernandez, Berbatov made just eight starts from February onwards and another two month barren spell followed before he turned in a last minute winner at home to Bolton Wanderers.

Although he had missed several games he still managed to finish the season with 20 League goals, sharing the golden boot award with former colleague Carlos Tevez. Despite enjoying his best season at the club, he was surprisingly excluded from the squad for the Champions League final, which United lost to Barcelona. This led to intense speculation about his future.

Leading League Scorer in:
2010-2011 -20 goals, 32 appearances

The Reds' record goalscorer Viollet (below) and his nearest rival Ronaldo (left).

LEADING LEAGUE GOALSCORERS
MOST GOALS IN A SEASON

Continuing our theme of leading League goalscorers, here are United's top twenty highest goalscorers in a League season (including the Alliance). Fifties star Dennis Viollet tops the all-time list, although his goals per game ratio is bettered by the second and third highest scorers Cristiano Ronaldo, John 'Jack' Picken and Denis Law. The best ratio of the top twenty strikers is Bob Donaldson with 1.32 goals per game during the Alliance season of 1891-92.

	Year	Division	Number of Goals	Games	Goals Per Game Ratio	Player
1	1960	One	32	36	0.888889	Viollet
2	2008	Premier	31	34	0.911765	Ronaldo
3=	1906	Two	30	33	0.909091	Picken
3=	1952	One	30	40	0.75	Rowley (Jack)
3=	1964	One	30	30	1	Law
6=	1892	Alliance	29	22	1.318182	Donaldson
6=	1959	One	29	38	0.763158	Charlton
8=	1965	One	28	36	0.777778	Law
9=	1968	One	28	41	0.682927	Best
10=	1947	One	26	37	0.702703	Rowley (Jack)
10=	1957	One	26	39	0.666667	Whelan
10=	2010	Premier	26	32	0.8125	Rooney
13=	1908	One	25	30	0.833333	Turnbull (Sandy)
13=	1956	One	25	33	0.757576	Taylor
13=	2003	Premier	25	34	0.735294	Van Nistelrooy
16=	1966	One	24	37	0.648649	Herd
16=	1988	One	24	40	0.6	McClair
18=	1948	One	23	39	0.589744	Rowley (Jack)
18=	1963	One	23	38	0.605263	Law
18=	1967	One	23	36	0.638889	Law
18=	2002	Premier	23	32	0.71875	Van Nistelrooy

All figures are accurate up to the end of the 2010-11 season.

The Football Season Daily Reminder

May

Well, here is the final section of *The Big Book Of United's* Football Season Daily Reminder. As we said earlier, we don't highlight every anniversary, but this section completes our aim to provide one snippet for every single date in the period 1st August through to 31st May.

1st May 1976

Second Division Southampton stunned the football world with their 1-0 victory over United in the FA Cup final.

2nd May 2010

A 28th minute goal from Nani was all that separated United and Sunderland when they met at the Stadium of Light.

3rd May 1958

An emotionally charged atmosphere saw Bolton defeat United 2-0 in the FA Cup final at Wembley.

4th May 1957

Matt Busby's United were defeated 2-1 in the FA Cup final by Aston Villa.

5th May 1945

A wonderful header from close range by Port Vale's Alf Bellis, appearing as a guest player for United, gave United an equaliser in the first leg of their Northern War League Cup semi-final against Chesterfield. The game was watched by 32,013 at Maine Road. United progressed to the final after winning the second leg 1-0.

6th May 1991

Steve Bruce scored his 19th first team goal of the 1990-91 season in the League game with Arsenal. This was said to be a record for a defender at the time and comprised of 13 League goals, four in the ECWC and two in the League Cup.

7th May 1949

A crowd of 49,808 witnessed a 3-2 United win over Portsmouth in their

5 May 1971 "This Is Your Life, Sir Matt Busby."

Viollet scoring in the 2-1 win over
AC Milan on 8 May 1958

last home League game at City's Maine Road stadium.

8th May 1964

Denis Law scores a hat trick against City in the Duke of Edinburgh Cup. The competition was organised to raise money for children's groups and Prince Phillip attended a rain-sodden Maine Road.

9th May 2010

Despite a 4-0 victory over Stoke the Reds missed out on the title by a point to Chelsea. The difference was the 2-1 Chelsea win when the two sides met on 3rd April.

10th May 1947

A Stan Pearson goal ensured a point at Preston before 23,278. Despite winning the final two games of the campaign, the Reds ended the season second – one point behind Liverpool.

11th May 1996

United defeated Liverpool 1-0 with a goal from Eric Cantona in the FA Cup final at Wembley.

12th May 1979

The Reds were defeated 3-2 by Arsenal in an amazing FA Cup final. The Gunners were winning 2-0 by half time, but late goals from McQueen (86) and McIlroy (88) suggested United would go on to win the match. Sadly, Alan Sunderland scored

Arsenal's third goal a minute later.

13th May 2007

Despite losing 1-0 on the final day of the season at home to West Ham, United won the Premier League. They finished the season six points clear of their nearest rivals Chelsea.

14th May 1994

Two goals from Cantona helped United achieve a 4-0 FA Cup final victory over Chelsea at Wembley Stadium. Mark Hughes and Brian McClair scored the others.

15th May 1981

Patrice Evra was born in Dakar. On his tenth birthday United defeated Barcelona 2-1 to win the ECWC.

16th May 1999

United defeated Tottenham 2-1 with goals

from Beckham and Cole. The victory gave United the title by a point – Arsenal finished second.

17th May 1990

Alex Ferguson won his first trophy as United manager when the Reds defeated Crystal Palace 1-0 in the FA Cup final replay.

18th May 1985

United defeated Everton 1-0 with a goal from Norman Whiteside in the 110th minute (the game had gone into extra-time).

In the 78th minute of the game Kevin Moran was sent off for a foul on Peter Reid, but ten-man United seemed more determined as a result.

19th May 2001

Despite successive defeats by Southampton (13/5) and Spurs (19/5) United won the Premier League title by ten points. United had 80 points with Arsenal second on 70.

20th May 1953

United defeated Liverpool 3-1 in the penultimate game of the season at Old Trafford. The match was watched by 20,869 – the second lowest home League crowd of the season.

21st May 2008

Ryan Giggs breaks Bobby Charlton's appearance record with his 759th first team game for the Reds. The match was United's Champions League final

victory over Chelsea in Moscow.

22nd May 1946

George Best was born in Belfast. On the same day in 2011 United celebrated their record breaking 19th League title success.

23rd May 1942

The final game of the wartime season saw the Reds defeat City 3-1 at Maine Road.

24th May 1966

Eric Cantona was born in Paris. Five days earlier United's season had ended with a 1-1 draw at home to Leeds.

25th May 1963

The FA Cup final ended in a 3-1 United victory over Leicester City.

26th May 1945

United drew 2-2 with Bolton in the second leg of the Northern War League Cup final. The first leg had ended in a 1-0 Bolton

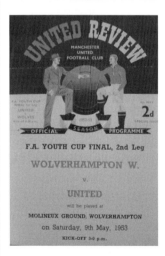

had shelved plans to bid for United: "Wealthy Manchester United fans are understood to have shelved plans to buy the club after they decided the price was too high. The consortium of businessmen, dubbed the Red Knights, had been expected to table a formal bid of up to £1.2 billion for the club before the start of the World Cup in June."

after extra time the replay would have been held at Highbury on this date. A few programmes were produced and in 2001 a reprint of the programme for 'the game that never was' was issued.

win and so they won the trophy on aggregate, however the second leg was regarded as possibly the most thrilling northern wartime game. The Maine Road attendance was 57,395. 54 Years later the Reds defeated Bayern Munich 2-1 in a dramatic Champions League final.

27th May 2009

The Reds were defeated 2-0 in the Champions League final at Rome.

28th May 2008

Bruce Springsteen and the E Street Band played a concert at Old Trafford as part of Springsteen's world tour.

29th May 1968

United beat Benfica 4-1 after extra time in the European Cup final at Wembley Stadium.

30th May 2010

The Daily Star reported that the 'Red Knights'

31st May 1968

Had the European Cup final ended in a draw

SEASON 1967-68

EUROPEAN CHAMPION CLUBS' CUP FINAL REPLAY

The European Cup

MANCHESTER UNITED
v
BENFICA

FRIDAY, 31st MAY   KICK-OFF 7.30 pm

ARSENAL STADIUM

Official Programme

1/-

THE FINAL WORD

In preparation for the 1958 Christmas period the "Boys Book Of Soccer 1959" was published. That annual, like the versions for the previous couple of seasons, carried an article by one of United's – and England's - leading stars. The difference being that by the time the article for the 1959 annual was published the author had died.

The Munich Air Disaster was a terrible tragedy that sent Manchester into an unprecedented period of mourning. The story of the day and its impact on Manchester has been well documented over the years (the full story can be read in The Big Book Of United's sister publication "Manchester: A Football History" by Gary James). However, we feel it is appropriate to re-publish the text from the article written for the Boys Book Of Soccer by the legendary United star Duncan Edwards.

The editor of the Boys Book Of Soccer 1959 explained the significance and circumstances behind the article at the time of publication: "Duncan Edwards wrote this article only a few days before taking off with the rest of the Manchester United team on their fateful flight to Belgrade, to play Red Star in the quarter-finals of the European Cup: the flight from which he was not to return.

"Duncan gave me the article at the hotel in London - within a stone's throw of the headquarters of the Football Association - where the team were staying before their League match with Arsenal on the previous Saturday.

"The usual throng of boys with autograph albums lay in wait outside the hotel; inside, the players looked the embodiment of health and strength, youth and life. Two were old friends of mine. Tommy Taylor had written an article for the Boys' Book of Soccer last year, and Roger Byrne the year before that. Duncan Edwards was carrying on the tradition: and now all three are dead. They died, with others, when the world-famous team known as 'Busby's Babes' was broken by a cruel air crash.

"Broken, but not destroyed. Manchester United immediately rose again. The spirit, which is the main thing, survived untouched. That is why I am publishing this article just as Duncan Edwards wrote it, less than a week before he began his own brave but unavailing fight with death. It explains why Duncan and other boy football stars chose to join Manchester United; and, I think, why many more youngsters in the future will choose the same."

Here at "The Big Book Of United" we believe Duncan's views at that time deserve to be recalled, and we can think of no more appropriate way than to end this edition of our book with Duncan's comments from 1958.

WHY I JOINED MANCHESTER UNITED
BY DUNCAN EDWARDS

I joined Manchester United because - well, first of all - because they asked me. It was, I thought, a great honour to be asked, immediately after leaving school, if I would like to sign on with a famous club like Manchester United. That in itself was almost a good enough reason: but - to make the honour even greater - I was invited to join other clubs at the same time. Wolves were interested, and so were West Bromwich Albion and other Midland clubs. I was born and bred in the Midlands, so to them I was a local boy.

But I must pause a moment to explain that all these clubs were not exactly fighting over my young body. I should hate to seem to be boasting that half the clubs in the country were begging me to sign on with them when I walked out of school on the last day of my last term.

Football clubs do not chase after schoolboys quite like that.

"I think you've a chance to make a go of it." That was what the Manchester United scout said. The representatives of the other clubs put - it in much the same way. They thought I had a chance. These clubs would give me a chance. Whether I took it or not - whether I made a go of it - was largely up to me. Time would tell. Because a boy has been capped for a few schools internationals it does not mean that he is set fair for a football career.

I had received nine schoolboy caps, and played at Wembley twice - once before I was fifteen. Schoolboy internationals are watched by scouts from League clubs, although boys cannot be approached until they have left school. I had a pretty good idea that I might be approached, and before I left I had resolved to try to make football my career.

But why should a Midlands boy go to Manchester, when clubs like Wolves and the Albion were willing to take him on?

Well, perhaps it was partly because I thought I might be better away from my home territory. But the main reason, beyond all doubt, was the reputation Manchester United had as they still have - for bringing on youngsters. I had heard about it, and read about it; and whenever I asked, I heard much the same sort of answer. Old Trafford was the place for boys. They looked after you, taught you and trained you - and gave you plenty of opportunities to show what you could do.

So I went... and the first time I entered the dressing-room, to meet the other players on the club's books, I almost felt as if I was back at school. The place was packed with youngsters, several of them hardly older than myself.

Duncan Edwards and future England manager Bobby Robson during an England training session.

MANCHESTER UNITED F.C.

[Photo courtesy *Manchester Evening Chronicle*]

Standing (*left to right*) : Mr. M. BUSBY (*manager*), E. COLMAN, R. WOOD, M. JONES, W. FOULKES, D. PEGG, D. EDWARDS, Mr. J. MURPHY.
Front Row (*left to right*) : J. BERRY, R. BYRNE, T. TAYLOR, D. VIOLLET, W. WHELAN.
Insets (*left*) : J. BLANCHFLOWER, (*right*) : R. CHARLTON.

Soon I met the older players, such as there were; and I was heartened by the warm welcome they gave me.

This was the first thing I discovered at Old Trafford. There was no jealousy between the older and younger players. Instead there was a real team-spirit and friendliness. Youth and experience met on equal terms. The club was well named United.

I found also that there was nothing phony in those stories about the encouragement to youngsters.

I was soon playing in the club's Under-18 team - in which I won a medal; and, only nine months after leaving the school classroom, the big moment arrived when I was called to the manager's office, and Mr. Busby told me quietly that I had been picked for the first team.

Four other boys in their 'teens had made their debuts with the United already that season - outside right John Scott, centre forward Eddie Lewis, inside forward John Doherty and outside left David Pegg - so you can see what chances there were. Our opponents were Cardiff City. We lost 1-4. That was the only time I played for the first team that season.

But half-way through the next season I won a permanent place. For this success I owed more than anything to the man whose place I eventually took: a great international wing half-Henry Cockburn. A great player, and a wonderful friend to me. For quite a long time he was on the injured list, and attended our League games only as a spectator. Regularly, when we played at home, he would come into the dressing-room just before the kick-off to give me some tips about my opponent that afternoon.

It would have been a fine gesture even if his advice had been only in the form of encouragement. But it was more than that - he gave me practical tips that proved invaluable on the field of play. This was all in the Old Trafford tradition. The same thing is being done today by another great player and grand sport - outside right John Berry. And his shrewd advice is being given freely to our brilliant young right winger Ken Morgans.

Now that I am nearly in the veteran class(!) I also am expected to help the new boys to settle down and fit into the playing staff. It's a pleasure and a privilege - for, believe me, some of the lads coming up at Old Trafford now are really top-class.

Ken Morgans, still in his 'teens, is an outstanding example of the quality of the intake that followed mine. Others, even younger, have the makings of first-rate players. At the moment they are unknown: any time, when the opportunity occurs (and it keeps occurring at Old Trafford), they will burst into fame.

'Busby's Babes', as the newspapers sometimes call us, do not need any advertisement from me. But if any youngster with talent has the chance to begin his career with Manchester United - if he is tempted because of what he has heard of the way youngsters are treated, but hasn't quite made up his mind-well, to him I say, 'Don't think about it - do it'. You won't regret it, for what you've heard is true.

One other word to boys who may have ideas of following a football career: you must keep at it, keep trying to go one better than you have gone so far. When you're in your school team you should be aiming to play for the town, then for the county - then in a schools international. Chances will not come to you if you just sit back and wait for them.

I do not mean that you must be pushing or always telling people how good you are. I mean simply that you must be ambitious, seek chances and snap them up when they come.

Of course I have been lucky. Things worked out for me wonderfully well. So well, in fact, that at the age of eighteen and a half I was actually capped for England. I shall never forget my first full international match. Not just because we won (we beat Scotland 7-2). Not just because it was only three years, almost to the day, since I had played on the same ground in a schools international. But also because of the way the other England players made me welcome in spite of my youth.

I felt the same atmosphere as at Old Trafford, although some of the players were old enough to be my father. Indeed, one of them had been playing for England before I was born! Yes, of course, that was Stanley Matthews; and it was a great honour for me to be playing in the same England team as this immortal footballer.

So I have been lucky - lucky especially to play for a club at a time when it was winning honours both at home and abroad.

The club that, in 1956-57, nearly won the Cup-and-League double. . . . That is for the future. I'm sure we'll pull it off.

It is worth noting that "The Boys Book Of Soccer" indirectly inspired James Ward to publish this book on United. The 1959 edition was edited by Patrick Pringle and published by Evans Brothers Limited. Copies of this book and others in the series are highly collectable.

SUBSCRIBERS

The publisher would like to acknowledge the following as subscribers to this volume. Your support of this project is appreciated.

	Subscriber	Favourite United Goalscorer
1	Manchester United F.C.	
2	The British Library	
3	The National Football Museum	
4	The Football Association	
5	Trevor Hartley	
6	Fred Burden	
7	Edward Garvey	
7	Alex Wormall	Ole Gunnar Solskjaer
8	Tim Ashmore	Andrei Kanchelskis
9	Paul Nagel	Denis Law
10	Iain McCartney	
11	Gary James	
12	Peter Wormall	Bobby Charlton
13	Alan Ashmore	Denis Law
14	David Fowler	Mark Hughes
15	Vera Wormall	Lou Macari
16	Joanne Morris	Alan Smith
17	Martin Short	Ole Gunnar Solskjaer
18	Natalie Rostron	Mark Hughes
19	Simon Shakeshaft	Ryan Giggs
20	Mark Fletcher	Andrew Cole
21	Ben Rostron	Denis Irwin
22	Kim Burdett	Eric Cantona
23	Stephen Irish	Mark Hughes
24	Griffy Rostron	Danny Welbeck
25	Dan Burdett	Bryan Robson
26	Ian Short	Eric Cantona
27	Sarah Acton	Wayne Rooney
28	Martin Baloch	Ryan Giggs
29	Mark Skelton	George Best

BIBLIOGRAPHY

This list is not meant to be a comprehensive review of all Manchester United publications, but it is intended as a guide to further reading. In addition, many of the works featured here have been consulted during the production of this book.

General

The Book of Football, various, 1905
Association Football & The Men Who Made It, various, 1905
A History Of British Football, Percy M Young, 1968
The Rothmans/Sky Sports Yearbooks, 1970-2012
Football Through The Turnstiles Again, Brian Tabner, 2002
The Complete Record of The FA Cup, Mike Collett, 2003
Manchester A Football History, Gary James, 2008 & 2010

United Specific

Manchester United, Alf Clarke, 1951
Manchester United Football Club, Alf Clarke, 1951
Charles Buchan's Salute To Manchester United, 1959
Manchester United, Percy M Young, 1960
Manchester United: Barson To Busby, Eric Thornton, 1971
The History of United, Tony Pullein, 1974
The Manchester United Story, Arthur Barker, 1977 & 1979
There's Only One United, Geoffrey Green, 1978
The Manchester United Football Books, David Meek, 1966-1980
Matt Busby's Manchester United Scrapbook, Matt Busby, 1980
Winners & Champions: The Story Of Manchester United's 1948 Cup Final and 1952 League Championship Winning Teams, Alec Shorrocks, 1985
Manchester United A Complete Record, Ian Morrison & Alan Shury, 1986, 1990 & 1992
Manchester United A Pictorial History & Club Record, Charles Zahra, Joseph Muscat, Iain McCartney, & Keith Mellor, 1986
Heathens & Red Devils, Keith Mellor, 1987
Illustrated History of Manchester United, Tom Tyrell & David Meek, 1988 & 1994
Red Devils In Europe, David Meek, 1988
Manchester United Player By Player, Ivan Ponting, 1989
Manchester United The Betrayal of a Legend, Michael Crick & David Smith, 1989
Back Page United, Stephen F Kelly, 1990
The Gibson Guarantee, Peter Harrington, 1994
The United Alphabet, Garth Dykes, 1994
United - The Story Of Manchester United in the FA Cup, Steve Cawley, 1994
United We Stood, Richard Kurt, 1994
Are You Watching, Liverpool?, Jim White, 1995

The Official Manchester United Official History, Justyn Barnes, Adam Bostock, Cliff Butler, Aubrey Ganguly, Graham McColl & Mark Wylie, 2001 onwards.

The Tartan Reds, Iain McCartney, 2002

Manchester United The Top 11 of Everything Red, Jim White & Andy Mitten, 2005

United: A History of Manchester United (The United Opus), Justyn Barnes, 2006

Manchester United: The Biography, Jim White, 2008 & 2009

Glory Glory! Man United in the '90s: The Players' Stories, Andy Mitten, 2009

Manchester United: The Forgotten Fixtures, Iain McCartney, 2009

Manchester United: Thirty Memorable Games from the Fifties, Iain McCartney, 2010

We're the Famous Man United - Old Trafford in the '80s: The Players' Stories, Andy Mitten, 2011

The Munich Air Disaster

The Day A Team Died, Frank Taylor, 1960

Munich Air Disaster: Captain Thain's Ordeal, Stanley Williamson, 1973

The Team That Wouldn't Die, John Roberts, 1975

Duncan Edwards, Iain McCartney & Roy Cavanagh, 1988

Tommy Taylor of Manchester United & Barnsley, John Kennedy, 1994

Roger Byrne, Iain McCartney, 2000

Harry's Game, Harry Gregg & Roger Anderson, 2002

Bill Foulkes – Manchester United & Beyond, Bill Foulkes & Ivan Ponting, 2003

The Lost Babes, Jeff Connor, 2006

General Manchester Footballing Works

My Story, Matt Busby with David R Jack, 1957

Living For Kicks, Denis Law with Kenneth Wheeler, 1963

Piccadilly Radio Soccer Book, Tom Tyrell, 1975 & 1976

A-Z of Manchester Football: 100 Years of Rivalry, Derek Brandon, 1978

Denis Law: An Autobiography, Denis Law with Ron Gubba, 1979

Football Wizard: The Story Of Billy Meredith, John Harding, 1985

Manchester FC – 125 Year History, Len Balaam, 1985.

A Strange Kind Of Glory: Sir Matt Busby & Manchester United, Eamon Dunphy, 1991

What A Game, Fred Eyre & Roy Cavanagh, 1983

The Pride Of Manchester, Steve Cawley and Gary James, 1991

Free The Manchester United One, Graham Sharpe, 2003

Venue Specific

Old Trafford Theatre Of Dreams, Iain McCartney, 1996

Farewell To Maine Rd, Gary James, 2003

Engineering Archie (Archibald Leitch – football ground designer), Simon Inglis, 2005

Old Trafford: 100 Years At The Theatre Of Dreams, Iain McCartney, 2010

There have also been a large number of fanzines, academic works, websites, forums, blogs and other publications consulted. Where possible these have been referred to in the main text.

JAMES WARD

Publisher of limited edition football books

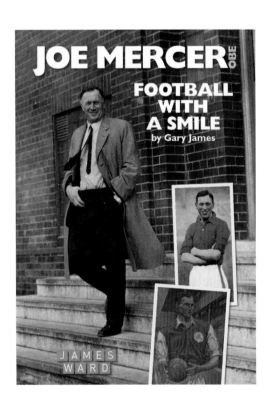

RECENT MANCHESTER PUBLICATIONS

Joe Mercer, OBE: Football With A Smile

£19.95, published April 2010, 304 pages including 16 page colour section,
ISBN 9780955812743

"The book is wonderfully illustrated, impeccably researched and has plenty of enjoyable anecdotes to recount." Ian Farrell, When Saturday Comes

The Big Book Of City

£19.95, published October 2009, 296 pages including 8 page colour section,
ISBN 9780955812729

Manchester: A Football History

£24.95, published December 2010, 544 pages plus 8 page colour section,
ISBN 9780955812736

"It is a real achievement and the first time the history of the game in the region has been told", Joyce Woolridge, When Saturday Comes

"BOOK OF THE WEEK - For all the ink that has been spilled in the name of Manchester United, only now do we learn the definitive - some say fateful - date on which the planet's most famous sporting institution spluttered into life, as Newton Heath FC was consigned to history... and it says everything about his immaculate piece of scholarship that James reveals the club to be two days older than it seems to think it is", Ian Herbert, The Independent

For up to date information on future Manchester related publications see our website and facebook page. Become a 'fan' on facebook and receive the latest information on all our books.

PO Box 822, Halifax, West Yorkshire, HX1 9FX

www.manchesterfootball.org

www.facebook.com/Jameswardpublishing

The Big Book of United is dedicated to
every Manchester United supporter.

Photographer Edward Garvey captures the scene outside Old Trafford in February 2008.